THE NEW
PSYCHOTHERAPIES

ROBERT A. HARPER, in private practice for over twenty years, has taught at several universities and also directed clinical training programs. A former president of the American Academy of Psychotherapists and the American Association of Marriage and Family Counselors, Dr. Harper is now serving in the governing structure of many professional organizations and as a consulting editor for their publications. He has written numerous articles and is author or co-author of six books, including *Psychoanalysis and Psychotherapy: 36 Systems, 45 Levels to Sexual Understanding and Enjoyment*, and *A Guide to Rational Living*.

THE NEW PSYCHOTHERAPIES

Robert A. Harper

A SPECTRUM BOOK

PRENTICE-HALL, INC., ENGLEWOOD CLIFFS, N.J.

Library of Congress Cataloging in Publication Data

HARPER, ROBERT ALLAN.
    The new psychotherapies.

    (A Spectrum Book)
    Includes bibliographies.
        1. Psychotherapy. I. Title. [DNLM: 1. Psy-
chotherapy. WM420 H295n]
    RC480.H29   616.8'914   75-5754
    ISBN 0-13-615419-0
    ISBN 0-13-615401-8 pbk.

1   2   3   4   5   6   7   8   9   10

PRENTICE-HALL INTERNATIONAL, INC. *(London)*
PRENTICE-Hall OF AUSTRALIA PTY., LTD. *(Sydney)*
PRENTICE-HALL OF CANADA, LTD. *(Toronto)*
PRENTICE-Hall OF INDIA PRIVATE LIMITED *(New Delhi)*
PRENTICE-HALL OF JAPAN, INC. *(Tokyo)*
PRENTICE-HALL OF SOUTHEAST ASIA (PTE.) LTD. *(Singapore)*

For
MAKUCHAN
Sleep well, black and gallant knight

CONTENTS

PREFACE

This book is a sequel to *Psychoanalysis and Psychotherapy: 36 Systems*, which appeared in 1959. In the period of time since its publication, tremendous changes have been made in the broad and increasingly amorphous area of psychotherapy. Certain tidy conceptions about psychotherapy that could be held with cool confidence in the late fifties sound like the weak and soulful notes of an orthodox isolate in the sixties and seventies. When, for example, in *36 Systems*, I wrote about dealing with the "various systems of psychic treatment which depend mainly on verbal interchange," I made sense for that time. Now (1974) we must consider much that goes under the category of psychotherapy that often shuns the verbal and, instead, emphasizes what is going on in the body of the patient and communicated by him through touch, screams, gestures, posture, and other nonverbal means.

I have tried to avoid duplication. However differently I might today write a few sections of *36 Systems*, none of the systems seems to me to be so inadequately treated that it screams for revision. My judgment in this matter is confirmed by the many colleagues who have commented to me about that book's consideration of various forms of psychotherapy and psychoanalysis. Two apparent duplications are really not such: Reichian vegetotherapy and gestalt therapy. The former was dismissed with a word or two in the earlier book (because it did not meet the criterion of emphasis on verbal communication); and gestalt therapy, under the auspices of the late genius-showman, Fritz Perls, and his many capable followers, has so changed and grown since the late fifties that it calls for consideration in the new context of the body psychotherapies at the present time.

Although, as I have said, the field of psychotherapy no longer resides quietly within clearly marked borders, the areas where great changes have occurred in the last fifteen years can be fairly neatly delineated. They are the behavior therapies, the body psychotherapies, family therapies, and group psychotherapies. These areas account for seven of the ten chapters of the book. The chapter on family-related therapies deals with treatment methods which cannot all be considered strictly developments of the past decade and a half (child, adolescent, sex, and marriage therapies), but which are important trends that did not fit into the framework used in *36 Systems*. The ninth chapter is a kind of roundup of other approaches brought to professional and public attention since 1959.

Group psychotherapy in various shapes and forms had, of course, made the scene quite noticeably in the late fifties, but it has gone through many stages of change and growth in the ensuing years. Group therapy systems treated in the earlier book (see Chapter 9 of *36 Systems*) have not, as far as I can observe, greatly altered their theories or practices in the interim and are thus skipped in the current volume. Some of the group therapies dealt with here predate the sixties and seventies, but have come into prominence recently. Transactional analysis (already developing on the West Coast in the late fifties, but not known nationally until later) is included among the group therapies because it is usually practiced in a group setting, but is given a chapter to itself because of its prominence today as a psychotherapeutic system.

Family therapy just barely existed in the late fifties (a pioneer form of it created by Dr. C. F. Midelfort is discussed in Chapter 9 of *36 Systems*). Now it is a major treatment modality and has assumed many ingenious varieties.

Behavior therapy, too, had poked up a blossom or two (see discussions of Salter's and Wolpe's work in Chapter 7 of *36 Systems*) in the late fifties. Today it is probably the greatest "growth stock" in the field of psychotherapy. Much of its strength seems to be related to its research orientation and its close interaction with various psychological learning theories.

In the preface to *36 Systems*, I expressed the hope that students of the behavioral and social sciences (as well as intelligent laymen) would find that book a helpful map to the then-existing psychotherapeutic maze. Testimonials have accumulated through the years that that small volume so served and continues to be of value to a large number of people of diverse educational backgrounds.

If *The New Psychotherapies* has similar worth to many people, I shall feel rewarded for my long swim through what retrospectively seems like an incredible amount of written material to emerge with the relatively few words of this volume. In the course of the reading and writing processes, I never stumbled upon any objective criteria regarding what to include or exclude in recent approaches to psychotherapy. I tried, however, to keep subjectivity in leash: I have included material which very much runs against the grain of my own biases, but which seemed to me to be an important or influential part of the contemporary psychotherapeutic scene; and I have excluded points of view that coincide closely with my own in instances where they seem to be falling on the deaf ear of the psychotherapeutic community.

As for my own prepossessions, I still echo my eclecticism of fifteen years ago. Both the technical and theoretical blends have changed a little, but I still believe basically that both the explanations and treatment of human behavior are circumstantial and that no psychotherapeutic theory or treatment method fits all therapists and all patients. In terms of the many points of view represented in this book, I think more help for more people will, in the long run, derive from the more cognitive systems (group and individual), from the behavior therapists, and from the pragmatically oriented family therapists than from the body and emotion-centered therapists (again, group and individual). So all this makes me something like a cognitive-behavioral-pragmatic eclectic.

The way I ended the preface to *36 Systems* seems to me an appropriate and desirable way to conclude this one: "However this book may be received, the process of writing it has added a great deal to the author's understanding of a very complex and very important aspect of contemporary life. And for this increased understanding, I am grateful."

R. A. H.
Washington, D.C.

1

FAMILY
THERAPIES

Ackerman, Satir, Zuk, and Bell

Although various kinds of work in therapeutic situations with families have existed for several decades and some focus of attention on conjoint family therapy began to develop in the late fifties (see a description of Midelfort's pioneering work in *Psychoanalysis and Psychotherapy: 36 Systems*, pp. 135–37), family therapies in variety and plenitude are a phenomenon of the sixties and seventies. Many approaches go under the general label of family therapy, but the ones that have come in the last decade to dominate the field and the only ones to which we shall direct our attention in this discussion fall into the general category of "conjoint family therapy."

Conjoint family therapy is to be distinguished from a collaborative type of family therapy, on the one hand, where two or more family members are in separate treatment with two or more therapists who occasionally consult about family matters (characteristic of child guidance clinics) and concomitant treatment, on the other hand, where one therapist sees two or more members of the family, but often separately. In conjoint treatment most (and often all) sessions include most (and often all) family members in a single collection. As we shall observe later, more than one psychotherapist may, however, be involved in the conjoint treatment of a particular family.

Most family therapists agree that the fundamental way family therapy differs from individual therapy is that the former has *changes in the family system* as its major goal. Changes in the behavior of individual family members are, of course, inevitably needed to effect family system changes, but individual changes are secondary to the focus on family patterns.

Like most desirable (and some undesirable) things in psychotherapeutic history, awareness of the importance of the family background can be traced to Freud, who took the family into account in his understanding of anxiety. The patient's environment, often more specifically his family environment, was brought much more sharply into focus by Adler, Horney, Sullivan, Fromm, and their followers. But the individual, not the family, was the object of treatment in all these instances.

The idea that the patient could be treated in a setting other than the exceedingly private and rather sacrosanct one-to-one relationship inherited from psychoanalysis sprang from marriage counseling and group psychotherapy. In the former, conjoint sessions of the counselor with husband and wife were quite common, as was the conception that the counselor was treating the marriage rather than two individuals who happened to be married (although this conception was not accepted by all marriage counselors—perhaps not even by a majority—it was nevertheless widespread). There was still quite a jump left, however, from the idea of the treatment of a marital dyad to the inclusion of children (and possibly other family members) in the process of dealing with the family as a treatment unit.

In group psychotherapy, although attention is still centered on the individual, many potential family therapists are offered the opportunity of becoming comfortable in working in other than a tête-à-tête situation. However, a number of aspects of therapeutic procedure are quite different. It is not possible for the family therapist, for example, to select members for the group so that a manageable balance of personalities and problems among participants can be effected. Also, while nonfamily therapy groups are temporarily and artificially created, the family group is together in one way or another all the time. Still another difference is that in group therapy, where strictly individual problems predominate, group members can join the therapist in providing perspectives of relative objectivity or emotional detachment for other group members' difficulties. In family therapy, however, the therapist stands alone as a presumably uninvolved and neutral outsider.

The most fundamental of the foregoing differences is that in family therapy the group life persists throughout the week that usually intervenes between therapy sessions. Instead of individuals receiving treatment *in* a group, family therapy is treatment *for* a group which then keeps right on functioning *as* a group without the therapist.

This ongoing process can have both advantages and disadvantages therapeutically. In nonfamily group therapy, an unfinished or poorly resolved problem of group functioning can, in effect, be put on the shelf until the next time the group meets, at which time a new look can be taken at what has been held suspended for group attention and action. (It is true that the *individuals* must go on with their lives, but the group therapeutic process remains unmolested from one session to the next.) In family therapy, however, regardless of where the therapeutic process may have left the group in unresolved dilemmas, the group goes on living with its difficulties without therapeutic aid until the next session. Constructive changes, on the other hand, initiated in family sessions, can take direct and immediate effect and get reinforced on a full-time basis. In other words, considerable positive or negative transformations can be effected by the family as a group between sessions.

These transformations of the family as a group—that is to say, the positive ones—constitute the definite and agreed-upon purpose of family therapy. Individual change is viewed as a secondary (although often necessary and desirable) consideration in relation to the goal of changing the family system of interaction. Psychotherapists inexperienced in family therapy find this the most difficult adjustment to make.

Real assistance in the process of effecting changes in the family system comes to the psychotherapist from family members not only in some of the between-session work referred to earlier but also in therapy sessions where characteristic maneuvers, avoidances, pretenses, or fantasies of one family member will be more expertly and forthrightly revealed than the therapist by himself could do. Such exposure of defensive and evasive tactics on the part of one family member in the full view of both the therapist and the rest of the family will often initiate important changes in other parts of the family system. These changes, which start really as breakdowns of some of the old and unconstructive patterns of family relationship, can be used by the alert family therapist as the basis for building new and more constructive modes of interaction.

In addition to receiving assistance, the therapist, of course, sometimes gives it. This is particularly true in the broad area of communication, with which some trouble exists in any family that presents itself for therapy. Not only can a competent family therapist often discern blocks to communication and initiate corrective measures, but he can also help the family to provide a model of effective communication within therapy sessions. This model, in turn, may be so rewarding that improved communicative procedures are carried over in home interactions.

In the first of these two chapters on family therapy, we briefly examine the work of four early and well-known systematists: Ackerman, Satir, Zuk, and Bell. Ackerman is sometimes called the "grandfather" of family therapy and shares with Midelfort honors for undertaking pioneer explorations of the whole family approach. Bell came on the scene at almost the same time as Ackerman and Midelfort and wrote one of the earliest treatises on family therapy. Ackerman, Midelfort, and Bell all worked independently of each other, as do all good frontiersmen, and yet arrived at some remarkably similar points of view as a result of their separate work.

Virginia Satir made the scene of family therapy a little post-pioneer, but was part of the first wave of early settlers. Her skill, wisdom, and clear thinking as a theoretician and her equal skill, wit, and charm as a practitioner have set her firmly at the top of the family therapy field.

Zuk was selected to become the fourth "star" in this family therapy panorama because of his vigorous championship of a nonpsychoanalytical approach. In his many publications, he clearly espouses what he calls triadic-based family therapy. Zuk sees the family therapist in the roles of mediator and side-taker in applying leverage against pathogenic relating in families.

After looking at the systems developed by these theorists we will turn our attention in the next chapter to further systematic developments (some of them quite ingenious) of the whole family therapy concept.

ACKERMAN'S FAMILY DIAGNOSIS AND THERAPY

The late Nathan W. Ackerman, a New York psychiatrist who did probably more than anyone to develop and widely establish family psychotherapy among professionals, stressed the interdependence of the procedures of diagnosis and treatment. He pointed out that diagnostic judgment determines the clarity and appropriateness of the choice of therapeutic goals and the specificity of the techniques of family psychotherapy and that the family interview, of course, is the pathway to diagnosis. He thought the lack of interest in diagnosis in family therapy derived partly from the effort to unshackle the procedure from the medical model of illness, to counteract the criticism of psychiatric labeling, and to avoid excessive claims of accuracy in the therapeutic process. He also contended that diagnosis, compared to spontaneous interaction with a family, is hard work and that this markedly reduced its popularity with many of his colleagues.

It was all right with Dr. Ackerman if his colleagues preferred to call diagnoses "evaluations," but he wanted to make sure that trainees did not get the impression that there was any way to avoid the responsibility of conceptualizing and categorizing family types. Therapists inevitably, Ackerman showed, formulate judgments regarding the families they treat. He believed that to compare and contrast families and thereby to draw meaningful clinical distinctions, a clinically oriented classification of families is necessary. Without such, there is a danger of family therapy becoming an expression of the idiosyncratic talent of individual therapists.

In search of a classificatory system of family ills, Ackerman and his associates (first at the Child Development Center, then the Family Mental Health Clinic of the Jewish Family Service, and finally the Family Institute), over a quarter of a century, designed and kept modifying a normative standard of family health, which Ackerman insisted was an essential component of a system of diagnosis. "As long as we lack a concept of a well family, we may easily deceive ourselves about what really constitutes a sick family. The one perspective carries meaning only in relation to the other," Ackerman said.

In his last formulation of the parameters of a normative standard of family well-being, Ackerman set forth the following: (1) the biological and transcultural core of the human family phenomenon; (2) the common denominators of family life in the human and near-human species; (3) (a) the family's adaptation to society and to social change and (b) society's adaptation to the family; and (4) the role of values in the preservation of the family. Distinction is made in (3a) between those forms of adaptation which are on the side of growth and life and those which lead to family disorganization and decay; in (3b) between the societal supports for family viability and those damaging to same; and in (4) between healthy and pathogenic values as these mold the family's destiny.

With these parameters in mind, Ackerman saw the goals of family therapy as the alleviation of emotional distress and disability in order to enhance the level of health of the family as a group as well as its individual members; the strengthening of the individual against destructive forces within himself and within the family; and the strengthening of the integrative capacity of the family. To pursue these general aims, the family therapist had to work along the lines of these more specific principles: (1) to help the family achieve a clearer definition of the real content of conflict; (2) to counteract inappropriate displacements of conflict; (3) to neutralize the irrational prejudices and scapegoating that are involved in the displacement of conflict; (4) to relieve an excessive load of conflict on one victimized part of the family; (5) to lift concealed interpersonal conflicts to the level of interpersonal relations, where they can be dealt with more effectively; (6) to activate an improved quality of emotional complementarity in family role relationships; and (7) to replace the lacks in the patterns of family interaction through the appropriate and selective use of the therapist's personality. "This means," Ackerman said, "a discriminating injection of healthy elements of emotional interaction to replace sick ones, as the alignments in family relationships shift."

Ackerman conceived of the role of the family therapist as an active, open, forthright one. As movies made of his work testify, he pitched in with the family and implemented the emotional elements that were missing in family interaction. In the words of Beels and Ferber, "Ackerman mobilized family interaction, watching it for non-verbal gestures and interactional clues to the more primitive relations of sex, aggression and helpless dependency in the group. . . . He cut through denial, hypocrisy, and projection, forcing the members to be more open to him than they were to each other."

In his conception of the way to initiate family therapy, Ackerman stressed a simple and casual manner. Troubled families know that "things" for them are in a mess, that there is multiplicity of disturbance, and that any clinical approach that is likely to work must be responsive to the contagious state of disorder existing among members. Ackerman believed, therefore, that long explanatory dissertations from the therapist were both unnecessary and nontherapeutic; he preferred that the therapist get down immediately to problem solving with the family.

In Ackerman's view the responsibilities of the family therapist are multiple and complex and require a flexible and undefensive use of self. The therapist has as his major function the fostering of the family's use of his emotional participation in the direction of achieving a favorable shift in the homeostasis of family relationships. "He loosens and shakes up preexisting pathogenic equilibria," Ackerman wrote, "and makes way for a healthier realignment of these family relationships. In this role, his influence may be likened to that of a catalyst, a chemical reagent, a re-synthesizer." The family therapist, as seen by Ackerman, mobilizes those forms of interaction that tend to lead to the undoing of distorted percepts of self and others, to the dissolving of confusion, and to eventual awareness of underlying conflicts and their solutions.

Beels and Ferber have written that Ackerman made so much use of nonverbal material in his very successful therapeutic approach to families that he had real difficulty transmitting his skills to colleagues and students. He wrote that family therapy requires a continuous correlation of the inside of the mind and the outside (that is, the ongoing "interconnections of intrapsychic and interpersonal experience") and necessitates "a continuous juxtaposing of conscious and unconscious, real and unreal, inner and outer experience, individual and group."

To such a description of the work of the family therapist, the reader is not inclined to offer up critical or disputatious commentary, but rather to say, "Great, but how do you do it?" Although Ackerman called for and made efforts to produce a scientific base for his approach to family therapy, he remained primarily the talented artist whose particular "system" of family therapy died with him. Some of his basic theoretical ideas, however, along with diagnostic formulations and research, are being carried forward by the Family Institute (which now bears his name).

SATIR'S CONJOINT FAMILY THERAPY

In writing of Virginia Satir as a therapist, Beels and Ferber (who studied the styles, techniques, and theories of a large number of family therapists) have compared her to the late Nathan Ackerman. She too enters directly, vigorously, and authoritatively into the sessions with family members. As Beels and Ferber put it, "Both generally made more statements than any family member during the course of a session, and although the aim and effect was to promote interaction between family members, they did it by establishing a star-shaped verbal communication pattern with themselves as the center."

Satir, however, relies less on nonverbal communication, cues regarding the unconscious, and mysterious changes of pace in her approach to a family than did Ackerman. Hence, although her great success as a therapist and a teacher of therapists is certainly not wholly independent of her personal charisma, a high percentage of Satir's methods are directly communicable by her to others (which, as we noted, was not true of Ackerman's work). Beels and Ferber say that Satir "makes herself the embodiment of clarity and perception in communication, using simple words, keeping up a running explanatory gloss on what she is doing, and arranging encounters between family members according to her rules." They go on to point out that she does much more than this as she translates into her own language many of the more traditional theories of family dynamics. But fundamentally, Beels and Ferber state, Satir is a teacher of a method of communication and considers treatment accomplished when she has passed on a good portion of her communication skills to the family members.

Satir's evaluation of herself, however, is that "although I naturally believe in my own methods, and hope that others may find it helpful to read about them, I do not mean to imply that they are the last and only word in therapeutic procedure." She stresses that each therapist must find his own style and should not "sacrifice his particular flavor to some kind of professional, impersonal ideal." In her own style, informality of approach is quite important in establishing an atmosphere of cooperation, hopefulness, and good will in the family.

To teach a family how to communicate, the therapist must, of course, start at the existing level. "It is often astonishing to an inexperienced therapist," Satir writes, "how frequently family members cannot ask even simple, fact-finding questions of each other and must be shown how." The therapist's different perspective on the family's problems and interactions often effectively sinks in with family members by her simple, direct, and repetitious interrogation technique.

In making the initial appointment, Satir usually insists on both husband and wife being present for the first interview, stressing the need for both the male and female point of view in obtaining information about the family's problems. She begins the first interview by asking questions to establish what the family wants and expects from therapy and then pointing out briefly the nature of family therapy. She explains that each family member has a contribution to make that cannot be duplicated by another member and that each family has a pattern of operation in dealing with difficulties that the therapist needs to understand before changes can be suggested that will ease these difficulties.

By following her preference (which she reluctantly yields if the family is so dysfunctional that mates cannot bear to look at their own relationship) of seeing the marital pair for at least two sessions without the children, Satir believes she emphasizes the importance from the outset of the husband and the wife as persons and as spouses instead of strictly as parents. She writes that in dysfunctional families the mates have usually abandoned their marital roles and have come to focus on their children because they are afraid to focus on each other. If, on the other hand, the identified patient is a "child" who is over 21 (often a schizophrenic) and treated as a child by the parents, Satir includes this person from the outset by making it clear that she is dealing with three adults who have difficulties relating to each other.

Early in the first interview Satir starts compiling a family life chronology. She feels that such active structuring by the therapist reveals not only valuable information from the past but also a lot about present interactions. Because their marital difficulties have caused them to "parent" according to their own needs rather than to the child's growth needs, marital therapy is a large component of family therapy as Satir undertakes it. In the course of this history taking, she spends considerable time on each mate's relationship to his or her parents as a means of introducing new concepts in a relatively unthreatening way about the mate's functioning as a parent in the present family. Such concepts as differentness and how it is handled, disagreements and pain and coping with them, and learning to have fun as a family can be introduced in this phase of the therapy.

In bringing the children into therapy, Satir is partly guided by age: if children are four or older, they stay in family therapy for most of the sessions; if they are under four, usually only for two or three of the early sessions (partly so that the therapist can see how the parents perform their parenting function). Because Satir's approach tends consistently to be a direct, active, and authoritative one, she encounters few problems in keeping children under control; they usually become as engrossed in the therapy process as their parents.

The opening sessions with the whole family, like her initial interviews with the parents, are used by Satir for both diagnostic and information-gathering purposes, on the one hand, and for therapy, on the other. Concepts are instilled in the children and reinforced in the adults similar to those emphasized in the marital therapy: that people are individuals and differ from one another (in dysfunctional families the pretherapeutic concept is usually that it is bad to be different, thus inviting feelings of being unloved); that disagreements over perception and opinion commonly occur in families and are not to be viewed with alarm; and that clear communication about what family members see, think, and feel is desirable and leads (soon, if not immediately) to desirable effects in family relations.

Satir asks many questions in a family interview not only because both information and behavior are revealed in the answers but also because she believes warm, specific, matter-of-fact questioning is itself therapeutic. As she has written, this may be the first time that the children have been treated as people with perceptions and opinions, and it is desirable for both them and their parents to experience this.

More specifically, in trying to help the family communicate more effectively, Satir both helps parents to understand their children and receive feedback from them, and children to understand their parents and themselves as children. She asks children to explain a parent's behavior in order to challenge strictly negative interpretation, and she asks parents to explain their own behavior toward children. She also helps children express covert questions openly and asks the parents to answer these questions. While generally supporting parental authority, Satir helps parents to recognize that children are increasingly able to make good judgments and decisions for themselves. In addition, she helps parents to separate themselves from their own parents, to strengthen the marital relationship, to equalize the parental responsibilities, to strengthen same-sex parent-child relationships (dysfunctional families tend to be overly strong on mother-son and father-daughter relationships), and to help mates attend to each other more and to the children less.

Satir considers treatment completed in family therapy when most of the following conditions are fulfilled: family members complete transactions, interpret hostility, see how others see them and how they see themselves, disagree, make choices, learn through practice, free themselves from harmful effects of past models, and are generally congruent in their behavior (with a minimum of hidden messages and of difference between feelings and communication). When one family member can tell another what he hopes, fears, and expects from the other and when such statements are direct, clear, and delineated, Satir believes the family is ready to leave therapy.

ZUK'S TRIADIC-BASED FAMILY THERAPY

Gerald H. Zuk, a Philadelphia psychologist, has developed a system of family therapy based on the interactions of three or more persons in the family rather than the dyad. He believes that much of family therapy to date has been dominated by the psychoanalytic point of view, which emphasizes dyadic interaction. Even when the analytically oriented family therapist or researcher deals with the triad, Zuk points out, it is often treated as if it were made up of dyads: mother-child, father-child, mother-father.

Triadic-based family therapy consists of a clinical application of the concepts of coalition, mediation, and side-taking. Zuk sees the family therapist as taking the roles of mediator and side-taker in applying leverage against pathogenic relating in families. Pathogenic relating, as he describes it, refers to silencing strategies, scapegoating, threats of physical violence, selective inattention, unfair or inappropriate labeling, myths or rituals (origin and accuracy uncertain), and creation of distractions. In order to dislodge pathogenic relating, Zuk becomes the go-between or side-taker who exerts pressure on family members to redefine and restructure their relationships to one another and to shift relationships in directions that he considers desirable.

Destructive processes (pathogenic relating) that erupt in the therapist's presence are often triadic-based, as Zuk points out, because they involve the coalition of two or more family members against another. One of the most frequent and persistent types of pathogenic relating is what Zuk has termed "silencing strategies." These are complexly motivated techniques designed to punish a family member for some transgression by isolating him in silence. The message (for example, from parents to child) is to comply or be isolated in silence. The victim's response may be to conform, and then he proceeds in the good graces of the family. If he rebels, however, his rebellion may take two forms. One is his agreement to the isolation; the other is babbling—he makes no verbal sense as an alternative to conforming either to the original desired behavior or to the punishment of silence. Zuk says that "it is not unusual for the perpetrators of the silencing strategy to see the defiance of their victim everywhere. In this they are dominated by their 'private' level motivation, which is to project their own feelings of being bad or inanimate onto him." The perpetrators exert strong pressures to shut up the victim or cause him to babble, and then denounce him for being stubborn or spiteful. Having been compelled to submit to silence or babbling, the victim learns that he has acquired power in so functioning. "Quite unconsciously the victim has absorbed, despite his conscious resistance, some of the negative feelings projected onto him by his silencers, and he employs these feelings as motives to justify use of his powerful new-found weapon against his silencers," Zuk writes. The therapist must carefully intervene to break up the power struggle between the silencers and the silenced (or babbling) one. Zuk warns that with the silent patient the therapist may himself get involved in a massive silencing strategy; but by judicious mediation and side-taking, he can help extricate both the silencers and the silenced from the family's breakdown of communication.

The go-between process is Zuk's idea of an alternative to the psychoanalytic insight-centered model to effect desirable changes in family therapy. He sees the family and the therapist as antagonists, especially on the questions of whether or not there is really something wrong with the family and what can and should be done about it. "Some families," he writes, "in their eagerness to convince the therapist at the onset that there is nothing wrong with them, will actually bring about some improvement. The change need not be perceived as the result of insight but as a function of the 'bargaining' transaction between family and therapist on the question, 'Is there something wrong with us?' " The family change is calculated, Zuk says, to be the least necessary in order to obtain a change in the therapist's expected position. "By means of judicious siding," Zuk writes, "by taking the role of go-between, or by shifting between these two positions, the therapist hopes to control the 'bargaining' transaction in accordance with his therapeutic goals."

In his work with many families over the years, Zuk has observed two partial paradoxes in their response to therapeutic efforts. One is that the family will work to follow the therapist's direction, but at the same time resist any direction that seems to promise to undermine the status quo. They are saying, in effect, "We want very much to do what you say that we need to do to improve, but don't ask us to do anything that will alter the way things are now." An important aspect of "the way things are now" as the therapist views the pathogenically functioning family is a complete denial of its responsibility for the condition of the "identified patient." One of the difficult jobs of the therapist, as Zuk sees it, is to dispossess the family somehow of its conviction that it is not implicated in the illness of the identified patient.

Zuk's second paradox, a corollary of the first, is that families often say that they really want the identified patient to get better and will do anything the therapist says to help the patient improve, but in actuality they fight the idea that the member's improvement depends in any way on their acceptance of their involvement as a cause of his condition. This, too, calls for subtle maneuvering by the therapist.

In commenting on Zuk's therapeutic theory and practice, Beels and Ferber state that he (like Haley and Jackson, whom they consider in the same general category of "reactor," as distinguished from "conductors" like Ackerman and Satir) seems sometimes theoretically cynical or disingenuously artful in engaging in a kind of power struggle with the family and in devising a strategy by which he will emerge as a covert leader. "The curative agent is the paradoxical manipulation of power," Beels and Ferber write, "so that the therapist lets the family seem to define the situation, but in the end it follows his covert lead." They believe that this is a rather chilling *idea* of the therapist as trickster and is contrary to the warm and concerned work with actual families they have observed Zuk (and also Haley and Jackson) perform.

Zuk, however, thinks that such criticisms of his theory derive from adherence to an outmoded psychoanalytic point of view. He believes that the main struggle today in family therapy is between those who hold to a psychoanalytic model "with their special focus on the exploration of the unconscious, their attempt to reconstruct the historical sequence of pathology, their attachment to such notions as transference and countertransference and Oedipal situations, and attraction to the concept of therapeutic insight" and those who advocate some kind of systems approach. The latter, like Zuk himself, he says, center their attention on "comprehending sources of power and leverage in the immediate field of action," have a preference for explanation not tied to a linear cause-and-effect relationship "but rather put in terms of negative and positive feedback," and believe that insight is not necessary for therapeutic change "but rather that change may be an outcome of the bargaining or negotiation that goes on between therapist and family members."

BELL'S FAMILY GROUP THERAPY

John Elderkin Bell, a California psychologist, may be considered, along with Nathan Ackerman and C. F. Midelfort (discussed in *Psychoanalysis and Psychotherapy: 36 Systems*), one of the actual founders of family therapy. He calls his form of therapy "family group therapy" because he conceives of it as the application of small-group theory from social psychology to the natural group of the family. In his words, "The therapy which led to the development of the theory and which is also, in its later stages an outgrowth of theory, is an effort to apply knowledge of the operation of small groups to the production of change in the family unit."

Bell defines the working family group in therapy as children about nine and older (younger ones usually can't handle the verbal and intellectual demands of therapeutic communication), the parents, and any other individuals (not necessarily biologically related) who constitute the functioning group in the household. He emphasizes that anyone who is excluded is likely to work against changes that are being effected in therapy.

Once he has defined the family group and its problems, Bell insists on full attendance on the basis that the group cannot be changed unless it is dealt with as a whole. He postpones meetings in case a member cannot attend, and he refuses to be drawn into individual consultations with any of the family members. All relations between him and family members must be in the group and tuned into by all of them. He does not engage in activities other than therapy with the family in whole or in part. He likewise avoids taking over functions that any member performs or may be expected to perform for the family. In short, he functions in relation to the identified family group in a way calculated to strengthen it as a group.

Bell sees his primary task as examining the interactions among family members to see how these can be more effectively handled. He sets up procedures to analyze problems and the factors that create them and to develop and test solutions to the problems. Much of Bell's role at first, even in identifying and analyzing the family's problems (and later in working toward solutions), is to help expand and improve communication between family members. "An immediate task," he has written, "is to put into words what before has been left unexpressed or said in such circuitous ways that its meaning has not been transmitted." But unlike some forms of therapy which imply that communication is somehow a great value in and of itself, Bell's therapy uses increased family communication only as a method toward accomplishing the task of solving the family problems.

In the Bell system of family therapy, the therapist must develop and maintain a clear definition and presentation of his own functions in order to promote participation of family members. By providing as unambiguous a model as possible, he facilitates the group's ability to structure itself into a functioning conference. Social action is patterned after the therapist's own methods of participation. In Bell's words, "He conducts relationships—now with one, now with two, now with all—in the presence of the others. He disrupts unsatisfactory patterns of relationship as he permits individuals to reaffirm old intentions that have been frustrated. He calls up new intentions. He encourages the family to clarify its goals, to choose more appropriate group goals for the whole family and more suitable personal goals for use in life outside the family's direct involvement." The therapist is seen as an agent who works to begin and maintain a problem-solving program. Bell writes that the therapist "works with the family on the means of study and of problem solving. Consistent with keeping outside the family group, he does not determine the goals for the family nor make its decisions for it. He helps them into the position where they recognize their goals and are free to make such decisions as are demanded in the movement towards attaining them."

Bell has found that most families are concerned with reaching goals represented in their present value systems rather than stretching for new values. They want the experience of success in achieving known goals before considering new ideas about family life. The most immediate and pressing goal of the family in treatment, of course, is to emerge safely from its present crisis.

In dealing first with the crisis and then gradually with less acutely pressing problems, Bell relates to family members and encourages them to relate to him in a way that demonstrates to the family that it can be more flexible in the roles and functions it permits its members; more open, direct, and clear in its communication; and more disciplined in its choice and forms of relationships. The therapist, Bell writes, "prevents any family members from evading the implications of their relationships with him and others. He demonstrates forms of relationship that can be transferred to other interactions in the family. This leads the family to the conviction that change is possible and desirable and may bring about a greater measure of behaviour that the family would interpret as positive."

Because he is an outsider, the therapist can elicit from family members kinds of behavior (what he calls public patterns, as differentiated from familial patterns) that they ordinarily would be anxious about using only in the presence of one another. As he brings out such "new" behavior, the family members are forced to alter stereotyped conceptions they have about one another. And as they respond to each other with new attitudes, they are changing their own ways of functioning. In Bell's words, "together they test out, thereby, potentialities for relationship, incorporating changes that prove useful, and rejecting those that fail."

Bell believes that his form of therapy encourages a family to develop its own potential for change, which not only comes out in the course of treatment but also helps the family to carry on in problem-solving and behavior-improving ways subsequent to treatment. As the family members consolidate changed patterns that they have developed in the treatment situation, they work together to inhibit their former patterns. Thus both the individual and the group changes in an interacting process. All these changes depend on the presence and control of the therapist, who uses his own personal and social skills to help the family achieve a type of relationship that has much greater satisfaction for each family member and for the external community.

SUMMARY

In conjoint family therapy, discussed in this and the next chapter, most (and often all) sessions include most (and often all) family members in a single collection. Conjoint family therapy differs from both individual and group psychotherapy because its major emphasis is on changes in the family system rather than in the individual. It nevertheless partially derives from group psychotherapy (and to some extent marriage counseling).

Of the four outstanding family therapists considered in this chapter, Nathan Ackerman, recently deceased, was the earliest and most notable. He placed great emphasis on the importance of diagnosis, feeling this was the only route toward a scientific and manageable discipline rather than an expression of idiosyncratic talent. However, he was, as he often admitted, largely frustrated in working out a stable classificatory system. Ackerman saw his role as beyond simply clear evaluation or diagnosis of the specific problems; he wished to help the family achieve a clearer definition of the real content of conflict, to counteract inappropriate displacements of conflict, to neutralize the irrational prejudices and scapegoating that are involved in the displacement of conflict, to relieve an excessive load of conflict on one victimized part of the family, to lift concealed interpersonal conflicts to the level of interpersonal relations, to activate an improved quality of emotional complementarity in family role relationships, and to replace the lacks in the patterns of family interaction through the appropriate and selective use of the therapist's own personality.

Although Ackerman was active, open, and forthright in his approach, his style was simple and casual in initiating an interview. He believed in a flexible and undefensive use of the therapist's self rather than involved explanations in getting down immediately to problem solving with the family.

Virginia Satir's therapeutic approach is similar to Ackerman's in that she takes a direct, vigorous, and authoritative entrance into sessions with family members. She relies, however, much less on nonverbal communication and unconscious cues and is articulate in communicating her therapeutic methods to others.

Teaching the family to communicate is seen by Satir as the therapist's most important concern. To this end she uses such techniques as compilation of a family life chronology, the introduction of new concepts such as that of differentness, the importance of mature communication between children and parents, and better ways of coping with pain and disagreement. Successful treatment is considered to be completed when the family members are better able to understand and cope with one another in positive ways.

In his triadic-based family therapy, Gerald Zuk uses go-between and side-taker roles in his efforts to dislodge pathogenic relating. This process is his alternative to the psychoanalytic dyadic insight-centered model to explain desirable changes that may occur in family therapy. He sees the family and the therapist as antagonists, especially on the questions of whether or not there is really something wrong with the family and what can and should be done about it. Zuk, in his aggressive therapy, helps the family accept the responsibility for its state of imbalance and/or for the problems of an identified patient and thus to be able to effect positive changes.

John E. Bell defines his working family therapy group as consisting of children (usually nine and older), parents, and any other individuals who are part of the functioning household group. This group, once defined, is required to be in attendance at all sessions, and Bell relates to group members only in the presence of the rest of the group.

Much of Bell's emphasis, especially early in therapy, is on communication as the necessary method toward accomplishing the task of solving family problems. In dealing with the family group and its problems, Bell relates to family members in a way that enables them to learn to be more flexible in the roles and functions they permit one another, more open, direct, and clear in their communication, and more disciplined in their choice and forms of relationships.

SELECTED READINGS

ACKERMAN, NATHAN W., "Family Diagnosis and Therapy," in Jules H. Masserman, *Current Psychiatric Therapies*, Vol. 3. New York: Grune & Stratton, 1963.

———, "Family Psychotherapy and Psychoanalysis: The Implications of Difference," in Nathan W. Ackerman, ed., *Family Process*. New York: Basic Books, 1970.

———, "The Growing Edge of Family Therapy," in C. J. Sager and H. S. Kaplan, eds., *Progress in Group and Family Therapy*. New York: Brunner/Mazel, 1972.

BEELS, C. C., and ANDREW FERBER, "What Family Therapists Do," in Andrew Ferber, Marilyn Mendelsohn, and Augustus Napier, *The Book of Family Therapy*. New York: Science House, 1972.

BELL, JOHN E., "A Theoretical Position for Family Group Therapy," in Ackerman, ed., *Family Process*.

———, *Family Group Therapy*. Washington, D.C.: U.S. Dept. of Health, Education and Welfare (Pub. Health Monograph No. 64), 1961.

———, "Recent Advances in Family Group Therapy," in John G. Howells, *Theory and Practice of Family Psychiatry*. New York: Brunner/Mazel, 1971.

BLOCH, DONALD A., *Techniques of Family Psychotherapy: A Primer*. New York: Grune & Stratton, 1973.

FRAMO, J. L., ed., *Family Interaction: A Dialogue Between Family Researchers and Family Therapists*. New York: Springer, 1972.

SATIR, VIRGINIA, *Conjoint Family Therapy: A Guide to Theory and Technique.* Palo Alto, Cal.: Science & Behavior Books, 1964.

ZUK, GERALD H., *Family Therapy: A Triadic-Based Approach.* New York: Behavioral Publications, 1971.

2

FAMILY
THERAPIES

A Variety of Systems

In this chapter, we will take a look at what imagination and industry can produce in the way of fruitful proliferation of methods of working with families. All of the systems described herein have shown promise, and some have preliminary research to substantiate the clinical optimism of their practitioners. None, like the four approaches we examined in the previous chapter, has clearly proved the superiority of their theories and techniques to those of other therapeutic systems.

Although he is not alone in having made an effort to apply the principles of behavior theory to family therapy, R. P. Liberman makes a cogent case for it. His is the first system to be treated in this chapter.

We then move to the earliest and most-cited team approach to family therapy. The leader of this particular application of psychological, psychiatric, and social work principles to work with families is Robert MacGregor. The term applied to the system is "multiple impact therapy."

Next we view what Ross V. Speck calls "social network intervention." Speck and his co-therapists assemble all relatives, friends, and neighbors of the problem-presenting family who seem to have a significant influence on that family. This is the social network and the "treatable entity" with which Speck and his associates deal. It is only with families in crisis that social network therapy is undertaken.

Another type of crisis intervention on a somewhat less massive scale was developed in the mid-sixties at the Colorado Psychiatric Hospital by D. G. Langsley and D. M. Kaplan. Crisis family therapy, designed to be brief and immediate and to open the way for families to handle their own problems and (where needed) more effectively to use the long-term facilities of the community, varies with the particular crisis of the particular family; the training, personalities, and therapeutic philosophy of the intervening professionals; the kind and policies of the institution they represent, and other factors. These conditions make crisis family therapy difficult to describe, but certain generalizations about the work of Langsley and Kaplan are presented.

The last type of family therapy that we inspect is a system which treats four or five hospitalized patients and their families in a group. What was started by H. P. Laqueur and his associates as an expedient in a hospital situation in which there was an insufficient number of family therapists soon developed into a treatment of choice. The term Laqueur uses to designate this type of treatment is, logically enough, "multiple family therapy."

BEHAVIORAL FAMILY THERAPY

Robert Paul Liberman, a California psychiatrist, has applied many of the theories and procedures of behavior therapy to working with families. He believes that typically, families that seek treatment have dealt with the maladaptive and deviant behavior of one or more family members by responding to it for a long time with such things as sympathy, anger, babying, nagging, and other forms of attention that have had the effect of reinforcing the deviance. Even superficially punitive behavior thus can come through to the deviant family member as positive concern and interest—the message that is transmitted is, in effect, "You will get our special attention as long as you continue to misbehave." Sometimes such behavior is produced with full awareness (here the patient is viewed therapeutically as "consciously manipulative"), and sometimes it occurs without the individual's insight and is therefore considered unconsciously motivated. In either case it can often be difficult to eradicate because of the perpetuation of intermittent reinforcement from the family (and sometimes from school and other sources).

Liberman therefore defines the behavioral approach to family therapy in terms of changing the contingencies by which the patient gets acknowledgment and concern from other members of his family. The therapist can set up conditions by which social reinforcement (verbal and nonverbal means of giving attention and recognition—what is called "strokes" in transactional analysis) is made contingent on desired behavior instead of the continuation of symptomatic behavior. He writes, "It is the task of the therapist in collaboration with the family or couple to (1) specify the maladaptive behavior, (2) choose reasonable goals which are alternative, adaptive behaviors, (3) direct and guide the family to change the contingencies of their social reinforcement patterns from maladaptive to adaptive target behaviors."

In applying behavior theory to family therapy, Liberman has emphasized three major areas of concern: the creation and maintenance of a positive therapeutic alliance which permits the therapist to function as an effective social reinforcer and model; the diagnosis of the family problems in behavioral terms; and the implementation of the behavioral principles of reinforcement and modeling in the context of ongoing interpersonal interactions.

Regarding the need for what he calls a positive therapeutic alliance with the family, Liberman differs from some behavior therapists who have tended to minimize the importance of the patient-therapist relationship. He considers that accurate empathy, nonpossessive warmth, and genuine concern are necessary attributes in behavior therapy as well as in other types of approaches to patients and their families. Although some critics of behavior therapy have suggested that his is a kind of teaching-machine approach to personality change, Liberman stresses that just as in other modalities, therapists who are applying behavior theory to family therapy are most effective when they express themselves in a comfortable, human style.

In making his behavioral evaluation, Liberman asks each family member in turn what changes he would like to see in others in the family and how he would like to be different himself. Using the answers to these questions as a guide, he is able to make a careful choice of specific behavioral goals.

At the next point in his behavioral or functional analysis, Liberman looks for the environmental and interpersonal contingencies that currently support the problematic behavior that is causing the problem. "The mutual patterns of social reinforcement in the family," he says, "deserve special scrutiny in this analysis since their deciphering and clarification become central to an understanding of the case and to the formulation of therapeutic strategy." Behavioral analysis does not end after the initial sessions, but continues throughout the course of therapy as problem behaviors themselves change. "New sources of reinforcement for the patient and family members must be assessed. In this sense, the behavioral approach to family therapy is dynamic."

Among the tactics Liberman employs for reinforcement are role playing (sometimes called behavioral rehearsal) and shaping. The latter is a process developed in operant conditioning where gradual approximation to the desired behavior are reinforced by the therapist (with approval and spontaneous and genuine interest). Liberman uses modeling as a behavior therapy method in his work with families. The model may be either the therapist or a family member held in esteem by the patient. If the model demonstrates the desired adaptive behavior and is observed to receive positive reinforcement for this behavior from others, the patient is likely to imitate him. In Liberman's words, "the amount of observational learning will be governed by the degree to which a family member pays attention to the modeling cues, has the capacity to process and rehearse the causes, and possesses the necessary components in his behavioral experience which can be combined to reproduce the more complex, currently modeled behavior."

The third area of technical concern emphasized by Liberman is the choice and implementation of the interpersonal transactions between the therapist and family members and among the family members that are best designed to alter the problem behavior in a more adaptive direction. He views these tactics of treatment implementation as "behavioral change experiments" in which the therapist and family "re-program the contingencies of reinforcement" operating in the family system. "The behavioral change experiments consist of family members responding to each other in various ways, with the responses contingent on more desired reciprocal ways of relating."

Liberman contends that the experimental nature of the behavioral approach to family therapy is one of its greatest strengths. Unlike the psychoanalytic approach in which he feels that there is a tendency for the therapist to view failures as caused by patients who are inappropriate candidates for the technique, the behavioral approach places the burden on the therapist to devise more effective treatment. In addition to thus being potentially more effective for greater numbers of patients, the behavioral approach is seen as being faster and less likely to bring about the adventitious reinforcement of contradictory behavior patterns. The latter is true because of the more systematic and specific guidelines of behavior therapy as compared with most other approaches.

Like other family therapists who are moving toward a total systems approach, Liberman's behaviorally oriented family therapist does not restrict himself to the here and now of the therapy sessions, but is also involved in collaboration with adjunctive agencies such as schools, rehabilitation services, medication, and work settings.

Although Liberman admits that many of his contentions about a behavioral approach to family therapy remain to be proved by systematic research he has the hope that "further clinical and research progress made by behaviorally oriented therapists will challenge all family therapists, regardless of theoretical leanings, to specify more clearly their interventions, their goals, and their empirical results."

MULTIPLE IMPACT THERAPY

Robert MacGregor, a psychologist, and his former associates at the University of Texas Medical Branch Hospital in Galveston, Texas, have developed a method for treating families with a disturbed adolescent in crisis which they call "multiple impact therapy" (MIT). MacGregor has referred to MIT as a kind of expanded intake procedure which involves the insinuation of a whole orthopsychiatric team into the family group in a way that communicates a strong helping force for the family. MIT tries to utilize and assist the natural processes in the patient and the family to move toward improved functioning.

Before beginning multiple impact therapy with a family, there is a thorough orientation of the referring agency and other persons in the community who have worked with the adolescent or the family (probation officer, physician, etc.). The MIT team assembles before the family arrives, speculates freely on the data at hand, and makes tentative plans as to what team member will see which family member individually after the initial team-family conference.

Two and a half days are reserved for MIT (although usually the work is accomplished in two days), and the "impact" starts in a team-family conference early in the morning of the first day. The family includes parents, the adolescent primary patient, siblings and other relatives (when deemed relevant), and often a community representative who has worked closely with the patient and family. The MIT team may include psychologists, psychiatrists, other physicians, social workers, ministers, and others.

After opening pleasantries in this first conference, one team member often offers a challenging statement such as, for example, his conception of the family's tendency to overprotect and infantilize the adolescent. Questions, comments, and retorts are likely to ensue that enable the team to show the family how defective communication often underlies the inadequate social development of a person like the patient. If the family is still reluctant to talk (which happens in some instances), the team members may engage in a pointed discussion of the family or team-family problems. This almost invariably brings family participation in a "corrective" initiation of their points of view.

However this first collective interview goes, plans for seeing each family member individually (including possible alterations in who is going to see whom, based on what has happened in the initial meeting) are discussed by the team in the presence of the family. MacGregor reports that family members usually show relief that they are going to be given an opportunity to have private interviews with the therapists. He also indicates that it is important that private conferences other than the scheduled ones not occur between therapists and that all changes in evaluation and strategy occur out in the open.   After the individual interviews have progressed for a while, there is usually an overlapping session in which the interviewer of the teenager joins the interview of one or another of the parents. The original therapist of the parent reviews for the teenager's therapist what has been learned, and the parent has the opportunity to listen to the summary and make corrections and clarifications. The entering therapist comments on how this material fits in with what he has learned from the teenager.

At the end of these interviews family members are told that the team will talk about the whole situation at lunch, and they are encouraged to do likewise. The afternoon starts with individual interviews with switched personnel (very often the wife's therapist of the morning becomes the husband's of the afternoon and vice versa). The adolescent patient (and siblings, if any) are kept busy during the afternoon with tests and further interviewing so that the parents feel free to focus on their individual and interactional problems. Overlapping sessions like the one mentioned earlier become more frequent in the pursuit of certain interpretations and understandings.

Late in the first day all of the team and the family are reassembled. In MacGregor's words, this conference has the following purpose: "Whereas the family members in individual or multiple-therapist situations may have maintained a resistive attitude toward team members, they now face each other as well. Team members, by openly telling of revised attitudes about the family and their situation, provide a climate for change. This is often furthered by a therapist's accepting from others, or offering as self-criticism, information on how his own involvement in the material interfered with understanding."

The pattern of the second morning is a variation on the procedures of the first afternoon. The family often has emotionally charged material to offer from reflections and attempted discussion of their evening together. Most of this material is dealt with in individual conferences (although a team-family conference may be called). The emphasis of the individual therapeutic sessions is on dealing with factors that interfere with family communication in general and with husband-wife intimate communication in particular.

The second afternoon often starts with each individual returning to a conference with the therapist with whom he began. This session deals with what has been learned by the patient and the therapist about family members and interactions; each person then discusses what he thinks are the next steps. This afternoon's work, according to MacGregor, is directed toward a final team-family conference. "By that time the relevant recurring patterns tend to be sufficiently well into awareness so that their repetition yields suitable warning signals to all. Normal convergence of dynamic interpretations has been aided by a noon staff conference with supervisors of psychotherapy."

Specific questions about practical procedures to be followed until the follow-up visit (two to six months later) are dealt with in the final conference. Although occasionally after two days the outlook is not promising and the extra half day is invoked, in general families are given a vote of confidence by the therapists by being put on their own after two days to apply what they have learned.

Research to date indicates that this method of treatment has effective and durable results. Beels and Ferber have written that MIT "is a very intensive, powerful experience—historical, prescriptive, and future-oriented. The team brings to bear the power of their number, the solidarity and depth of their relationships to each other, and their experience with their own and other families. They are explicitly conveying the values of the culture, as well as the understanding of the idiosyncratic position from which the family starts."

SOCIAL NETWORK INTERVENTION

Psychiatrist Ross V. Speck and his associates have developed a massive approach to family therapy. Most of their work in this new form has been in situations where problems of schizophrenia have developed, but Speck has also recommended this type of treatment with troubled and depressed adolescents. A problem of considerable and pressing family and community concern is obviously needed to assemble the large group of people involved in this form of therapy.

Speck has defined a social network as "that group of persons who maintain an ongoing significance in each other's lives by fulfilling specific human needs." In social network intervention Speck and his associates assemble all relatives, friends, and neighbors of the problem-presenting family who seem to have a significant influence on that family. The meetings are held in the family's home, and they usually involve about forty people. These people meet with a team of "network interveners" (three or more people), each of whom knows the others and their ways of working well enough to do a coordinated job.

The role of the leader in social network intervention has been compared to that of a director of a theatrical production. In the words of Speck and Attneave, the leader needs "a sense of timing, empathy with emotional highpoints, a sense of group moods and undercurrents, and some charismatic presence." He should also have the ability to delegate and diffuse responsibility, efface himself, and give network members the glow of accomplishment that they are really running things themselves (which soon, to some extent, they are).

Similar characteristics are desirable in other team members. In addition, where several generations are involved in a network intervention therapy session, a team member from both ends of the age continuum is desirable. Youth and the elderly tend to be distrustful of a group of people who seem to them to be too old and too young, respectively.

Goals of network intervention have been variously stated, but include the creation of conditions for a climate of trust and openness among all assembled, a facilitation of interpersonal relationships that will continue after the meetings, the strengthening of bonds and the loosening of binds, the opening up of new perceptions and communication channels, and the activation of latent strengths within the network and various groups (including the original family) within the network.

Creating a group atmosphere conducive to improved interaction has led Speck and his associates to utilize encounter group techniques with their emphasis on feeling and nonverbal communication. As Speck and Attneave have written, "Not only are the nonverbal reactions of the group extremely sensitive cues and clues for the intervention team, but when the team plays upon them to build a nonverbal network experiences a ritual takes place." The network members get a sense of union from things like handclasping in a circle and huddling like a football team and a release of tension from running and jumping and shouting.

Although there have been some variations in the number and length of meetings held by Speck and his co-workers, six evening sessions of about four hours each have often been held. They are generally spaced a week apart.

The nuclear family with the family member or members around whom the crisis is centered are given the responsibility for the arrangement of space and the extending of invitations to immediate family members, relatives, friends, and neighbors who have any interest or involvement in the crisis. There is usually no difficulty in assembling "the tribe" because the crises are usually so grave (schizophrenic breakdown, flagrant drug abuse, murderous assaults or threats, depression with suicidal attempts or threats, etc.) that hospitalization or police intervention are the only alternatives. The invited people are told that the purpose of the tribal meeting is to help the nuclear family in its crisis and that professional persons will be present to assist them in working out solutions to the problems related to the crisis.

Out of pre-network discussions with the family (when it is first determined by the psychotherapist that network intervention will be undertaken), information is gathered that provides the basis for the network team's construction of strategy for the first meeting. A usual procedure is to have a short pre-session in which the therapists install the tape recorder, mix with the incoming group members as well as the immediate family, listen to gossip, and generally acquire further information about the group. The therapeutic team members provide feedback to the leader regarding what they learn, including information about moods and subgroupings.

In Speck and Rueveni's typical network meetings, their procedure is to act as co-therapists with two to four other professionals as consultants. The consultants are often in training as network therapists, but also function as reporters and mixers in the fashion described in the foregoing paragraph. "The network members are told at the beginning that this is not similar to most conventional psychotherapies, that we are dealing with the tribe, that there are no secrets or collusions which will be treated in a confidential manner," Speck and Rueveni report. When confidences are made during one-to-one relationships with the therapists during or between sessions, they are broken as quickly as possible by the therapists in order to make network communication constantly as overt as it can be.

After a brief introduction by the leader, the tribe is often divided into two concentric circles. The inner group, usually composed of eight or ten of the younger and more outgoing persons quickly selected by the therapists, is instigated into action by the leader along discussional lines. (There have already been warm-up encounter group activities of a nonverbal sort for the whole tribe.) Such questions as "How many of you have used drugs?", "What is it you think the older people of this tribe fail to understand?", and "What do you think is *really* wrong with this family?" get the discussion going and often polarize issues along generational lines or in some other way dramatize the tensions that exist. The idea is to increase tension, for this leads to deeper interpersonal involvement and tribe commitment. When tension between the two groups becomes very strong, a process of synthesis occurs in which the cohesiveness of the whole tribe is achieved. In the words of Speck and

Rueveni, "When the outer group says that the inner group is superficial, a negation dialectic is set up so that it provokes the inner group to try harder. The interaction between inner group and outer group makes the outer group try harder in turn. This forces all persons to try to heal each other." When one synthesis has been achieved, the therapists push on to a new polarity with a dialectic that sets up a movement again toward a new synthesis. Each polarization is designed to move deeper into the conflicts and issues faced by the tribe.

Speck and his associates have found that in every network some members (whom they call activists) will assume leadership roles and help to keep the network plugging away at its problems. Professionals have to be flexible enough to turn responsibilities over to the activists and remain more in the background themselves as consultants.

Although the practice is not as common as that of creating a new social network via the group meeting method, network intervention sometimes utilizes pre-existing groups which possess the necessary membership variety. Minority groups in our society sometimes depend upon tribal-style assemblies, and occasionally a family in distress will be intimately related to a tribelike group within a church or temple. Sometimes, though rarely, block organizations serve as networks. Peer networks of adolescents and work associations are also sometimes used.

Therapists who employ the tribal approach contend that there is an important phenomenon, largely nonverbal and unconscious, which accounts for much of the impact of network intervention. They call this the "network effect" and compare it to the kind of euphoric high that is found at revival meetings, peace marches, civil rights activities, tribal healing ceremonies, and other such gatherings where a kind of mystical, hypnotic spell knits people closer together. The network effect is a turn-on phenomenon of group interaction that begins once members realize that they are now part of a special human cluster. The members of the network become involved with one another in new ways, with new feelings and a new sense of common bond.

This leads us into the most pertinent criticism of network intervention: namely, that the therapeutic effect may be as transitory as the network effect. There seems to be no doubt that most of the participants in these tribal gatherings emerge from the series of meetings with better understandings and more accepting feelings toward other members of the tribe. But do the good results last or are they as ephemeral as the new understandings and comradeship that follow upon the achievement of other types of "highs"? Network intervention has not been going on long enough in a sufficient variety of situations to answer that question. Even if it had, there has been no precision research designed to measure the therapeutic effects over a long time span.

It is only fair to state, however, that the desirable effects of network therapy are not necessarily temporary. It is possible that some of the changes that are begun in these sessions gain momentum and keep moving in a way that helps the participants to steer around some future problems and deal more adequately with those that are unavoidable. Such problem-solving momentum might particularly be maintained with the nuclear family around whose distress the tribe was originally assembled. The spotlight of attention and caring and problem solving may be sufficiently intense for this group to keep it and its members functioning more adequately in post-network times ahead.

CRISIS INTERVENTION

Donald G. Langsley, a psychiatrist, and David M. Kaplan, a psychologist, are usually credited with the development of the first extensive treatment of families in crisis with the establishment of the Family Treatment Unit at Colorado Psychiatric Hospital in 1964. Crisis therapy was used by them and their associates for families which included a member who would ordinarily be admitted for immediate treatment to a mental hospital. Their intervention in the family situation was based on the assumption that the removal of an individual from his family to a hospital was more likely to complicate than aid the situation. Placement of the troubled individual in a hospital, as Langsley has said, "removes one member from a family, permits extrusion and scapegoating and avoids the family problem which may have precipitated the crisis. This action denies that the family can be helped to solve its own problems."

As the term implies, crisis family therapy is designed to be brief and immediate. The goals are to help the family resolve the crisis and if possible to help the family member whose condition had suggested hospitalization to return to functioning at his previous level of adaptation. Though referrals may be made for longer-term therapy for individuals within the family, the duration of the crisis intervention is usually only a few weeks and half a dozen visits (at least one of which is a home visit).

The particular nature of a crisis intervention depends on the context of the particular family; the crisis within which the family finds itself; the training, personalities, and therapeutic philosophy of the intervening professionals; the kind of institution they represent and its policies; and many other circumstances. In this examination of some of the points made by family crisis therapists, it would be desirable for us to keep in mind the caution of Richard Rabkin, a prominent New York psychiatrist who is involved in both family crisis therapeutic training and practice: "Crisis intervention can probably be taught only by example. The usual supervisory method in which the student and teacher meet once a week and student works with the family" is too dangerous in crisis work. Rabkin likens it to turning a medical student loose in major surgery with the injunction that he should come back and talk to his supervisor about it the next week. In his words, "there is no hope of teaching crisis intervention unless it is possible for people to see a competent crisis intervention team *at work.*"

We obviously cannot provide an opportunity for readers of this book to see a crisis intervention team at work. The best we can do is to summarize some of the work of professional people who have engaged in this modality.

One thing they agree upon has already been suggested: namely, that crisis intervention requires a team effort. The intensity and the variability of the demands are too great for one person to handle alone. Rabkin indicates that a full 80 percent of crisis intervention is simple go-between or brokerage work and that the other 20 percent is too specific to the particular situation to warrant generalization. He points out that it is necessary to know whom to call for what sort of problems—schools, social agencies, churches, city and state and federal departments and bureaus, employment and unemployment resources. It is also important for the therapeutic team to know its own limitations and the limitations of the crisis intervention approach well enough to realize *when* as well as where to turn for help from outside sources.

It is evident that crisis intervention does not deal with the vague and mysterious. Concepts like "mental illness," "Oedipal conflict," and "depth causation" are of little concern to the family crisis therapist. Specific, soluble problems that people have with each other and with their social institutions constitute the main focus of this kind of therapy. There is much more concern about the things family members do (and how these things relate to the crisis) than about uncovering reasons as to why they do them. From the first, the family is made aware of the short-term nature of the intervention, but is told that the team will be available for future crises (which presumably both the team and the family are interested in preventing if possible).

Langsley and Kaplan have outlined family crisis treatment under seven main headings: immediate aid, defining the crisis as a family problem, focus on the current crisis, general prescription, specific prescription, identification of role conflicts and renegotiation, and management of future crises. The material that follows is a brief summary of the way family crisis therapy proceeded within these seven categories at the Colorado Family Treatment Unit.

Therapy began as soon as the family was accepted for treatment. The patient (and whatever family members were present) was seen immediately and told help would be available on a 24-hour basis.

From the first contact the idea was conveyed that the problem involved the whole family. The therapist implemented this definition by quickly calling together all available family members for the first meeting. Other caretakers (like ministers, physicians, and social workers) who had been involved were also immediately contacted and invited to work with the intervention team and to continue their relationship with the family after the crisis.

Very early in the first session, the therapist focused the family's attention on the specific nature of the current crisis. Missing details or distortions in the picture painted by the identified patient were usually corrected by other family members (especially children, who are less inclined to keep family secrets). Areas of agreement, disagreement, and distortion were likely to be revealed in this first meeting, which was quickly (usually within 12 hours) followed by another. Also within the first 24 to 36 hours, the treatment team scheduled a visit to the family home, regarding which Langsley and Kaplan reported: "This is especially valuable in observing parent-child interaction. Information about the family composition and family functioning is obtained in the home which may be overlooked or unavailable at a family group session in our own offices." They believed it also reinforced the therapeutic alliance, for the family tended to be convinced by the home visit that the therapists really did care.

As far as what Langsley and Kaplan call the "general prescription" is concerned, the goal of family crisis therapy is to reduce the level of tension and upset in the family that is inevitably associated with bringing one of its members to a mental hospital; also to interfere with regression; point out to the rest of the family that the psychotic symptoms of the identified patient represent his attempts to communicate (which communications the therapists will interpret for the rest of the family); and to encourage more adaptive behavior and more adaptive styles of communication. Drug medication is also used at this stage for family members if it is needed.

The "specific prescription" depends, of course, on the nature of the crisis. Langsley and Kaplan could hypothesize that a series of events had brought about a change in family equilibrium (due, perhaps, to a change in role performance of some member or a change in circumstances requiring a new role—e.g., a physical illness on the part of one family member) and that this had led to the decompensation of a susceptible family member. Family tasks would be proposed that were directed toward the resolution of the specific crisis. Whenever possible, the task would be an activity in which the whole family could participate, and this would help the family to focus on the task rather than on the symptoms and the conflicts.

By the time the therapy reached the stage of identification of role conflicts and renegotiation, the calming effects of emotional support, reassurance, drugs, and catharsis hopefully had changed the clinical picture. By about the middle of the third week (although the therapists reported that there was considerable variation in both directions on the time length), contacts with the family (phone calls as well as visits) began to taper off as each member became aware of his responsibility to the family as a unit and saw the significant effect of his actions upon other family members. "The focus at this point may shift from the symptomatic member of the family (the identified patient) to a family member who is able and willing to make compromises. The family is confronted as a group with their responsibility for compromise and change to meet and cope with whatever the new problem may be."

As far as the management of future crises is concerned, Langsley and Kaplan and their associates dealt with any long-term individual or interactional problems by referral to other therapists or agencies. They also felt in many instances that the family itself had taken a first step toward more adaptive management of crises with at least the minimum understanding that future difficulties could be handled in other ways than putting a family member in the hospital. The therapists also emphasized that in case future crises turned out not to be manageable by the family even with the help of outside agency help (in case any was provided), the Family Treatment Unit would respond to a call for help. They told the family that, in any case, they would be in touch from time to time for research purposes.

Such research, incidentally, has demonstrated that the crisis therapy of the Colorado unit succeeded quite well in its fundamental aim of avoiding hospitalization and the attendant promotion of regression and chronicity. An 18-month follow-up study comparing patients who were part of families treated by the Family Treatment Unit with carefully matched patients who had been hospitalized according to standard procedures showed only half the number of days spent in the hospital by the experimental group. The studies have also indicated that the family crisis therapeutic method tends to blunt some of the weapon value of symptoms and to help families to find less drastic (financially and otherwise) methods than hospitalization to deal with future crises.

Salvador Minuchin and Avner Barcai have extended the idea of family crisis therapy by emphasizing the desirability, in certain cases, of capitalizing on accidentally occurring crises and, as well, by actually inducing crises in families with which they are working. These therapists point out that crisis is defined as a situation that presents elements so different from the usual that the family is forced to change in order to deal adequately with the situation. This means that crisis presents the opportunity for change and can be precipitated by the therapists in case it fails to develop out of the existing situation; they induce change from within the family by forcibly entering the system and temporarily rendering it unstable. They then remain as interim regulators and negotiaters while preparing the family for a more autonomous existence. In at least the first week of this type of intervention, Minuchin and Barcai report seeing the family several times a week and for sessions ranging between three and four and a half hours.

MULTIPLE-FAMILY THERAPY

H. Peter Laqueur, a psychiatrist and the inventor of "multiple family therapy" (MFT), has written that it was developed out of necessity. Finding an insufficient number of therapists available to conduct family therapy sessions in the state hospital where he was working, Laqueur and his associates started treating four or five hospitalized patients and their families in a group. What started as an expedient developed into a treatment of choice as Lacqueur and his colleagues came to believe that MFT could induce desirable changes in interactional patterns faster and more effectively than was usually possible with single-family treatment.

Particularly when there is a schizophrenic member of a family being treated (which was generally the case in the families about which Laqueur has reported), MFT provides a better setting than single-family therapy, Laqueur believes, because the presence of other families and other hospitalized patients stimulates the schizophrenic person to struggle more actively toward self-differentiation and independence rather than clinging to the symbiotic relationship to his family that has probably contributed in a major degree to the development of his illness.

Laqueur also speaks of a kind of code of communication peculiar to each family and of distorted language of schizophrenic persons. He finds other families useful as "translators" between therapist and a particular family and other schizophrenics helpful in the same way between therapist and a particular patient (and sometimes also to make meanings clearer between a patient and his own family).

After the initial MFT situation in a New York hospital, Dr. Laqueur moved to Vermont, where he has continued to practice the MFT techniques. When he brings together four or five families (from his own private practise or referred to him through the community mental health clinic or the hospital), he explains to them that their problems will be dealt with jointly (but each family is to feel free to return or not after the first session and to talk only when they feel comfortable in talking); and that each family will be treated as if each family member needs help as much as the one officially referred as "the patient."

Families are mixed as much as possible in educational and socioeconomic backgrounds. Laqueur believes in a random mixture, for people of very similar backgrounds tend to be superficial and sterile in their interactions. "The daughter of a taxidriver and the son of a professor," Laqueur has written, "can cause their parents much more efficiently to talk about parent-child relations than pre-programmed people of similar backgrounds."

MFT families that do not drop out in the first several sessions are likely to stay for the duration of treatment. Twelve months was the length of time required for termination by the therapist in some government research groups with which Laqueur worked, but he thinks eighteen or more months are necessary before most families are ready to be sent out on their own. He reports that most families go through such stages as first wondering why they are in the group and how it can help them to talk about their problems in front of other families with problems, then finding understanding and emotional support from at least one other family in the group (which reduces the pain of exposing their problems), and finally facing the quite painful realization that they are causing many of their own difficulties.

Laqueur has enumerated some of the mechanisms of change he believes are involved in MFT. First, as mentioned in the foregoing quote, the MFT therapist makes use of less disturbed families as co-therapists. Because all families in the group have one problem in common (a person officially declared seriously disturbed), MFT offers them an opportunity in this frame of reference to improve communications and achieve better understanding. Under these circumstances, one family is likely to be accepting (after initial resistance) of another family in the co-therapeutic role.

Second, Laqueur believes that competition among several families in the MFT system produces changes faster in the earlier stages of treatment. Cooperation replaces competition in later stages.

Third, MFT helps to communicate the idea that an individual family member must be understood in terms of his behavior in the context of the actions, reactions, and general behavior of other people in his environment. "The therapist uses this concept of the field of interacting forces to bring into the open the feelings, problems, and needs of participants that had previously been denied or covered up, and to explore new ways of handling them."

Fourth, MFT group members are provided many opportunities to observe analogous conflict situations. To see that other families have had comparable problems and have somehow emerged is helpful in a supportive way. But perhaps even more important, the observing family can learn new and more successful ways of dealing with a comparable problem from another family.

Fifth, MFT, according to Laqueur, offers many opportunities for what he calls learning through identification. He refers here to what a person insecure in his role can pick up about more effectively handling this role by observing others in their relationships: married couples relate better to each other after observing other married couples interact; children and parents can cope more effectively with one another after watching other parent-children relationships. (Laqueur also extends the matter of identification in two further points: what he calls the "identification constellation," which is apparently the close grouping of persons with similar problems, and "tuning-in"—the identification of one situation with another.)

Sixth, the MFT experience provides family members opportunities to try out new modes of behavior to see how other people respond to them with less resulting turbulence than such trial-and-error experimentation would evoke in their own family situation. In the MFT setting, in which family relationships are pooled, both designated patients and other family members sense a broader and safer atmosphere within which to try out adaptive behavior and new role relationships than is possible in a single-family therapeutic situation.

Seventh, modeling as a learning procedure is effectively employed in MFT, according to Laqueur, partly because of the open-ended nature of the groupings which make for families at different stages of treatment. He states that the persons with the most severe symptoms (the originally designated patients) are usually the first MFT group members to develop changes based on models, and that attitude changes of other group members come later as they see the more mature behavior of the primary patients.

Eighth, MFT offers an alert therapist the opportunity to use a new and more realistic type of behavior shown by one individual or family as a basis for focus of excitation for the whole group and as a challenge for other families and individuals to move ahead more realistically in a more effective handling of their situations.

Laqueur has pointed out that MFT groups are rather volatile and shaky as transitory aggregations and can readily fail unless the therapist has considerable agility in handling new situations, ability to adjust quickly to cases of unusual malfunctioning, initiative in the choice of hitherto unused approaches in critical situations, and a sense of timing. When the therapist is well-equipped with these characteristics, how well does MFT succeed? Laqueur admits the need for more precise evaluative and follow-up studies (which he reports to be in progress), but has come to the following tentative conclusion about MFT (based on the first 600 families who have experienced this therapy under his supervision): "The introduction of MFT has reduced the frequency and length of hospitalization, enhanced the potential for preventing future crises, and facilitated the restructuring of intrafamily relationships to permit greater mutual understanding and more realistic confrontation of family problems."

SUMMARY

In his behavioral approach to family therapy, Liberman thinks in terms of changing the contingencies by which the patient gets acknowledgment and concern from other members of his family. The therapist sets up conditions whereby social reinforcement is caused by desired behavior instead of the continuation of symptomatic behavior (as has been the case in maladaptive family situations.)

The three areas for technical concern in behavioral family therapy are considered by Liberman to be the creation and maintenance of a positive therapeutic alliance which permits the therapist to function as an effective social reinforcer and model; the diagnosis of the family problems in behavioral terms; and the implementation of the behavioral principles of reinforcement and modeling in the context of ongoing interpersonal interactions.

One of the strengths of the behavioral approach to family therapy, according to Liberman, is its experimental nature, which causes the therapist to devise more effective interventions. Other advantages are its relative speed and the decreased likelihood of bringing about the adventitious reinforcement of contradictory behavior patterns.

Multiple impact therapy has been described by its originator, Robert MacGregor, as the insinuation of a whole orthopsychiatric team into the family group in a way that communicates a strong helping force for the family. In a two-day intensive treatment experience, MIT tries to utilize and assist the normal drives of the patient and his family to move toward improved functioning.

The various therapists involved in the MIT process work with the family both collectively and in different combinations of individual interviews. Team conferences and team-family conferences help to keep a kind of ongoing validity check on the progress that has been made and that needs to be made.

In R. V. Speck's social network intervention, many people (relatives, friends, and neighbors) are assembled in the family's home. The leader and his professional associates must get such conferences started in a constructive direction, keep in empathic touch with emotional trends and developments, and gradually turn the operation of the processes they initiate over to network members. In general, six evening sessions of about four hours each are needed to deal with the family crisis and to get long-term improvements of family interaction underway.

The family crisis with which social network therapy usually deals is the troublesome and distressing presence of an identified patient. The initial effect sought by the network team is to increase tension, for this leads to deeper interpersonal involvement and tribe (an alternate word used to refer to the network group) commitment. There are often subdivisions of the assembled network into inner and outer circles which relate to each other in a kind of competitive healing fashion.

Other forms of family crisis intervention have been developed independently. The best-known system, that developed by Langsley and Kaplan at the Colorado Psychiatric Hospital, is described as having seven main components: immediate aid, defining the crisis as a family problem, focus on the current crisis, general prescription, specific prescription, identification of role conflicts and renegotiation, and management of future crises.

Family crisis therapy concerns itself mainly with the things family members *do* (and how these things relate to the crisis) rather than uncovering reasons as to why they do them. The family is made aware of the short-term nature of the intervention and is told that long-term individual or interactional problems (if any) will be referred to other therapists or agencies.

Considerable research has been conducted in connection with the Colorado Psychiatric Hospital crisis intervention; it indicates that the fundamental aim of the project—namely, avoiding hospitalization with its tendency to promote regression and chronicity—is met successfully.

Impressed with the effectiveness of crisis family therapy, Minuchin and Barcai have developed a method of actually inducing crises by forcibly entering the family situation and deliberately rendering it unstable. They then remain as interim regulators and negotiators while preparing the family for a more autonomous existence based on the new patterns that have emerged in the course of the crisis.

Using as a method of choice what first developed as a hospital expedient,

Laqueur treats groups of families of patients selected from hospitals, clinics, and his private practice. Families chosen for this multiple-family therapy are as diversified as possible in educational and socioeconomic backgrounds. Laqueur believes that the mutual aid and feedback processes in a group of families make MFT a very effective treatment modality.

SELECTED READINGS

LANGSLEY, D. G., and D. M. KAPLAN, *The Treatment of Families in Crisis.* New York: Grune & Stratton, 1968.

LANGSLEY, D. G., et al., "Family Crisis Therapy—Results and Implications," in Nathan W. Ackerman, ed., *Family Process.* New York: Basic Books, 1970.

LAQUEUR, H. P., "Mechanisms of Change in Multiple Family Therapy," in C. J. Sager and H. S. Kaplan, eds., *Progress in Group and Family Therapy.* New York: Brunner/Mazel, 1972.

————, "Multiple Family Therapy," in Andrew Ferber, Marilyn Mendelsohn, and Augustus Napier, eds., *The Book of Family Therapy.* New York: Science House, 1972.

LIBERMAN, R. P., "Behavioral Approaches to Family and Couple Therapy," in Sager and Kaplan, *Progress in Group and Family Therapy.*

MacGREGOR, ROBERT, "Multiple Impact Psychotherapy with Families," in John G. Howells, *Theory and Practice of Family Psychiatry.* New York: Brunner/Mazel, 1971.

MacGREGOR, ROBERT, et al., *Multiple Impact Therapy with Families.* New York: Grune & Stratton, 1964.

MINUCHIN, SALVADOR, *Families and Family Therapy.* Cambridge, Mass.: Harvard, 1974.

MINUCHIN, SALVADOR, and AVNER BARCAI, "Therapeutically Induced Family Crisis," in Sager and Kaplan, *Progress in Group and Family Therapy.*

RABKIN, RICHARD, "Crisis Intervention," in Ferber et al., *The Book of Family Therapy.*

SPECK, R. V., and C. L. ATTNEAVE, "Social Network Intervention," in Sager and Kaplan, *Progress in Group and Family Therapy.* (Also under the title of "Network Therapy" in Ferber et al., *The Book of Family Therapy.*)

SPECK, R. V., and URI RUEVENI, "Network Therapy—a Developing Concept," in Ackerman, *Family Process.*

3

FAMILY-RELATED
PSYCHOTHERAPIES

None of the therapies discussed in this chapter originated as recently as the sixties and seventies. All, however, have come into increasing public and professional attention during this period and have special features to distinguish them from one another and from other forms of psychotherapy. The four types of therapy reviewed in this chapter concern childhood, adolescence, sex, and marriage. Problems in these four areas often derive from and have a bearing on family life. Hence, "family-related psychotherapies" are not to be confused with the various forms of family therapy considered in the first two chapters.

PSYCHOTHERAPY WITH YOUNG CHILDREN

Frederick H. Allen, long considered the dean of American child psychiatrists, has said that every child enters psychotherapy in one way or another organized against being changed. He says the oppositional direction is overtly acted out by some and well disguised by others. "He may move in almost totally," Allen has written, "and thus neutralize the assumed power of this new force; or move away into a corner and refuse to communicate, or be openly hostile, thus disguising his anxiety. He may state his problem with the assumption that this person will take over and correct the situation, or he may deny having any difficulty. In a variety of ways he reacts with his own feeling to this new experience and in reacting he is engaged in a beginning relation that has a potential for being helpful."

Allen goes on to state that in the important beginning phase of therapy the child finds a person interested in and understanding of how he feels. He also receives help in expressing himself about being afraid, withdrawn, hostile, etc. "For the therapist," Allen says, "this beginning phase provides an important diagnostic opportunity. He sees the child as he is and not just the person described in a variety of ways by the parents. Here is a living entity. The therapist is able to get impressions about the degree of accessibility, what the child presents as his own problem, and the way he can express feeling

35

engendered by this new experience. The therapist observes how the child leaves the parent to come with him and how he returns to the parent at the end of each session. In a variety of ways, the therapist gets a tentative diagnostic picture, while opening the door to a therapeutic journey which may follow."

D. W. Winnicott, a much-honored British psychiatrist, concurs, contending that it is often possible to undertake very effective deep-going therapy in the first interview with a child. Psychoanalytic treatment (in which Winnicott is trained), where caution is believed to be appropriate at the beginning, wastes a great deal of opportunity for deep therapy, he believes, in a short series of sessions with children. To illustrate Winnicott presents the case history (see the reference cited in the selected readings at the end of this chapter) of a boy whose home and school behavior was rebellious and obnoxious. In the course of the interview reported, Winnicott used his "squiggle" technique—a game in which the therapist makes a quick drawing, which the child then can turn into something if he wants to. Then the child makes a squiggle for the therapist to turn into something. While the game is going on, the therapist and the child talk about what the squiggles mean and anything else that occurs to either of them. Winnicott considers this one-shot approach particularly effective in situations in which "the family and the school are ready waiting to be used if the child is enabled to get past some block in his or her development so as to be able to use them. In this particular case there were unfavorable signs at the beginning of the consultation, restlessness indicating that the child had a great fear of deep feelings. Gradually, by the technique employed, the boy was able to gain confidence in the relationship and so to be able to play. Thus, he not only could remember a significant and frightening dream, but he could reach back to a reliving of the time when he was having it, at the age when he was highly disturbed by the birth of the twins. . . ." Apparently the cathartic effect of discussing the dream that referred to the period when his previously good relationship with his mother had begun to sour enabled the child to proceed in his home and school adjustments without the severe emotional block he had shown prior to the session.

In summing up both the case and his therapeutic method, Winnicott has written, "The immediate clinical result was satisfactory and indicated a real change in the boy's personality. Incidentally, the changes in the boy produced favorable changes in the environment, and the general result was beneficial.

"In this work the therapist cashes in on the child's capacity to believe in human reliability. The therapist remains a subjective object, and the work is unlike that of psychoanalysis in that it is not done in terms of nascent transference neurosis samples.

"Interpretation is minimal. Interpretation is not in itself therapeutic, but it facilitates that that is therapeutic, namely, the child's reliving of frightening experiences. With the therapist's ego support, the child becomes able for the first time to assimilate these key experiences into the whole personality."

A differing aspect of child therapy theory is considered by Herman S. Belmont, a psychoanalyst and child psychiatrist, who has written that great care must be exercised in distinguishing between past and present environmental influences on children. "The fact that there has in the past been a developmental interference, deriving from qualitative or quantitative environmental disturbance, does not mean that now, in the present, all the consequences can be erased by simple compensatory modification of the child's environment today. . . . With a thorough dynamic-genetic formulation as a basis, we can then better ascertain the therapy or combinations of types of therapy most appropriate. The choice will be related also to treatment goal, whether we are aiming for extensive personality reorganization or symptomatic change, whether for circumscribed and limited changes in the present or projected long-range goals."

Belmont goes on to describe the varieties of therapies of childhood. He points out that psychotherapy may be administered by one person almost exclusively or by a team of therapists. The therapists may have backgrounds primarily in psychology, education, medicine, or social work. The child may be seen alone or within a group (family or otherwise), and the child and parents may be seen separately by the same or different therapists (and if the latter, in varying degrees of collaboration). Sessions may vary from fifteen minutes to several hours at a time and from five or six times a week to weeks apart. The therapist may consult with the child in an office or institutional setting (such as a day school), a hospital or a residential center, or even in the child's home. There may or may not be primary or supplemental medical approaches and treatment efforts through modification of the environment.

Belmont believes that "considering the infinite variety of contributory variables in a child's mental health and social adjustment, alongside of the already currently utilized numerous forms of treatment, and all of the backgrounds, skills, and personalities of psychotherapists, the probability of inappropriate or ineffectual treatment efforts is great. . . . There is a distinct need for training of those personnel of all disciplines concerned with treatment of children, not only in the dynamics and genetics of the entire range of diagnostic categories, but also the entire range of treatment methods. . . . Further, there must be some kind of rationale of diagnosis and treatment so that we can get away from a tubular vision approach to psychopathology. Random and aimless expenditure of effort with poorly defined goals cannot be considered an adequate basis for treatment innovations."

Quite in disagreement with Belmont's view that strictly disciplined diagnostic and treatment methods are necessary for effective psychotherapy with children is the approach of nondirective play therapists. Founded by Virginia Axline (who based much of her therapeutic philosophy on the general client-centered ideology of Carl Rogers), nondirective play therapy is based on the belief that the child has within him the answer to his problems and that the therapist's task is to present empathic understanding and accurate reflection (and sometimes clarification) of the emotional expression of the child.

According to Axline, the psychotherapist should do no defining or diagnosing or active treating of the child. The latter has the responsibility of making choices and instituting change: "The child leads the way; the therapist follows. . . . The therapist establishes only those limitations that are necessary to anchor the therapy to the world of reality and make the child aware of his responsibility in the relationship."

Underlying the nondirective approach to play therapy with children is the concept of an actualizing tendency in the person. In Axline's words, "this force may be characterized as a drive toward independence, maturity, and self direction. It goes on relentlessly to achieve consummation, but it needs good 'growing ground' to develop a well balanced structure." The child's play, in the nondirective view, is thus considered his most revealing self-expression; if given a chance, he will play out his own conflicts. Structuring of the situation and diagnostic and treatment activities devised by the therapist can therefore do nothing more than inhibit and obstruct the child's efforts at self-actualization.

Nondirective therapists, however, have no monopoly on play therapy as the preferred treatment method for children. We have already noted the use of the squiggle game by Dr. Winnicott. Generally in analytic therapy, according to Kessler, "the child's spontaneous play is used as a way of gaining an understanding of his conflicts and feelings, a natural substitute for the technique of free association in the adult person. Some analysts, of the Kleinian school, feel that all play can be interpreted in the light of the unconscious; others, who follow Anna Freud's thinking, are more cautious in interpretation and watch for repetitions or unusual themes."

Gerald Weinberger has contended that traditionally psychotherapy with children has been dominated by the psychoanalytic assumption that the child's problems are symptomatic of underlying and unresolved conflicts which can only be removed through an understanding and resolution of these conflicts. To this end, the child is encouraged to express conflicts via symbolic play. (The nondirective play therapy approach, in its emphasis on a kind of unfolding of the self-actualizing propensities of the child, often amounts to practically the same long-term effect.) Most child treatment, he points out, is conceptualized as a long-term process owing to such factors as resistance, the intricacies of intrapsychic processes and their expression, and the need to develop a relationship of trust and closeness with the child. (In fairness, it must be noted that highly flexible psychoanalysts such as Winnicott have been able to overcome factors of resistance, deal with the intricacies of intrapsychic processes, and establish a relationship of trust and closeness with a child in a single session. What Weinberger says about the slowness of the process does, however, seem to apply to the vast majority of psychoanalyti-cally—and, I add, nondirectively—oriented child therapists.)

Weinberger has developed a brief therapy with children based primarily on a recognition of the fact, borne out by national statistics, that most cases are seen for only an average of four to six interviews. This simply does not permit a leisurely approach to probing the underlying conflicts of children. He further bases his approach on a model which sees children and their parents as basically coping and adaptive but experiencing "problems which may be caused by ignorance, inappropriate expectations, social surroundings, or other factors which do not implicate the parents as malevolent and pathogenically motivated."

Because children undergo therapy "by the grace of their parents," Weinberger considers it important to ascertain as quickly as possible what the parents conceptualize as the problem. As explicit a contract as possible is drawn up by Weinberger with the parents to specify what is expected. "In all cases," Weinberger writes, "this contract involves selecting out certain current behaviors which are troublesome, and endeavoring to effect change, in a delimited sense, and in a short period of time (at the author's clinic the time limit, set before the parents are ever seen, is a maximum of 6 weeks and 12 sessions for all family members seen, inclusive)."

Quite different in his methods from those of the psychoanalytically and nondirectively oriented, Weinberger focuses on current and explicit behavior and seeks to modify family relationships in such a way as to further generate new and more satisfying ways for family members to live with one another. "The therapist may suggest ways for parents and children to get what they want from each other; he may reduce anxiety by altering or making more realistic mutual expectations about what the child and the parent are capable of doing; and he may educate, give advice, and make suggestions as to what should be done."

Weinberger pays no attention to the sex life or marital relationship of the parents (or the nature of their relationship with their own parents) unless blatant problems which seem to stem from such sources act to prevent the parents from carrying out effective plans of action needed with the children. Children themselves are viewed not as passive recipients of parental conflicts but as actively engaged individuals, responsible for their own actions, who have become "ensnared in an unsatisfying relationship" with their family, other institutions, their peers, or between their own actions and their stated goals and desires.

To do brief therapy effectively, Weinberger writes, "it is crucial that one accept the notion that changes first in overt behavior can then lead to changes in understanding, attitude, self-concept, and self-esteem. These in turn lead to further behavioral changes in an ever-growing and widening spiral."

It is possible for child therapists, Weinberger says, to effect changes in overt behavior and in attitudes quickly and competently. These are not, according to him, mere "symptom removals" (as the psychoanalytically oriented allege), "but significant and maintained changes which generate, in both parents and child, enhanced feelings of competence, growth, and mastery over their own lives."

Bernard G. Guerney, Jr., a clinical psychologist, has developed a form of therapy designed both to make more efficient use of the professionally trained person's time and to reach children with emotional problems early in life. The procedure he has designed, called "filial therapy," consists of the training of parents of young children (in groups of six to eight) to undertake play therapy with their own children in a fashion modeled after client-centered play therapy.

After an initial training period of six to eight sessions (when both the therapist and the parents think they are ready), parents are equipped with standard play therapy equipment and sent forth to start conducting therapy with their own children. They are instructed to take notes following each session (usually starting at 30 minutes once a week and increasing to 45 minutes twice or more a week), which they discuss with the therapist and other parents in the group.

Guerney has written that "as therapy succeeds sufficiently to suggest to the parent that there is no longer a need for help, this is discussed by the group, and the parent, of course, is free to terminate." As groups thus become smaller, they merge with other groups that have been similarly reduced in size.

In accordance with the client-centered philosophy, parents are taught to encourage complete determination of the activities of the child by the child; this free expression and self-direction are supposed to release the child from tension-producing inner conflict. The parent is helped to develop empathic understanding of the basic needs and feelings the child communicates in this free play and to communicate immediately back to the child that these needs and feelings are understood. Although play is permissive, limits regarding destruction of play materials and infliction of pain to either child or parent are firmly enforced. According to Guerney, "the child is expected to learn that he and his feelings are accepted, but that certain overt acts are not tolerated. . . ."

Guerney tries to emphasize the importance of avoiding a mechanical approach to parents' therapy with their children. Specific client-centered therapeutic techniques are nevertheless taught and demonstrated by the therapist to the group parents by use of a one-way screen.

The filial therapeutic approach attempts to mobilize the parent's motivation both to help and to be helped, which eliminates much of the resistance encountered among parents who are wary of the usual clinical procedures used in therapeutic treatment of the child. The parent often interprets the ordinary treatment plan as meaning that he has damaged the child and that he must turn the child over to the therapist to clean up the mess he (the parent) has made. In filial therapy, on the other hand, parents are not made to feel that they are a destructive force, but indeed, that their help is essential in aiding the child.

In Guerney's words, "with very few exceptions, parents of nonpsychotic, young, emotionally troubled children, given a very *clearly defined* role to play for a *clearly limited* time of day, and given *corrective feedback* by the therapist and by other parents attempting to learn the same thing, may be expected to learn to play that role with the child reasonably successfully."

Areas of inflexibility and preconceptions about proper parent-child interactions are often revealed by initial difficulties parents encounter in undertaking a play therapy role with their children. These areas may be examined fruitfully in group discussion with other parents and the therapist. Guerney believes that the fact that parents are experimenting regularly, even for short spans of time, with new roles has a weakening effect on habitual negative patterns of interaction with the child. The parent can see and feel different ways of interacting with the child and this can facilitate his/her ability to make permanent improvements in the relationship with the child.

Even when parents do not succeed so well in carrying out their prescribed roles as play therapists with their children, they are at least attentively observing the children and thus learning more about them in a relatively free atmosphere. Such learning, plus the obvious interest and attention the children receive, has a therapeutically beneficial effect. Such an effect, Guerney argues, should be many times more powerful for children than that which is acquired in the usual clinical setting, for "anxiety should be much more easily extinguished in the presence of the precise stimulus (parent) under which it was originally induced than in the presence of a stimulus which only resembles it (therapist)." It would also seem probable that a relatively small amount of direct affection, attention, interest, and so on from the parent would be therapeutically beneficial to a child and that he could in this way be helped to reformulate a much more positive image of the parent than any which may have played a part in creating the child's disturbances.

Preliminary research into filial therapeutic results has led Guerney to assert that most parents develop and maintain high motivation and play their therapeutic role quite well. Children seem to respond with significant emotional release (including dynamic material) and to demonstrate reduction in various disturbances and improvement in general functioning.

Guerney and one of his associates, Andronico, have proposed that filial therapy be used by public school psychologists. Because of the small number of school psychologists and their heavy diagnostic loads (as well as the shortage of space), one-to-one psychotherapy is usually not feasible. By using parents as intermediaries (and training them in the fashion described earlier), the school psychologist could be reaching many more children with therapy and possibly more effectively than if he were to undertake the work directly.

These authors have also suggested that filial therapy principles have a possible application to teachers. Just as parents, once they have acquired the skill, have more opportunity to make significant improvements in their child's mental health than does the outside professional, teachers likewise (given the skill) are in a position to make very important contributions to a child's improved behavioral development. In addition to the direct help that both parents and teachers could give to problem children, therapeutic and empathic skills and understandings would be conveyed to all children, Guerney and Andronico contend, by filial therapy training program in the public schools.

PSYCHOTHERAPY WITH ADOLESCENTS

Psychotherapists agree that the treatment of adolescents is difficult and often discouraging. The dropout rate of adolescent out-patients has always been high, but has increased markedly in recent years in the United States. This appears to be partly because more adolescents who engage in antisocial behavior are recognized as having emotional problems (and hence, are more apt to be referred for psychotherapy than were adolescents of an earlier period) and partly because there has been an increase in mental health services available to the lower socioeconomic groups, who seem less adaptable to the psychotherapeutic approaches of psychiatrists, psychologists, and social workers who often have been recruited from the middle-class group and are carriers of middle-class values and language.

Albert Bryt, a New York psychiatrist, addresses himself to the communication problem with adolescents thus: "The assumption that one shares a semantic framework because he speaks the same language as the other person may be erroneous. . . . There is more to language than the use of words. The sociocultural, and especially the familial, backgrounds add affective flavoring. Thus distinct personal idioms come into existence in any language, occasionally only remotely related to commonly accepted semantic symbolizations." He writes that "it seems fairly well established that culturally deprived children use action for self-expression—'action-language,' even in using words, rather than verbal language—despite the use of verbal symbols. So long as a consensus has not been established between the two participants on the semantic framework within which therapeutic operations are carried out, it may be appropriate to take communicative cues from the patient's actions, verbal as well as nonverbal. In recent years much attention has been paid to these nonverbal cues. To this it may be appropriate to add the operational meaning of the spoken language itself, irrespective of content."

Many adolescents who get into some kind of difficulty at home, school, or in the community have not progressed to what Piaget has called the expected age level of hypothetico-deductive reasoning. There has not been an internalization of action behavior as an expression of intellectual and perceptual adaptation. Action behavior is directed toward immature, egocentric satisfaction without communicative purpose. Foresighted behavior is limited to the avoidance of immediate anxiety and displeasure rather than being directed toward long-range efforts of constructive planning. Speech is not used with the listener in mind, and semantic symbolizations are almost irrelevant.

Bryt more optimistically contends, however, that "there arises with adolescence an exquisite ability to repair some of the earlier damage. This may occur in a new social setting when the use of language is geared to convey needs and to share feelings. The therapeutic situation can be such a setting. However, it is probably unrealistic to expect that psychotherapy alone can suffice in even a majority of cases. The patient's milieu must contain the ingredients favorable to the pursuit of these goals, once their personal appropriateness has been discovered in the course of treatment. Therapy can provide only the impetus for the change. It can be structured to facilitate the socialization of language."

In addition to language problems, the initial defiance of many adolescents, as many clinicians and researchers have pointed out, makes it difficult to establish contact in any form of psychotherapy. If defiant noncooperation fails to work, many adolescents simply do not come to sessions. As Cohler has written, "a part of the problem in psychotherapy with adolescents arises from the fact that young people are trying to emancipate themselves from relationships in which they must rely so greatly on another at the same time that they are being asked to form such a relationship with a psychotherapist."

Cohler believes that the adolescent with serious emotional problems needs a well-structured environment that can offer support in his struggles with himself and society. Cohler describes the University of Chicago's Sonia Shankman Orthogenic School as providing the necessary positive therapeutic milieu: "In contrast to the psychiatric hospital, the school has a very simple organizational structure, one that can be understood by even the most confused adolescent. All the staff work directly with the children and have only one task, that of providing for a particular youngster the care most congruent with his needs. Typically, the adolescent lives in a group of six to eight young people, with two regular therapist-counselors who have been trained in a variety of skills that, together, contribute to the reconstruction of the young personality."

Great emphasis is placed in the Orthogenic School, according to Cohler, on trained personnel (most of whom are either candidates for advanced degrees or mental health professionals), who devote their entire effort to the young people with whom they work. Daily staff meetings are often focused around the staff member's inner attitudes and the meaning of his emotional reactions to the adolescents with whom he works rather than exclusively on the latter's problems.

Cohler concludes his report by saying that "the treatment philosophy of the Orthogenic School is based on a view of adolescence as a time of inner turmoil which, in a young person who has previously experienced conflicts in his own development, and who finds a lack of environmental support for his attempt to develop internal control, may lead to an emotional disturbance that is actually only a response to a life-threatening situation. Clearly, neither the manipulation of outward behavior nor the provision of a better facade of adjustment will succeed in helping the adolescent to resolve this disturbance and to achieve a better adaptation. However, reparenting, combined with intensive individual psychotherapy, in an environment structured around the adolescent's unique psychological needs, has led to a more effective adaptation in the vast majority of young persons with whom we have worked."

If seriously disturbed adolescents cannot be treated in a positive residential setting, group therapy is often believed to be the treatment of choice. Nicholas G. Frignito and Carlton W. Orchinik, a psychiatrist and a psychologist who, at the time of the writing of their account (see selected readings) were associated with the County Court of Philadelphia, have listed what they believe to be the advantages of the group method for apprehended delinquents on probation:

1. Group members serve in various roles and relationships to each other. This helps to point up areas of difficulty.
2. Because the delinquent acts in a socially deviant manner, the group experience comes closer to the social nature of the adolescent personality problems.
3. Group conditions and processes are especially advantageous in improving social skills and communication.
4. Communication verbally is in contrast with other forms of acting out which the adolescent more habitually employs.
5. The group increases the security of the individual when he feels threatened by adult authority.
6. The group allows clearer delineation of defenses and irrational processes. At the same time self-critical, inhibiting self-conscious tendencies decline so that the delinquent verbalizes these attitudes more openly.
7. The group enhances opportunity to form and modify identifications. It allows members to observe and study models with whom they can selectively identify.
8. The adolescent can experience more guided social interaction with opportunities to achieve greater self-understanding.

In treating delinquents in a residential community (Children's Village, Dobbs Ferry, N.Y.), psychiatrist Selwyn Brody has found many "untreatables" responsive to supportive therapy with emphasis on warmth and positive relationship. He has also found it useful to join forces with what he discerns as underlying desires of adolescent patients as they reveal them in therapy (as distinguished from overt defensive and often offensive behavior). Brody also sometimes reflects negative patterns of delinquents. He finds that this "encourages the ego to discharge hostility verbally. One of the most difficult problems is that of the non-verbalizing delinquents. Occasionally such dreary youths can be helped by the therapist's mirroring his silence." Finally, Brody has discovered that some of the most unresponsive delinquents can be helped to effective personality change by having therapists assigned to work with their families.

SEX THERAPY

During much of the twentieth century many psychotherapists have undertaken the treatment of a wide variety of sexual problems. Likewise, marriage counselors (some of whom have never considered themselves psychotherapists) have—in the United States and more sparsely in some other countries—devoted a great deal of their attention to the sexual difficulties of the married and unmarried. Physicians of various nonpsychiatric specialties have also long dealt with problems in the sexual area of their patients' lives. In the past decade or two there has been a tremendous upsurge of interest in the treatment of sexual dysfunction: the recently formed American Association of Sex Educators and Counselors (which brings into one organization members of many professions that have come to be involved in sex therapy and education) is one manifestation of this growth of interest and activity.

The work of many individual practitioners of the past and present in treating sexual problems could be very favorably cited. Both because it is based on the most extensive and intensive research and because it has most impressively influenced the whole field of sex therapy, however, the work of William H. Masters and Virginia E. Johnson will be described in this section of the chapter.

Three major aspects of human sexual response have been studied successively since 1954 by Masters (joined in 1957 by Johnson): sexual physiology, sexual dysfunction, and homosexual response patterns. The work began under the auspices of Washington University School of Medicine and switched in 1964 to the independent Reproductive Biology Research Foundation in St. Louis. "Established Foundation policy requires that at least a decade be devoted to each area of human sexual functioning under investigation before reporting work in progress to the scientific community."

One of the outstanding features of the Masters and Johnson therapeutic approach is the dual-sex therapy team. The plan, which grew out of Masters' and Johnson's earlier work on sexual physiology, is said to have the advantages of providing the man and woman who are being treated with an interpreter, a "friend in court," and a sense of not being "ganged up on" (which is apt to be the case for the patient who is the opposite sex from the therapist). For the intensive daily therapy (over a two-week period), problems of transference are likewise thought to be best avoided by use of the dual-sex team. And finally, the team of a physician and a psychologist seems appropriate for dealing with physical and laboratory examinations on the one hand and psychosexual problems on the other.

While one therapist of the team is taking an active role in talking with the couple in treatment, the other therapist listens carefully and watches for nonverbal cues. As topics of discussion change, the therapist roles are switched. The silent therapist at any particular time has the responsibility of determining whether the patients are accepting or rejecting the material under discussion.

An important technique employed by the dual-sex teams is what Masters and Johnson call "reflective teaching." During the therapy session from time to time the therapists restate for the couple in relatively objective terms what their problems are and how they are failing adequately to communicate about their problems. In the words of Masters and Johnson, "The co-therapists encounter a multiplicity of these problems to which they can respond by holding up a professional 'mirror' and helping the marital partners understand what it reflects. With the nonjudgmental mirror available, constructive criticism can be accepted in the same nonprejudiced, comfortable manner in which it must be presented."

Although other forms of therapy have often been directed at teaching the individual to do something, Masters and Johnson stress that all the patients at the Foundation need to do is cooperate in helping to eliminate the blocks; then nature can take its course. In their words, "This mode of psychotherapy presumes that human sexual functioning, like that of other animals, must be considered a natural process. It is not only unnecessary, it is impossible to 'teach' the human male to achieve erection, the female to lubricate, the male to ejaculate or the female to experience orgasm. The basic principle that must be accepted by patient and cotherapist alike is that physical expression of sexual tension is a natural function. From this platform of general agreement, therapeutic techniques can be activated which are designed to contribute to progressive removal of psychosocial blocks inhibiting sexual responsivity."

Masters and Johnson have found, however, that performance fears cannot be removed simply by exhortation against them. For this reason the co-therapists at the outset lay down a rigid reconditioning program, the first step of which is to forbid any sexual activity not instigated at their direction. The educative reflective process designed to help the couple understand their fears is begun, and then they are led gradually through a process to mutual and pleasurable sexual involvement and fulfillment.

The homework assignments that are given the couple in helping them to recondition themselves, along with their joint and individual reactions to other matters that derived from the previous day's sessions, are subject to daily review. "In this manner," Masters and Johnson have written, "the marital pair explores the appropriateness and reliability of combinations of verbal and nonverbal, sexual and nonsexual communication in producing mutually desired feelings and attitudes. They subsequently may accept or reject any particular experience (and its means of attainment) as it does or does not support their mutual values and goals."

Where Foundation treatment has been identified as having failed for a particular couple, no follow-up study is made. This is thought to encourage such a couple to seek help elsewhere. But there is a routine five-year study made of all couples not designated failures. If couples are not to be labeled Foundation failures at the time of the follow-up study, they must evidence a trend of continued or progressive improvement after termination of therapy.

Many couples have now been trained by Masters and Johnson at the Foundation, and great effort has been made to screen these trainees as to both their professional competence and personal skills and integrity. The sexual attitudes of the therapists is, of course, of great importance. In the words of Masters and Johnson, "It is vital that psychotherapists dealing directly with clinical symptoms of sexual distress react from a sense of confidence and comfort in their own sexuality and sexual functioning. There is a tendency for a sexually insecure therapist to lose objectivity when dealing with a sexually distressed patient, particularly one of the opposite sex. Any failure to maintain perspective has grave potential for undermining the effectiveness of the professional's therapeutic approach to the patient's complaint of sexual inadequacy."

The joint interviews of husband and wife by co-therapists, which, as we have indicated, are the characteristic procedure at the Foundation, have been preceded on the first two days of the couple's two-week therapy by individual medical examinations and intensive history taking. Masters and Johnson have emphasized that "the basic value systems of both the husband and the wife must be defined in depth sufficient to implement therapeutic effort successfully. A superficial scanning of the husband's or wife's set of personal values including their sexual value systems can indeed destroy therapeutic effectiveness. Superficiality of interrogation inevitably results in inadequate professional representation of the same-sex patient. The same-sex therapist must come to appreciate the patient's attitudinal approach to the psychosexual influences of our culture. Problems arise when a professional does not develop a history which adequately reflects patient values or life style, and, under pressure to meet demands of the therapy, imposes an interpretation based upon his or her own limited personal experience. With sufficient authoritative identification of the patient's individual value systems and of the context in which they function, it is far easier to keep the Foundation's educative program focused on those things truly desired by the individual rather than those possibly imposed by the therapist's own value system."

Specific techniques, which are always modified to fit the needs of the particular couple with whom the co-therapists are working, have been developed by Masters and Johnson for dealing with specific types of sexual dysfunction. The main areas of dysfunction that are frequently met with and treated in the Foundation clinic (and in comparable clinics now set up throughout the country) are premature ejaculation, ejaculatory incompetence, primary and secondary impotence, orgasmic dysfunction in women, vaginismus, painful intercourse, and particular difficulties of the aging.

While continuing with research with couples with problems of sexual dysfunction (and with homosexuals—publication on this subject had not yet been made at the time of this writing), Masters' and Johnson's major research commitment for the present decade is directed toward devising means for *preventing* sexual dysfunction.

MARRIAGE THERAPY

The treatment of troubled relationships between marital partners, premarital partners, and unmarried cohabiting partners, while never entirely ignored by psychotherapists, has often fallen into the hands of nonpsychiatric physicians, sociologists, and social case workers prior to the sixties and the seventies. With the development of family therapy and its emphasis on conjoint treatment and with the entrance of a growing number of psychiatrists and clinical psychologists into marriage counseling (there has been a tremendous growth of the American Association of Marriage and Family Counselors and of the Academy of Psychologists in Marriage and Family Therapy), the treatment of problems centered in and derived from the man-woman relationship has come to be considered a special emphasis within the general field of psychotherapy.

Jay Haley, a communications analyst, has studied what happens in various forms of psychotherapy, including marriage therapy. He has written that a marriage therapist provides a couple an opportunity for change in several ways: "He encourages discussion to resolve conflict rather than previous methods, such as withdrawal and silence; he provides a reasonably impartial advisor and judge; he encourages a couple to examine motivations which they might have outside awareness; he makes many maneuvers explicit and therefore more difficult to follow; and he engenders habits of dealing with sensitive topics."

In addition to these change-inducers, marriage therapists, according to Haley, use paradoxical strategies (similar to those used by therapists of individuals). While he offers benevolent help to a couple, the therapist at the same time requires them to go through a punishing ordeal of exposing their problems and conflicts and often most fully explores the very situations about which they are most sensitive. "Still another dimension of paradox occurs," Haley writes, "when the therapist encourages them to continue in their distress, while communicating to them at another level that he is helping them over that distress. Similarly, he assumes the posture of an expert and often declines to directly advise the couple as an expert would."

Paradoxical situations are likely to be necessary in therapy, however, because of the resistance of individuals (and couples) to change. Haley finds that people in a relationship tend to govern each other's range of behavior—"When one of them indicates a change the other tends to react against that change even when it might lead to less subjective distress. As it is sometimes said, if a wife wishes her husband to remain unchanged, she should set out to reform him." Because a couple, like an individual, tends to react in much the same way in the therapeutic relationship, the therapist needs to employ tactics that avoid indicating a change; he must find ways of inducing it without asking for it to occur. As Haley says, "when he paradoxically encourages an increase in distressing behavior, with a framework of alleviating it, he is most likely to bring about change."

Haley thinks understanding plays little or no role in bringing about improvements in marital relationships. Even though marriage therapists characteristically emphasize to couples their need for self-understanding, the most important thing they are doing is offering the couple a context in which they can learn alternative ways of behaving while being forced to abandon those past procedures which induced distress. "By advice, counsel, and example the therapist," Haley writes, "offers methods of resolving conflict. By imposing therapeutic paradoxes, the therapist both forces and frees the couple to develop new ways of relating to one another."

Other marriage therapy than that observed by Haley proceeds less subtly and paradoxically and with considerable alleged success. Ellis and Harper, for example, state that they believe in getting clients to face "the full realities—however black they may seem—about life in general and marriage and family life in particular. But we are equally convinced that no aspect of reality is so difficult or so negative that it cannot be somewhat (and often greatly) improved. Such improvement, as we have frequently reiterated, can usually be effected by a change in the individual's own attitudes. And such changes can often be brought about by his own intelligently directed actions."

Elsewhere Harper has presented a point of view (with which Ellis agrees) that much of the marriage therapist's time is desirably spent by very directively "helping the patient to recognize and alter the irrational patterns of thinking that are causing much of the disruption in his own emotions and, along with the irrational beliefs of his spouse, the disruption of his marital relations. The marriage counselor needs to listen to and observe both the husband and the wife (sometimes separately and sometimes together), but then he needs to formulate and communicate concrete recommendations for change. The therapist needs to make specific assignments of experiments, in thought and action, to be carried out between therapy sessions (homework). These assigned changes need to be practiced at times in the counseling situation as well. . . . But what these disturbed husbands and wives need most of the time is instruction in *thinking*, and hence feeling and acting, rationally and realistically."

Azrin, Naster, and Jones have correctly objected that such theories and approaches as those of Haley, Ellis, Harper, and a large variety of other writers on marriage therapy, are not based on experimentally derived principles. Azrin and associates present a study with a control feature that made possible an experimental evaluation of the results. Their approach, which they call "reciprocity counseling," is based on the principle of operant reinforcement. The experimental design was a comparison (within subjects, who were twelve married couples) of the reciprocity counseling procedure and undirected "catharsis-type" control procedure. These investigators have written that "the catharsis counseling was conducted for three weeks, followed by four weeks of Reciprocity Counseling. A test of marital adjustment . . . was given each day during this 7-week period to provide a continuous measure of change in marital adjustment. Since the test was divided into nine specific problem areas, it permitted evaluation of whether specific problem areas were improved. A second feature of the experimental design attempted to determine whether the Reciprocity Counseling improved the specific areas for which the client was being counseled, thereby determining whether the problem-oriented nature of the procedure was essential. This evaluation was made possible by restricting counseling to only three of the problem areas during the first week, an additional three problem areas during the second week and all nine problem areas during the third and fourth weeks. Improvement in the problem areas for which Reciprocity Counseling was given could then be compared with the areas for which Reciprocity Counseling had not yet been given."

The daily test consisted simply of a 10-point marital happiness scale on household responsibilities, rearing of children, social activities, money, communication, sex, academic or occupational progress, personal independence, spouse independence, and general happiness. There were two one-hour counseling sessions in both types of procedures (catharsis and reciprocity). During the reciprocity counseling various techniques were used such as feedback exchange procedure, appreciation reminder procedure, fantasy fulfillment procedure, and various homework assignments.

Little change in reported overall happiness resulted during the three weeks of catharsis counseling. In that period the average rating stayed right around the fifth point of the 10-point scale. "Reported happiness remained at that level through the first day of Reciprocity Counseling," Azrin et al. have written, "but increased to about 6.5 by the end of one week and reached a level of approximately 7 during the third and fourth week of Reciprocity Counseling. One month later, the follow-up test showed a further increase in overall happiness to a level greater than 7.5. . . .

"Analysis of the scores of the individual clients showed that 96 per cent of the clients (23 of the 24) reported a higher level of overall marital happiness during the last week of the Reciprocity Counseling period than on the day before Reciprocity Counseling. Similarly, for 88 per cent of the clients (21 of the 24), the reported marital happiness was greater on the 1-month follow-up date than on the day prior to Reciprocity Counseling. The reported happiness did not generally increase during the undirected catharsis-type counseling for most clients. Reported happiness on the last week of catharsis counseling was greater than on the first day for 33 per cent of the clients, actually less for 47 per cent of the clients, and unchanged for 20 per cent of the clients."

Azrin and associates found, further, that the increased happiness occurred in reciprocity counseling for each of the nine major areas of marital interaction. The greatest increase occurred for the two areas, communication and sex, in which the couples were least happy initially. "The specificity of the effect of the procedure," they have reported, "was evidenced by the greater increase of happiness in those areas that had been counseled than in the areas for which counseling had not yet been given. Yet, some generalization was evident in that (1) problem areas that had not yet been counseled also did increase and (2) happiness continued to increase during follow-up when presumably new problems were emerging. The evidence showed that the improvement during Reciprocity Counseling was caused by the specific nature of the procedure since a catharsis-type counseling of roughly comparable duration did not increase happiness and that at the same period in counseling, improvement was substantially greater for the specific interaction areas for which counseling was given than for the other areas for which direct counseling had not yet been given."

Azrin and associates describe the central role of the reciprocity feature whereby each spouse is reinforced for reinforcing the partner. "However," they say, "the reinforcement contingencies are not stated in terms of specific response-reinforcement relationships as in the Token Economy procedure, . . . but rather as a global 'package' of responses that produce a similarly global package of reinforcers. The approach does not attempt to teach the clients principles of reinforcement. Indeed, the instructions to the clients scrupulously avoided technical terms such as reinforcement, extinction, time-out and instead used more common lay terms, such as happiness, satisfaction, frustration, motivation, desire and appreciation. The approach is oriented toward specific behaviors as seen in its delineation of nine specific areas of behavioral interaction and the listing of specific behaviors within each area. Yet, the approach is non-behavioral in its reliance on 'happiness' as the focal attribute of the clients that was changed. The approach is quantitative, as are most behavioral approaches, but minimizes the need for the clients to keep records of their behavior."

As Azrin, Naster, and Jones have noted, practically no other method of marital therapy (or counseling) has received even minimal experimental evaluation. Reciprocity counseling needs to be tested much more extensively and intensively, but even at this point it seemed worthy of our special attention because of its demonstrated effectiveness in limited circumstances. The simplicity of the approach seems particularly appealing, but, as the authors point out, it "does not deny the central roles of such factors as personality, attitudes, expectation, role factors, communication, sex or social custom in determining marital happiness but rather provides a concrete method for changing personality, communication patterns, attitudes, etc."

SUMMARY

The four types of therapy dealt with in this chapter concern childhood, adolescence, sex, and marriage. Both Allen and Winnicott emphasize, in somewhat different ways, how much can be accomplished in the first (and sometimes only) interview with the child. Winnicott particularly, with his "squiggle" game, demonstrates an ability to help the child to achieve real personality change in one interview.

Belmont, referring to the many existing types of child therapy and the varieties of background and training of the therapists, stresses the need for strict training in the dynamics and genetics of the entire range of diagnostic categories in child psychopathology. Axline, on the other hand, as a foremost exponent of nondirective play therapy for children, emphasizes the point of view that answers to problems reside within the children themselves and that the therapist's role is primarily to provide empathic understanding and accurate reflection of their emotional expression. Play, by the nondirective view, is considered the child's most revealing self-expression. If he is given a chance, the child will play out his conflicts.

Somewhat similarly, in analytic therapy the child's spontaneous play is used as a way of gaining understanding of his conflicts and feelings. But, unlike nondirective therapy, great emphasis in analytic therapy is placed on the analyst's skilled interpretations as an important component of the route to emotional health for the child.

Weinberger, pointing to the unrealistic nature of long-term working out of problems through analytically oriented play therapy, has developed a brief therapy for children and their parents. He directs his attention toward effecting changes in overt behavior and in attitudes quickly and competently.

"Filial therapy" is the term Guerney has coined to refer to a method which consists of the small-group training of parents to undertake play therapy with their own young children in a fashion modeled after client-centered (or nondirective) play therapy. The filial therapeutic approach, according to Guerney, mobilizes the parent's motivation both to help and to be helped, which eliminates much of the resistance encountered among parents who are wary of the nature of the therapeutic treatment of the child under usual clinical procedures.

Psychotherapy with adolescents is generally agreed to be difficult, with a high dropout rate among out-patients. Bryt considers communication, one of the formidable problems in treating adolescents, as importantly affected by sociocultural background, noting that many culturally deprived children use action for self-expression. Consequently, therapists must take cues from patients' actions, nonverbal as well as verbal.

Cohler has noted that part of the problem in psychotherapy with adolescents arises from the fact that young people are trying to break away from an adult-child relationship at home at the same time that they are being asked to go into another adult-child relationship with the therapist. He describes as an effective answer for adolescents with serious emotional problems a well-structured environment that can offer support in his struggles with himself and society. He describes work at the Orthogenic School in Chicago where such an environment is provided.

Brody describes a residential community for adolescents where delinquents are effectively treated with a supportive therapy and an emphasis on warmth and positive relationship. He also uses the technique of mirroring negative attitudes and even silence in his treatment.

The most outstanding work in sex therapy (partly because it is most solidly based on research) has been that undertaken by Masters and Johnson and their trainees. The dual-sex therapy team is one of the outstanding features of their therapeutic approach. Masters and Johnson stress cooperation of their patients in helping to eliminate blocks and letting nature take over. This process, however, is not easy and requires a rigid reconditioning program and "reflective teaching" techniques.

In marriage therapy, ideas of Haley, Ellis, and Harper are initially discussed. Haley, in his studies of marriage therapy, observed that it generally provides a couple the opportunity for change. He notes the use of often necessary paradoxical strategies in the therapist's treatment and expresses his opinion that understanding plays little role in the marriage relationship; that it is the therapist's major role to offer the couple a context within which they can both learn alternative behavior and give up patterns that induce distress.

Ellis and Harper feel it is necessary for a couple to face the realities of life and marriage, however unpleasant, in order to be able to change. The therapist directively helps the patients to recognize and change irrational patterns of thinking that ultimately cause personal and marital disorganization.

Considerable attention was given to the experimental testing of marriage therapy techniques by Azrin, Naster, and Jones. In their "reciprocity counseling," each spouse is reinforced for reinforcing the partner. In experimentally comparing reciprocity counseling with a catharsis-type counseling over a seven-week period and a follow-up period, the authors found reciprocity counseling quite effective in increasing reported marital happiness for twelve couples who reported daily on a simple scale. Because of the experimental foundation and simplicity of the approach by Azrin and associates, this type of marriage therapy merits special attention.

SELECTED READINGS

ALLEN, FREDERICK H., "Child Psychotherapy," in J. H. Masserman, ed., *Current Psychiatric Therapies*, Vol. II. New York: Grune & Stratton, 1962.

ANDRONICO, MICHAEL P., and BERNARD G. GUERNEY, JR., "The Potential Application of Filial Therapy in the School Situation," in B. G. Guerney, Jr., *Psychotherapeutic Agents*. New York: Holt, Rinehart & Winston, 1969.

ARD, BEN N., JR., and CONSTANCE C. ARD, eds., *Handbook of Marriage Counseling*. Palo Alto, Cal.: Science & Behavior Books, 1969.

AXLINE, VIRGINIA M., *Play Therapy*. Boston: Houghton Mifflin, 1947.

AZRIN, N. H., B. J. NASTER, and R. JONES, "Reciprocity Counseling: A Rapid Learning-Based Procedure for Marital Counseling," *Behavior Research & Therapy*, (1973), 365–82.

BELMONT, H. S., "Theoretical Considerations in Child Psychotherapy," in S. L. Colpel, ed., *Behavior Pathology of Childhood and Adolescence*. New York: Basic Books, 1973.

BRYT, ALBERT, "Dropout of Adolescents from Psychotherapy: Failure in Communication," in Gerald Caplan and Serge Lebovici, eds., *Adolescence: Psychosocial Perspectives*. New York: Basic Books, 1969.

BRODY, SELWYN, "Community Therapy of Child Delinquents," in J. H. Masserman, ed., *Current Psychiatric Therapies*, Vol. III. New York: Grune & Stratton, 1963.

COHLER, BERTRAM J., "New Ways in the Treatment of Emotionally Disturbed Adolescents," in Sherman C. Feinstein and Peter Giovacchini, eds., *Adolescent Psychiatry*, Vol. II. New York: Basic Books, 1973.

ELLIS, ALBERT, and ROBERT A. HARPER, *A Guide to Successful Marriage*. Hollywood, Cal.: Wilshire, 1961.

FRIGNITO, N. G., and C. W. ORCHINIK, "The Therapy of Adolescent Offenders," in Masserman, *Current Psychiatric Therapies*, Vol. III.

GUERNEY, BERNARD G., JR., "Filial Therapy: Description and Rationale," in B. G. Guerney, Jr., *Psychotherapeutic Agents*.

HALEY, JAY, *Strategies of Psychotherapy*. New York: Grune & Stratton, 1963.

HARPER, ROBERT A., "Marriage Counseling as Rational Process-Oriented Psychotherapy," in Ard and Ard, *Handbook of Marriage Counseling*.

HARPER, ROBERT A., and WALTER R. STOKES, *45 Levels to Sexual Understanding and Enjoyment*. Englewood Cliffs, N.J.: Prentice-Hall, 1971.

KESSLER, JANE W., "Neurosis in Childhood," in B. B. Wolman, ed., *Manual of Child Psychopathology*. New York: McGraw-Hill, 1972.

MARCANTONIO, CHARLES, "Nondirective Treatment Methods," in Wolman, *Manual of Child Psychopathology*.

MASTERS, WILLIAM H., and VIRGINIA E. JOHNSON, *Human Sexual Inadequacy*. Boston: Little, Brown, 1970.

————, "The Rapid Treatment of Human Sexual Dysfunctions," in C. J. Sager and H. S. Kaplan, eds., *Progress in Group and Family Therapy.* New York: Brunner/Mazel, 1972.

MOUSTAKAS, CLARK E., ed., *Existential Child Therapy.* New York: Basic Books, 1966.

WEINBERGER, GERALD, "Brief Therapy with Children and Their Parents," in Harvey H. Barten, ed., *Brief Therapies.* New York: Behavioral Publications, 1971.

WINNICOTT, D. W., "A Psychotherapeutic Consultation in Child Psychiatry: A Comparative Study of the Dynamic Processes," in Silvano Arieti, ed., *The World Biennial of Psychiatry and Psychotherapy*, Vol. I. New York: Basic Books, 1971.

4

GROUP
THERAPIES

A Variety of Systems

In this chapter and the two that follow, we will consider the tremendous growth of all kinds of group structures and processes in what we refer to broadly and loosely as the field of psychotherapy. We concern ourselves in these three chapters with individual-centered groups.

The current chapter treats most of what has developed in the course of the expansion of various (more or less conventional) systems of individual psychotherapy into work with groups. Because psychodrama, analytic group therapy, client-centered group therapy, the (pre-marathon) orientation of George Bach, the approach of Hubert Coffey, didactic group therapy, and round-table psychotherapy were discussed in Chapter 9 of *Psychoanalysis and Psychotherapy: 36 Systems*, they are not included here.

Transactional analysis belongs to the same category of group therapies as those considered herein, but merits a fuller treatment and a chapter to itself. This "merit" could be debated if we were to stick strictly to theoretical and technical contributions as our basis of judgment. If, however, we expand our criteria of "importance" to include consumer response (and it obviously seems to me that we must), then TA is clearly one of the most influential of the current psychotherapeutic systems.

The third of our group therapy chapters is reserved for systems that are exciting and exotic. Many of the approaches considered there often label themselves as something other than psychotherapy: such as "individual-centered group education." If there ever was a discernible border between psychotherapy and individual-centered education, it has become so obscured by the proliferation of group activities of the sixties and seventies that only some future scholar will perhaps be able to rediscover its markers. The group therapies to which we turn our attention in the third of our chapters, then, will be those which carry such labels as personal growth, human potential, encounter, T-groups, marathons, mini-marathons, truth labs, humanistic confrontations, sensory awareness, etc. Some of the developments will be considered specifically (such as the Arica Institute), but most will be described generically.

But now we will look at the groups of the sixties and seventies that indisputably wear the psychotherapy tunic. These are systematic group approaches to help persons who are clearly engaged in self-defeating and/or socially reprehensible behavior to function more effectively and adaptively. In many instances, these approaches are the application of longstanding individual psychotherapeutic methods to the group therapy situation (principles from the systems of Adler, Horney, Sullivan, bio-energetics, behavior therapy, existentialism, and rational-emotive psychotherapy). In a few cases, we have the development of peer self-help therapies to consider (Mowrer's Integrity Groups, Low's Recovery, Inc., Synanon, and Alcoholics Anonymous). These, then, are what strike the author as the most important "traditional" systems (not encounter or T-group in origin) of group psychotherapy not previously discussed in Chapter 9 of *36 Systems.*

HORNEYIAN GROUP PSYCHOTHERAPY

Although Karen Horney did not practice group therapy, many of her followers do. One of these, Sidney Rose, has described how Horney's optimistic beliefs about the basically healthy urges of human beings can be considerably realized in a group psychotherapeutic atmosphere. Horney's notion that the individual can be freed from his neurotic patterns so that he may develop his strivings toward constructive integrating patterns manifests itself in the group, Rose says, in the mutuality and the group spirit that can eventually emerge, given correct therapeutic handling.

The Horneyian therapist, however, is aware that the group-unifying process must be turned in a healthy direction; it is possible for it to be misused in a neurotic way to relieve what Horney called "basic anxiety" (feelings of weakness and isolation; feelings that others are hostile). Group cohesiveness that caters merely to anxiety relief only encourages conflict and the emergence of anxiety. But when these negative emotions are out in the open, the therapist can help the members of the group to move toward a healthy feeling of belonging based on the essentially sound urges of each person.

A group conducted in a Horneyian fashion has a constant ebb (disorganization and disintegration) and flow (reorganization and reintegration in new directions) as it strives toward a cooperative mutuality. "The task of the analyst," Rose says, "is to feel the pulse of group movement and when the normal corrective processes fail to operate, he must act. Temporary phases of disharmony always occur and their recognition is important. The therapist rapidly scans the group process, shifting focus from the group atmosphere to interpersonal relatedness, to intrapsychic dynamisms. Intervention can be done on any of these three levels."

By its nature, of course, the group process is most sensitive to interpersonal difficulties and tends to reveal in detail the nature of self-perpetuating neurotic patterns. In the terms of Horney, the group member is thrown into conflict by having to face aspects of his behavior that lead to group friction. His false sense of unity, based on his idealized image, is threatened. In Rose's words, "The multidimensional nature and the self-perpetuating effects of neurotic patterns are illustrated repeatedly in the group process and the aim of therapy is to permit the experiencing of these patterns, and their consequences, and the encouragement of new ways."

Rose reports that the group gives the patient the opportunity to observe disowned self-aspects in others and his repetitive emotional reactions to them. These are sometimes similar to the disowned aspects in himself. As he is able to acknowledge these as his own, he begins to experience internal conflicts. Perpetuating reactions of both interpersonal and intrapsychic conflicts are eventually converted into beneficent actions and interactions. As the patient progresses in the group therapeutic situation, he comes not only to observe and later experience the neurotic nature of certain behavior in himself, but also reacts to the behavior of others more realistically rather than primarily in response to his own neurotic needs. As he comes to own more of his actual self (as revealed to him in interactions both with other group members and the therapist), he gradually gains the strength to give up the neurotic defenses (including much of his idealized self), to approach wholeness, and move onward toward self-fulfillment.

Although Rose believes that for long-range diagnosis and prognosis "other facets of the personality must be tapped" (presumably by other concepts than Horney's and by other modalities than group psychotherapy), he finds her concepts admirably suited for diagnosis and therapy (going hand in hand) in the group situation.

EXISTENTIAL GROUP PSYCHOTHERAPY

Thomas Hora, a New York psychiatrist who has long been associated with the existential point of view in psychotherapy, has reported that regardless of what diagnostic categories of psychopathology patients fall into, they suffer from "disturbed modes of being-in-the-world." In the group situation, these patients are deficient in their ability to communicate meaningfully with other members of the group. They suffer from a sense of isolation and frequently recurring conflicts. In Hora's words, "they are further afflicted by a limited capacity for presence; that is, they are in conflict with time, with their own intentionalities, striving, ethical codes and defensive attitudes."

When a group meets initially, the atmosphere is filled with emotional currents, and this undifferentiated state of emotional stimulation, experienced as group tension, creates a need to achieve a tension-relieving situation. Although talk is used as a means to effect this, little is communicated at this stage, for it is essentially a form of acting out, and it keeps group members from being aware of what is being experienced. Hora calls this "unauthentic behavior."

After the initial tension is discharged in this fashion, group members become curious about each other. They compare status and conditions in an effort not really to understand one another, but to relieve existential anxiety. They are preoccupied with each other as objects and want to master each other by a verbal form of manipulation and probing. As Hora says, "the human situation reveals itself in the therapy groups as a rather complex problem of adaptation, requiring man to fit himself into a world which he is thrown under rather difficult conditions."

This first phase of self-discovery in existential group therapy is followed by a gradually increasing amount of self-understanding. This causes the patient to be anxious while he experiments with learning to let go of his defensive strivings. Success in learning to accept one's anxiousness, according to Hora, "is an important step in the direction of accepting one's ontic condition, and is rewarded by a new phase of discovering oneself as being-in-the-world in an authentic fashion."

Because the group is considered an arena of existential encounter, outside issues, conceptualizations, and historical references are dealt with as relatively unimportant. The focus is on the effort at creative understanding of the here-and-now interactions in the group.

The group process itself is unstructured except, as Hora writes, "by the impact of the therapist's personality, which unavoidably and very meaningfully focuses on certain values reflected by his mode of being-in-the-world." Because he communicates in many nonverbal ways, the therapist's authenticity of being is of the greatest importance in existential psychotherapy—without this authenticity there will be a disparity between his verbal and his attitudinal communications.

Existential groups go through painful phases of long silences when group members have given up their habitual unauthentic expressions and ways of relating (personal need gratification and object manipulation) and have not yet developed authentic communing. In the periods as the group members learn to endure the existential anxiety they feel, they get bored. "Boredom," Hora says, "is a state of meaninglessness of existence which emerges whenever one attempts to renounce the pursuit of false meanings, or when the pursuit of such meanings is made impossible through psychotherapeutic illumination. The periods of silent boredom prevail for a while, until, one by one the group participants arrive at the edge of the 'wasteland' and begin to communicate in an increasingly authentic way."

Existential group psychotherapy is viewed by Hora as providing patients with an opportunity to recognize, understand, and liberate themselves from the obstacles which have hitherto stood in the way of their full and free participation in the process of existence. The therapist's attitude is desirably one of letting the group members' authentic individualities unfold. It is an attitude of what Hora calls "letting-be," which is "the open-minded wakeful receptivity to that which reveals itself without interference." This is part of Hora's contention that the existential psychotherapist does not "do" psychotherapy, but actually lives it. "He meets his patient in the *openness* of an interhuman existential encounter. He does not seek to make interpretations; he does not evaluate and judge; *he allows what is to be, so that it can reveal itself in the essence of its being, and then proceeds to elucidate what he understood.* In contrast to the interpretative approach, this is a 'hermeneutic,' (that is, clarifying mode) of *being with* a patient."

By his letting-be and being-with each group member, the therapist helps to make possible an unfolding process for the individual that eventually overcomes loneliness and isolation through self-transcendence. In terms of the therapy groups, "it means a mode of 'being-there' involving the total experiential sphere and communication potential of all participants. The capacity for this kind of presence is rooted in the attainment of authenticity of being."

ADLERIAN GROUP PSYCHOTHERAPY

Because Adler and his associates recognized man's problems and conflicts as social in nature (as distinguished from the intrapsychic emphasis of at least the early psychoanalysts who adhered to the teachings of Freud), they used a group approach as early as 1921 in their child guidance clinics in Vienna. In this country, the late Rudolf Dreikurs, also in the twenties, used what he then called "collective therapy" not only in child guidance work but also in the treatment of alcoholics. He later generalized the group approach to his private practice.

One of the values of group psychotherapy, according to Dreikurs, is that it facilitates the process of gaining insight. Because it is easy for neurotics to rationalize, it is difficult for them in the individual therapeutic situation to recognize their own goals and true intentions. In the group situation, however, the patient can more readily grasp the validity of the psychological interpretations and the difficulties of other group members to recognize the obvious about themselves. Dreikurs further believed that most psychological disclosures and interpretations made in the group are not for the benefit of the patient to whom they are directed, but for the benefit of the others who hopefully can learn from them. Although he thought there was a sufficient fundamental similarity in the faulty motivations and mistaken approaches among all human beings, he tried further to enhance commonality of experience through his selection of group members by arranging his groups in such a way that one or more common element was present along the lines of personalities, psychopathology, interests, age, or education.

"Reorientation" was what Dreikurs called the need for patients to discover methods of working out constructive change after they achieve insight into their self-defeating behavior. "This implies a change in the life style, in the fundamental attitude to life. These changes are not only expressed in improvement of functions, amelioration of symptoms and general well-being; they can be tested by characteristic changes in the early recollections of the patient, since these recollections always represent the basic outlook on life."

Even with the Adlerian point of view, it may be possible to escape social reorientation and the acceptance of new and better social values in individual psychotherapy. But the Adlerian therapy group, as Dreikurs conducted it, could not escape concerning itself with morals and values conducive to better social functioning. Adlerian group psychotherapy works, to a considerable extent, to offset aversive social stimuli that function from within the individual's cultural milieu.

The most important therapeutic factor in the Adler-Dreikurs concept of psychotherapy is the removal of inferiority feelings. This, stated positively, is the therapeutic goal of increasing the patient's self-respect. "Without increased self-confidence," he wrote, "without restored faith in his own worth and ability, the patient cannot improve and grow." In an Adlerian group, Dreikurs believed, there is a social atmosphere of equality that removes the need for distance. "The highly competitive atmosphere of our civilization produces a state of emotional isolation for everybody; revealing oneself as one entails the danger of ridicule and contempt. In the therapy group this danger is eliminated. For the first time the individual can be himself without fear and danger." The therapy group thus can provide subtle but all-persuasive encouragement for each member and permit an unrestricted feeling of belonging without necessary personal bonds or attachments. "Unlike personal and close relationships based on friendship or love, the feeling of solidarity is not based here on a union of personal aspirations," Dreikurs wrote. "Accordingly, the desire to help each other in the group springs from the deepest source of human empathy and fellowship, from a feeling of solidarity, of genuine humaneness." The Adlerian therapist, with his particular theoretical orientation, is especially well-equipped, Dreikurs believed, to maximize patient encouragement and other desirable changes through the group psychotherapy modality.

BEHAVIORAL GROUP THERAPY

In the first annual review of behavior therapy (1973), Franks and Wilson observe that in light of what they term "a curious melange of techniques" which "embraces an incredible range of ideas" that have grown up in group therapy and found ample expression in the literature, it is particularly strange that there is a lack of adequate writing on the behavioral approach to group therapy. They assert that behavior therapy, with its emphasis upon interindividual reinforcement schedules, is especially well suited to group adaptation.

"Systematic desensitization" is the behavior therapy technique that has been most often employed in a group setting. Although very successful results have been reported in the use of this technique with groups for various sexual problems (Lazarus), chronically anxious clients (Paul and Shannon), prison inmates (Thorne), speech anxiety (Meichenbaum et al.), and various other conditions, desensitization takes place primarily *in* but not *by* or *through* the group. As Lazarus, and Franks and Wilson as well point out, the lines of therapeutic communication are primarily from each individual to the therapist. The use of the group setting is mainly for economy of time and effort on the part of the therapist rather than to make use of the group process itself. The desensitization groups, too, are homogeneous regarding the behaviors that need to be modified, which is usually not the case with other types of therapy groups.

When systematic desensitization is undertaken in a group setting, members of the group are usually trained in relaxation, develop together a hierarchy of responses regarding their common condition (usually a phobia), and are encouraged to picture (intrapsychically, not in group discussion) the stimulus scenes as presented by the therapist. As Fensterheim has described it, "the entire group is relaxed when the first patient signals tension while picturing the stimulus scene; hence the group proceeds at the pace of the slowest (most anxious) patient."

Fensterheim goes on to say that group process could be used significantly in actual clinical use of desensitization (rather than the mainly experimental use of it to date). Group members could discuss the behavioral problem (rather than relying strictly on therapist-individual interaction), report positive changes in behavior, and look together at difficulties in the achievement of change. "Reports by individual members of their progress," Fensterheim says, "would receive positive reinforcement in the group, and the progress reported by others would encourage and serve as a model for those patients who find it more difficult to achieve change. Thus the fact that the group serves *in loco maternis* facilitates implementation of the therapeutic objective. Group processes such as universalization and social facilitation may be operative as well."

The objection that desensitization groups do not partake of the group process and depend strictly on lines of therapeutic communication between each individual and the therapist does not apply to another form of behavioral group therapy: namely, assertive training groups. In these the role of the therapist shifts from that of an instructor to a participant observer, and each patient becomes the therapeutic agent of others.

Fensterheim has observed that problems in assertion often underlie mood disturbances, hypochondria and some other phobic conditions, a low sense of self-worth, and mildly paranoid feelings about being pushed around and that, conversely, the individual's ability to assert himself appropriately is associated with an active orientation, feelings of mastery, and the ability to communicate effectively with others. As Lazarus has said, "the spectrum of assertive behavior extends from nonstylized displays and expressions of genuine love, warmth, gratitude and approval to forthright statements of resentment, indignation, displeasure and annoyance."

Lazarus goes on to make a clear distinction between assertion and aggression in anger-expressing responses and between affection and approval within the integrity of emotional expression and gushing, ingratiating, or overeffusive responses.

Reasons for an individual's apparent inability to act assertively may be a manifestation of anxiety (often about being rejected) or simply that he never learned this type of behavior. "Over-niceness" in childhood conditioning ("keeping a stiff upper lip," "revealing one's emotions is a sign of weakness," "good manners are more important than anything else," etc.) tends to produce adults who are hypocritical and defensive (nonassertive) in their behavior. Such persons are quite distrustful of their emotions and fearful of giving vent to them, and they find almost any kind of human contact (especially of the close and revealing type) an anxiety-inducing experience. These are the patients who often manifest lack of purpose or pleasure in living and who thus present themselves with so-called "existential problems" in therapy.

In the words of Lazarus, "assertive training groups afford a versatile reeducative milieu for the extinction of these maladaptive social anxieties, as well as the elicitation and support of adaptive social responses." The patient is encouraged in assertive training groups to actually experiment with assertive behavior under circumstances in which there is a broader base for social modeling and greater feedback than in individual assertive training. Fensterheim combines individual and group training in assertiveness; he uses the group mainly as a practice laboratory for what has been learned in individual sessions.

Both Lazarus and Fensterheim report setting up assertive training groups along roughly homogeneous lines of education, achievement, socioeconomic status, marital status, and age of members. Each has groups of eight to ten members. Fensterheim has his approximately equally divided as to sex, but Lazarus indicates that he achieves best results when group members are of the same sex. Both men function as teacher-expert and direct the course of each session; judging from their respective accounts, it is possible that Lazarus lectures more than Fensterheim. In each leader's group the emphasis is on the acquisition of specific behavioral skills to be employed in life situations and on the reports of individual attempts to use these skills. The general atmosphere of the group is friendly and supportive, with each member not only trying to learn but also helping other members to learn.

Each therapist employs special exercises, homework assignments, keeping of records (by the patients) of successes and failures in assertiveness between group sessions, etc.

Lazarus reports that termination is a problem with assertive training groups, because effective behavior patterns can be refined, reshaped, and reorganized indefinitely. Some of his groups have gone on meeting without a leader and report continuing gains. Lazarus believes, however, that the most significant learning and behavior changes occur within the first fifteen to twenty sessions. After twenty-five to thirty sessions, he says, the meetings tend to become repetitive and provide little more than social support and self-reinforcement.

Although systematic desensitization, as we noted earlier, does not lend itself as well to actual group process, it is much better adapted to specific behavioral outcome criteria than are assertive training groups. Lazarus is skeptical of many enthusiastic personal anecdotes and testimonials he has received from assertive training group members; he has probably done more work with these groups than any other behavior therapist and was the first to report on them in the literature. He says that "innumerable instances of specific gains and examples of improved functioning during and/or immediately following attendance in assertive training groups, perhaps provide little else than positive reinforcement for the therapist." From the standpoint of uncontrolled clinical observation, Lazarus nevertheless believes that these group sessions have elicited significant positive behavior change in nearly all the participants. "The majority report a transfer of assertive and expressive modes of behavior to all their interpersonal encounters. This tends to promote more positive, lasting, and satisfying human relationships."

In urging the desirable expansion of the behavior therapy influence in the field of group therapy, Franks and Wilson suggest that the group setting is an ideal one for the study of techniques like modeling, social reinforcement, the use of Masters and Johnson-type dual-sex co-therapist teams, discrimination learning, and behavioral rehearsal. "In this way," they write, "the extension of the behavioral model to group processes will do much to upgrade the status of the group psychotherapy literature," which is, as they and other observers have noted, in a very sorry state of observation and enquiry.

SULLIVANIAN GROUP PSYCHOTHERAPY

Harry Stack Sullivan's theories of human personality and psychotherapy seem to be particularly well suited to group psychotherapy. Sullivan believed that the analyst could function most effectively in a therapeutic situation in which he could sample those events that are characteristic of the patient's interactions with other people. "What better laboratory," as George Goldman has pointed out, "to observe and document these dynamic events than in the therapy group, where the analyst is, in the fullest sense of Sullivan's usage, participant observer of human interaction? Interaction, characteristic of the patient's interpersonal operations, is thus constantly under observation for its anxiety-laden overtones and for awareness of what else might have been going on other than what the patient assumed was happening."

These anxiety-laden overtones to which Goldman refers were a major focus of Sullivanian theory and practice. Sullivan conceived of much of the psychotherapist's work as consisting of acquainting the patient with the various maneuvers he uses to minimize or avoid anxiety. Many anxiety reactions arise from events in the early development of the individual—events that were part of human situations that occurred as interaction with the significant persons in the developing person's environment. Sullivan described in detail the stages of development through which an individual progresses and defined mental illness as interference with the progression through the stages and with the attainment of satisfactions and security along the way.

In the group situation, the Sullivanian therapist can explore with patients their dissatisfactions, feelings of insecurity, "stuck points" in stage progression, and what Sullivan labeled as parataxic distortions (where present relationships and intrapsychic reactions are blurred and twisted by the fantasies carried over from childhood). Because of the presence and participation of other group members and the impact of the here-and-now interaction with them, corrective effects are often deeper, more profound and lasting than in individual therapy alone. (Goldman's group therapy members are concurrently in individual treatment.)

Goldman believes the Sullivanian-structural group is a desirable place for patients to vividly act out patterns of interaction that are characteristic of their particular relatedness, which, in turn, bring out with unique clarity the reactions in fellow patients. Consensual validation based on thorough group discussion can reveal the parataxic elements in the various reactions.

In the group situation, Goldman goes on to state, the patient can become aware of unsatisfied strivings that are typical of some early developmental stage. The group is a place where the patient's imaginary or fantasied people come to life and are most vividly felt, and where he can re-experience the pain of the frustration of his desires. Such re-experiencing with its concomitant awareness of the feelings that have been dissociated presumably encourages growth. (This sounds very much like the abreaction of earlier Freudian and contemporary Janovian therapy, but it is more tempered in the way Goldman describes it: he says the patient does his re-experiencing of the pain "as close to the original situation as his chronological age allows with a minimum loss of self-esteem.")

The group directly meets some of the patient's needs for satisfactions and security, Goldman says, by giving him the feeling of being part of something and belonging that is often difficult to come by in present-day society. "His emptiness and loneliness are more directly alleviated in his contact with other people, who are, after all his fears and expectations, human and therefore more similar than different from himself." (Compare this with Dreikurs' statement about the group's providing fellowship, solidarity, and genuine humaneness in the Adlerian approach.)

RATIONAL-EMOTIVE GROUP PSYCHOTHERAPY

Albert Ellis, founder of rational-emotive therapy (RET), has written that it is particularly applicable to group therapy. In RET groups all the members are taught to apply its principles to the other members of the group so that they are thereby able to help these others to learn the principles better themselves and to get practice (under the direct supervision of the group leader) in applying them. A patient much more fully grasps and internalizes into his own behavior system a more rational and realistic way of handling one or more of his own life situations after he has gone through the process of helping a fellow group member to do the same.

In the RET group there is often more time to make and report on (and sometimes act out) homework assignments; to get assertion training (compare with the section in this chapter on behavioral group therapy); to engage in role playing; to interact with other people and to practice substituting more realistic behavior for self-defeating behavior; to learn by the experiences of others; to check through discussion the rationality or irrationality of one's interpretations of one's own and other people's behavior; and to have one's behavior directly observed by the therapist and other group members, instead of merely giving an after-the-fact report of it. These and other group processes are designed to carry out the basic purpose of RET in helping patients effect desirable change at the four behavioral levels of thinking, perceiving, feeling, and acting.

BIO-ENERGETIC GROUP THERAPY

Alexander Lowen, founder of bio-energetics, has made an application of the method to the group therapy situation. As in his individual therapeutic approach, Lowen emphasizes work with the patient's body. He has three justifications for focusing on the body of the patient: first, it gets at the whole person and offsets the mind-body split that he contends takes place; most other psychotherapeutic approaches concentrate strictly on verbal interchanges between patient and therapist. (This does not mean that group interaction on the verbal level is eliminated, however, for this takes place as part of the body work and at times independently.)

The second point in Lowen's rationale for the direct involvement of the body in the therapeutic process is that a new dimension is thus added. As he sees it, an experience that is both physical and psychological carries a depth of conviction that is not felt when words alone are used to provide insight to the patient.

Lowen believes, thirdly, that the therapist and the patient gain more immediate and profound access to the emotions through the body. In his words, "not only can the therapist reach the patient's emotions more effectively through the body, but the patient himself can, by working with his body, activate its curative forces on their deepest and most powerful level. The body heals itself when its natural motility is uninhibited."

In bio-energetic group therapy, men wear trunks and women wear leotards or something similar. This sufficiently exposes the body for interpretation of its expression and analysis of its form and movement. Nudity is avoided in the group situation because it focuses too much attention upon sex, to the relative neglect of the other bodily functions.

Bio-energetic group therapy provides techniques for reducing muscular tensions through the mobilization and release of feeling. In Lowen's opinion, every chronic muscular tension inhibits an impulse. At times bio-energetics works to eliminate the tension in order to release the feeling that is thus being blocked; at other times, by encouraging persons to express their feelings, bio-energetics reduces the tension. The latter is done—especially regarding the negative and hostile feelings—by having members of the group kick or hit some inanimate object (like a bed) and simultaneously to verbalize anger and other negative emotions. Lowen believes that the expression of positive feelings is not to be trusted until negative feelings have been well vented—otherwise, positive expression becomes a defense against the underlying negativity, which becomes further entrenched and will appear as resentment at the first disappointment. He also contends that the muscular tensions that bind an individual cannot be reduced without violent emotional expression.

Although all constructive group experiences produce some feeling of unity and rapport among group members, Lowen claims that it is never so strong nor so evident as when a group works directly on the body level. This is true, he says, because the body is humanity's common denominator. Bio-energetic group therapy members feel good and close to each other because they have abandoned their ego positions to relate to each other on the level that all humanity has in common—the human body.

PEER SELF-HELP GROUP THERAPY

There has been a widespread development of peer self-help groups of various sorts in our society. Some, like Alcoholics Anonymous (AA), have been very firmly established over the years and throughout the society. Others are new, local, and sometimes transitory. Those we briefly describe cannot be considered representative of hundreds that exist, but they will give the reader some idea of how this general form of group psychotherapy works.

ALCOHOLICS ANONYMOUS: The therapeutic nature of the AA organization is brought out in the literature handed out to prospective group members. This stresses the fellowship of men and women who share their experiences, strength, and hope with each other in order to solve their common problem and help others to recover from alcoholism. The recovery program of AA is based on twelve steps. The first three of these consist of the individual's admitting that he is not able to manage his life—that alcohol has definitely rendered him powerless—and that he is now turning over his life to God, in whom he presumably has faith. This is somewhat similar to the patient's turning his fate over to the therapist; in fact, in AA, one might say, God is the therapist. The fourth step is to make a moral inventory (good and bad traits) and might be considered a sort of homework personality analysis, which the member then reveals to a closed meeting of the group. Steps 5 through 11 consist of admitting the nature of wrongs, getting ready to ask God to remove defects of character, asking same, making a list of persons harmed by his or her drunken behavior, making direct amends where possible, continuing to take inventory and when wrong promptly admitting it, and getting and keeping in closer touch with God. The final step is carrying the message to other alcoholics and practicing all twelve steps regularly.

Many meetings are held for AA—some open to the public and some closed. Study groups are also available to members, as are informative and supportive groups for relatives and friends of the alcoholic (ALAnon) and for children with alcoholic parents (ALAteen).

What Dreikurs called a fundamental aspect of the Adlerian group would seem to be operating here: AA is giving the alcoholic an opportunity to regain his self-respect by stopping his drinking, focusing his attention on constructive social concerns, and becoming understood by and re-established with his relatives and associates. By continuing encouragement and giving the alcoholic a sense of social usefulness (step 12), AA attempts to render the psychotherapeutic gains permanent.

SYNANON: Synanon, a neologism, was founded as a social movement in 1958 by Charles E. Dederich. He patterned some aspects of it after AA, but because of the more intense work he felt was needed with drug addicts, he developed Synanon into a fulltime live-in community. The synanon itself is an informal meeting which consists of ten to fifteen patients and a synanist (moderator). The synanist, himself an ex-addict (Dederich was a longstanding AA member), leans heavily on his own insight into his own problems in trying to help patients face themselves. As with AA members, he is able to sense a patient's devices at avoiding and evading reality.

Each Synanon member participates in a synanon about three times a week (*Synanon* refers to the group structure, and *synanon* is the group psychotherapy session). Though special synanons are called to deal with problems of work, organization, education, status-seeking, and prejudice from time to time, intrapsychic and interpersonal difficulties of the day-in and day-out variety are the usual subject matter of the synanons.

Attack therapy may be considered the type most frequently employed in the synanon sessions. A main value held to in the sessions is extreme and uncompromising candor. The verbal attack method involves exaggerated statements, ridicule, and analogy. In the course of these interchanges, often conducted in hyperbole, emotional catharsis seems to be achieved by both attackers and attacked, and information and insight appear to be the result.

Norms of the Synanon society are transmitted, too, in the course of the synanon sessions. The synanon seems to have the generalized effect of socializing a person (all of whom are addicts and ex-convicts in the early Synanon communities) and to help him learn interpersonal relationship skills.

The synanons are set up in such a way that there is a constant turnover of membership. The leaders believe that this prevents the development of what they call a "therapeutic contract" (not to be confused with the positive use of this term in transactional analysis), which involves a reciprocal agreement that two or more people make not to expose or attack each other's most sensitive psychological areas. A member cannot get away with ruses unknown to a different group, for there is an open sharing of synanon-revealed material within the Synanon community (but no further).

Although there are no limits to verbal attack in the synanons, strong and abusive interchanges are not encouraged outside the meetings. Ordinary "beefing" or "bitching" is considered an acceptable way of relieving inner tension, however.

Observers have noted that the sharing of emotional experience in synanon sessions seems to lead to a tolerant and permissive attitude generally in Synanon living. A sharp and rigid line is drawn, however, regarding the use of any form of addictive substance except tobacco. The general point is made that no addictive personality can be subjected to anything that will affect mental functioning.

Synanon has had quite a good success record, both short- and long-run, with a hard-core criminal-addict population. More recently, Synanon has expanded to include individuals who were never criminals or addicts. Yablonsky reports that for these relatively successful members of the community, Synanon seems "to be resolving a variety of frustrations, feelings of loneliness, alienation, and relationship conflicts. This part of the program, for people with 'average' human problems, has been incorporated into the over-all Synanon operation and seems to be functioning with a considerable measure of success."

RECOVERY, INC.: The late Dr. Abraham Low of Chicago directed most of his practice toward the preparation of patients of psychiatric hospitals for independent and productive lives in the outer community. In order to reach more patients, he devised a vocabulary understandable to lower-class patients of poor education for various psychological mechanisms and a group approach which he soon found patients could operate to a considerable extent themselves. His book, written to serve as a guide for groups to follow, is included in the selected readings.

Low died in 1954, but Recovery, Inc., has gradually spread from the Chicago area. The groups are maintained on a nonsectarian, nonreligious, and nonpolitical basis. (Nothing was found in the literature about race or ethnic considerations, but I have the word of several persons connected with Recovery, Inc., that there is no discrimination toward any such group on pseudo-group grounds.) Churches, lodges, synagogues, schools, community centers, etc. are used as meeting places for the groups, which are kept down to thirty or less in number and subdivide along geographical lines whenever that number is exceeded. A continuous program of leader training is undertaken in most communities under the sponsorship of psychiatric social workers, psychiatric nurses, and psychiatrists whose functions (according to Recovery, Inc., literature) are "to maintain a kind of security in the purpose of the movement and to help avoid the pitfalls of going beyond the purposes of rehabilitation and resocialization. The movement is strictly oriented to assist and follow-up on the work of the psychiatrist but under no circumstances to replace him."

The Recovery, Inc., therapy sessions follow a prescribed pattern. They start with the playing of a tape made by Low (or the reading of a chapter from his book) which presents examples of symptoms treatable by the Recovery technique. The tape (or chapter) also contains various comments and suggestions by Low.

Next the meeting turns to "examples" presented by group members ("example" is one of Low's special words and means "an emotional and psychologic reaction involving disability and discomfort to the patient and preventing his normal participation in work or social activity"). Comments from the group members and leader follow upon presentation of examples. Such discussion lasts about an hour and is followed by an informal social period. The social period is arranged in such a way that the less assertive group members have an opportunity to talk with other group members and the leader about things that may be troubling them.

INTEGRITY GROUPS: O. Hobart Mowrer has founded what he originally called integrity therapy and now refers to as Integrity Groups or the I. G. Process. I shall go a bit further and refer to IGP (Integrity Group Process).

IGP is based on three cardinal principles: honesty, responsibility, and involvement. Members commit themselves to these three principles as a condition of entrance and continued participation in the group; they may be challenged at any time for possible deviation from these principles.

There is no time limit to participation, and Mowrer says that for many members the groups become a distinctive subculture and way of life. IGP is not concerned directly or primarily with changing others, only with self-change. "However," Mowrer says, "in changing oneself in desirable ways, one almost invariably begins to evoke more positive behavior from others and one also learns how to help others achieve self-change."

Professional persons (other than Mowrer) may or may not be involved in any particular IGP that is set up in a community. Mowrer has set forth some very specific ground rules and guidelines that can be followed by any group of persons who want to set up their own IGP.

Mowrer believes that IGP is part of the small group movement that has come into being because the traditional primary groups of home, church, school, and community have undergone fundamental changes that have left a void in many people's lives. He feels that IGP provided something of the family (or tribal) function of intimate association, the moral guidance of the church, the interpersonal learning type of function of the schools (not the academic role), and the neighborly and fellowship function of the small community.

SUMMARY

This chapter deals with the systems having a relatively conventional approach to group psychotherapy not previously discussed in *Psychoanalysis and Psychotherapy: 36 Systems.*

Horney's belief in the essentially healthy urges of a human being lends itself well to group therapy. The perceptive therapist observes and handles the ebb and flow of the group's attitudes and behavior, taking care that the cooperative mutuality toward which the group naturally strives does not become merely anxiety-relieving but is structured to achieve individual deep-analysis and constructive, integrative patterns of behavior.

Thomas Hora describes unauthentic ways people relate to each other to ease tension and gratify their personal needs. The existential group psychotherapist helps the group gradually to focus on the effort at creative understanding of the here-and-now interactions mainly by the values he communicates with the impact of his personality. An important part of his role is "letting-be," which is "the open-minded wakeful receptivity to that which reveals itself without interference"; this helps make possible the unfolding process for the individual which overcomes loneliness and isolation through self-transcendence.

Adler and his followers in Vienna used a kind of group therapy approach in their child guidance clinics in Vienna as early as 1921. An Adlerian group psychotherapeutic approach in a fuller sense was developed in the United States by Rudolf Dreikurs. Although he thought group therapy helped many patients to gain insights into their behavior (more so than individual therapy), he felt that Adlerian group therapy was particularly well suited to stimulate the patient to relinquish the faulty premises on which he had previously operated and to adopt new and sounder ones. The most important therapeutic factor in the Adlerian group psychotherapeutic approach is to help the patient to overcome his inferiority feelings and to achieve self-respect. This is done mainly by various forms of encouragement to group members.

Behavior therapy, most notably desensitization, has been applied in groups by many investigators and therapists, although there is a paucity of writing about it. Behavioral group therapy, in the sense of utilizing the full interactional group process, has been undertaken more sparingly, but Lazarus and Fensterheim both report its successful application in group psychotherapy for treating problems of assertion. Both report setting up assertive training groups in which the patient is encouraged to experiment with assertive behavior; within the group there is a broader base for social modeling and greater feedback than in individual assertive training. Both report significant positive behavior change in most of the participants.

The theories and techniques developed by Harry Stack Sullivan have also been applied to group psychotherapy, where, because of Sullivan's emphasis on the participant observer role of the therapist, they seem well suited. In the group situation, as reported by George Goldman, the Sullivanian therapist can explore with patients their dissatisfactions, feelings of insecurity, "stuck points" in stage progression, and parataxic distortions.

Albert Ellis' rational-emotive therapy is particularly applicable to group situations. Members are taught to apply RET principles to other group member's situations and hence learn to practice these principles more effectively themselves. Homework assignments, assertion training, role playing, and other psychotherapeutic aids tend to work more effectively in the group than in the individual treatment situation.

Work with the patient's body is an outstanding feature of both individual and group bio-energetic therapy. Alexander Lowen, originator of this system, believes that such emphasis offsets the mind-body split that occurs in most other psychotherapies, adds a new dimension to insight, and provides more immediate and profound access to the emotions for both therapist and patient. Bio-energetics works to eliminate tension in order to release blocked feeling and also to reduce tension by encouraging persons to express feelings. Group unity and rapport is greater, Lowen says, when work is done directly on the body level.

Alcoholics Anonymous, Synanon, Recovery, Inc., and Integrity Groups are described as examples of peer self-help groups in our society. Hundreds of this kind of group exist and constitute an important form of group therapy for serving needs of many thousands of people.

SELECTED READINGS

BELLWOOD, LESTER R., "Alcoholics Anonymous," in R. R. M. Jurjevich, ed., *Direct Psychotherapy*, Vol. II. Coral Gables, Fla.: University of Miami Press, 1973.

DREIKURS, RUDOLF, "Group Psychotherapy from the Point of View of Adlerian Psychology," in Hendrik M. Ruitenbeek, ed., *Group Therapy Today*. New York: Atherton, 1969.

ELLIS, ALBERT, "Rational-Emotive Therapy," in Raymond Corsini, ed., *Current Psychotherapies*. Itasca, Ill.: F. E. Peacock, 1973.

———, "The Group as Agent in Facilitating Change toward Rational Thinking and Appropriate Emoting," in Alfred Jacobs and W. W. Spradlin, eds., *The Group as Agent of Change*. New York: Behavioral Publications, 1974.

FENSTERHEIM, HERBERT, "Behavior Therapy: Assertive Training in Groups," in C. J. Sager and H. S. Kaplan, eds., *Progress in Group and Family Therapy*. New York: Brunner/Mazel, 1972.

FRANKS, CYRIL M., and G. TERENCE WILSON, *Annual Review of Behavior Therapy Theory and Practice: 1973*, Section VII, *Behavior Therapy in Groups*. New York: Brunner/Mazel, 1973.

GOLDMAN, GEORGE D., "Some Applications of Harry Stack Sullivan's Theories to Group Psychotherapy," in Ruitenbeek, *Group Therapy Today*.

HORA, THOMAS, "Existential Psychiatry and Group Psychotherapy: Basic Principles," in George M. Gazda, ed., *Basic Approaches to Group Psychotherapy and Group Counseling*. Springfield, Ill.: C. C. Thomas, 1968.

LAZARUS, ARNOLD A., "Behavior Therapy in Groups," in Gazda, *Basic Approaches to Group Therapy and Group Counseling*.

LOW, ABRAHAM A., "Recovery Incorporated: Mental Health Through Will Training," in Jurjevich, *Direct Psychotherapy*, Vol. II.

LOWEN, ALEXANDER, "Bio-Energetic Group Therapy," in Ruitenbeek, *Group Therapy Today*.

MASLOW, ABRAHAM H., "Synanon and Eupsychia," in Ruitenbeek, *Group Therapy Today*.

MOWRER, O. HOBART, "Integrity Groups Today," in Jurjevich, *Direct Psychotherapy*.

ROSE, SIDNEY, "Horney Concepts in Group Psychotherapy," in Ruitenbeek, *Group Therapy Today*.

THORNE, FREDERICK C., "Group Behavior Therapy with Offenders," in Jurjevich, *Direct Psychotherapy*.

YABLONSKY, LEWIS, "Synanon," in Jurjevich, *Direct Psychotherapy*.

5

GROUP THERAPIES

Transactional Analysis

The late Eric Berne once said that transactional analysis was born as a result of his starting, after twenty years of psychoanalytic training and practice, to listen to his patients rather than to his teachers. What he heard in his patient-listening was sometimes a child, other times a parent, and still other times an adult "talking out of the same patient." Berne asserted that everything in transactional analysis stems from the premise that human personality consists of Child, Parent, and Adult ego states.

Although transactional analysis as a method is not limited strictly to group treatment, its concepts and techniques derive from and considerably lend themselves to group therapy. It is usually in that setting that TA is practiced.

Probably more than any other contemporary psychotherapy, TA has reached the masses. Eric Berne's book, *Games People Play*, came out in 1964 (but was a "sleeper" and did not become a best seller until two or three years after publication) and fascinated the general public with the ideas and terminology of TA. Then Thomas A. Harris' *I'm OK—You're OK* appeared in 1969 and has reached a tremendous number of people with a kind of try-it-on-yourself-and-your-friends presentation of TA.

Because of Berne's long association with the psychoanalytic movement and because of both Freud's and Berne's tripartite division of the personality, it is not unusual to dismiss TA as "just another offshoot of psychoanalysis." Close examination of the two systems, however, certainly reveals many more dissimilarities than similarities. Freud's id, ego, and superego, for instance, are psychic agencies, hypothetical constructs, or inferred entities and not amenable to direct observation. Parent, Adult, and Child, however, are "complete ego states," aspects of the ego at particular times and in particular situations which can be directly reported upon phenomenologically and observed in interaction by others. Berne's ego states also have what he called "civic identities"—that is, real persons past or present who serve as prototypes for each PAC (Parent, Adult, Child). As Berne himself pointed out, each of

75

his ego states (PAC) may be thought of as being influenced by the hypothetical constructs of ego, id, and superego.

Another basic difference between psychoanalysis and TA is that "the unconscious" is notable by its absence in the latter system. A kind of unawareness that corresponds more to what Freud called the "preconscious" appears in a concept that Berne called "exclusion." Exclusion is a denial or disowning process in which a person fails to perceive and express entire ego states.

Berne, however, seemed singularly free of bitterness toward psychoanalysis (whose official body, the Psychoanalytic Institute, had rejected him prior to his own renunciation of psychoanalytic affiliation) or any other system of psychotherapy. He contended that psychoanalysis was well suited for individual treatment of phobias, hysterias, and obsessional neuroses (as Freud himself had frequently said), and that TA was preferred treatment for the areas in which psychoanalytic treatment is notably weak—especially, in Berne's view, all group therapy.

STRUCTURAL ANALYSIS

As we have already observed, Berne believed that each person possesses and uses three ego states. Berne thought of an ego state as "a coherent system of feelings with its related set of behavior patterns" and called the process by means of which ego states are identified and clarified in a given person "structural analysis." Structural analysis is the foundation on which the system of transactional analysis rests. We shall now examine these three ego states out of which subsequent TA theory developed and multiplied.

THE CHILD: Transactional analysts are clinically agreed that the Child is never more than about eight years old and can be as young as a newborn infant. These therapists describe the Child ego state as having been preserved pretty much intact from childhood; according to their observations, when this ego state is dominating the person sits, stands, perceives, walks, thinks, speaks, and feels as he did in childhood. (In Freudian terms, primary process thinking dominates at times when, in TA terms, the Child takes over.)

A person with his Child in control has relatively *little* control—that is, his behavior is impulsive or stimulus-bound rather than reflected upon or delayed. Statements or actions of others are not analyzed for inherent meanings, but responded to at face value. In short, an adolescent or adult in the Child ego state thinks, perceives, and acts very much as he did when he was actually a child.

A person who is often or crucially dominated by his Child ego state inevitably encounters difficulties with adult responsibilities (especially in such areas as family relations and job functions) and frequently behaves in irrational, unrealistic, and self-defeating ways. Transactional analysts seem to grow fond of this ego state in their patients. They speak of the Child as "the only part that can really enjoy itself" and as "the best part of the person."

THE PARENT: In TA terms, the Parent is the person's kind of photographic copy (inevitably containing what Harry Stack Sullivan called parataxic distortions—that is, subjective misrepresentations of how the actual parent *seemed* to be) of the real or surrogate parent of his childhood. The Parent ego state is almost as noncognitive as that of the Child, for it represents the person's perceptions without critical thought or analytical reflection of the rules, regulations, definitions, and limitations which the real parent symbolized. When adequate information is not available or when there is some kind of pathological block between the person and accessible reality, the Parent takes over as an ego state that is a kind of repository of "suitable" or "correct" behavior patterns to be followed.

THE ADULT: Although the Child and the Parent are ego states which have been kept relatively intact from the time of childhood, the Adult is a gradually developed ego state. As the person interacts with his physical and social environment over many years and (unless he is prevented from doing so by some serious emotional disturbance or constitutional inadequacy) cerebrally conducts validity tests or reality checks on himself as he interacts with this environment as well as on the environment, his Adult emerges. Berne thought of the Adult as a kind of computer in the personality, a logical data processor for making decisions and predictions, an unfeeling organ of the personality. As thus conceived, a person in the Adult ego state has no emotions, but may be capable of realistically appraising his Child or Parent emotions.

Structural analysis, then, may be considered the anatomical aspect of Berne's theory and transactional analysis the dynamic aspect, and the former is organized around the three ego states we have just briefly considered. Some of the problems people bring to the clinical situation are considered by the transactional analyst as mainly structural difficulties. The most elementary structural problem is where the individual is not capable of discerning his ego states and confusedly slips from one state to another. Berne, in fact, considered such confusion an outstanding characteristic of the presenting patient, but one that for which the therapist (helped by the group) could usually most readily instruct the patient in altering. As Holland has said (not, incidentally, in the simple language usually favored by Berne himself): "This is clearly a learning situation in which a person first develops a certain conceptual awareness which eventually becomes a sensitivity to those subjective phenomena and experiences which are crucial to the identification of his own experience in terms of the ego states concept." The patient, in other words, generally catches on to the PAC way of looking at himself, which the TA therapist considers most important for further patient progress.

Contamination, which exists when part of one ego state intrudes into another, is another common structural problem. The ego state that gets contaminated, of course, is the reality processor, the Adult. The latter holds as fact certain ideas which stem from the Parent or the Child. Various strong prejudices, defended and characterized as rational in nature and origin by the patient, are contaminations from the Parent; other irrational beliefs derive from the intrusion of the Child's fantasies into the Adult ego state.

Decontamination is an early and persisting therapeutic need in TA and calls for a carefully timed confrontation of the patient by the therapist with the unreality and distortion of the ideas that are causing the contamination. Decontamination is considered effected when the patient is able consistently to identify the ego state of origin for the sentiment expressed.

Exclusion is another structural problem and refers to a patient's rigid tendency to hold doggedly to one ego state and shut out the other two. The therapist (or group member) may be able to evoke another ego state in the patient by approaching with a complementary state (therapist's Adult can often evoke a patient's Adult, for example). Or the same effect can sometimes be achieved by giving the patient a homework assignment in interaction with a family member or friend that will evoke the desired P, A, or C ego state.

The term used to refer to the opposite of exclusion—that is, to the ability of the person easily and volitionally to change from one ego state to another—is *stabilization*. In many situations, the ego state most desirable for the person to be able to achieve at will is the Adult. This is true, of course, because the Adult is likely to have the least biased, best time-oriented, and most accurate touch with reality whenever an important decision must be made. On the other hand, if it is time for fun, the stabilized individual (in the sense that TA uses the term "stabilization") will be able to switch quickly and desirably to the Child.

TRANSACTIONAL ANALYSIS

Structural analysis both historically did and in usual therapeutic procedure does set the stage for transactional analysis. Just as the ego state is the unit of structural analysis, so the transaction is the unit of transactional analysis. A social transaction is composed of a social stimulus and the social response it elicits. In a simple transaction, there are only two ego states involved. For example, the Child of one student may energize the Child of another student: "Let's cut class and go to my room and smoke dope." "Great! Lead the way."

The most important question regarding the smoothness of the transaction is whether or not the transactional stimulus and response are complementary or crossed. In the foregoing example, both the agent and the respondent had the same ego states activated, and so the transaction was a complementary one. Another example: Agent: "Where does the Green Bay bus stop?" (Adult). Respondent: "At the corner of Arch Ave. and Verd St." (Adult).

This, too, is complementary because the same ego state is participating in both the agent and the respondent. It need not necessarily be the same ego state involved in agent and respondent, however, in order for the stimulus and response to be parallel or complementary. If the agent's ego state is Parent, for example, and he addresses the ego state of Child in the respondent, and the respondent not only receives the agent's stimulus as a Child but sends forth his response (which becomes a stimulus for the agent) in the Child role and addressed to the Parent in the agent, the transaction is still complementary.

As Berne has said: "It is evident . . . that transactions tend to proceed in chains, so that each response is in turn a stimulus. The first rule of communication is that communication will proceed smoothly as long as transactions are complementary; and its corollary is that as long as transactions are complementary, communication can, in principle, proceed indefinitely."

In any given series of transactions, a complementary transaction (and resultant satisfactory communication) can be said to exist if the response to a previous stimulus is addressed to the ego state that was the source of the stimulus and is emitted from the ego state to which that source addressed itself. Any other form of response will produce a crossed transaction and will lead to conflicted and often disrupted communication.

In one of our previous examples, when the Child in the first student said: "Let's cut class and go to my room and smoke dope," he was addressing the Child ego state of the second student. If the latter had responded with Parent ("Oh, heavens no; that stuff's illegal, you know") or Adult ("Let's sit down and discuss whether or not that idea is related to our long-term self-interest rather than just our immediate gratification"), the transaction would have been crossed. It would also have been crossed if the second student (respondent) had addressed another ego state in the first student (agent) than the Child ("Hey, Charlie, you had better reconsider; you may flunk this course if you don't snap out of it"—which would be appealing to either the Parent or the Adult in the first student).

Berne pointed out that simple complementary transactions occur usually in superficial working and social relationships. He, in fact, defined a superficial relationship as one that is confined to simple complementary transactions. Such relationships occur in procedures, rituals, and pastimes.

Transactions can also be complex and ulterior, and such a transaction has both social and psychological levels. More than two ego states are simultaneously activated in ulterior transactions, and usually the social level is a cover for the psychological meaning of the transaction. Ulterior transactions are the basis for games, which we will consider later.

THEORY OF SOCIAL INTERCOURSE

Before we can understand TA's conception of games, we need to have an understanding of Berne's view of human motivation and how it determines the nature of human interactions. He hypothesized, in addition to the biological drives related to survival, certain urges that he labeled stimulus hunger, structure hunger, excitement hunger, recognition hunger, and leadership hunger.

Stimulation seems to be one of the important needs of higher organisms. Stimulus hunger is satisfied at the simple biological level by stroking, which is the general term for intimate physical contact. At the post-infancy level of social intercourse, stimulus hunger gradually blends into recognition hunger. Berne used "stroking" to denote any act implying recognition of another's presence, and hence, an exchange of strokes as constituting a transaction.

The recognition hunger can be seen in children less complicatedly at times than in adults. When the child is making a bid for attention, he may—in his desperate recognition hunger—settle for very negative "strokes" rather than no attention at all. His sense of identity as a person seems to be dependent upon receiving periodical recognition of his existence—even if that recognition comes in the form of punishment.

Positive strokes, of course, tend to be in such forms as hugs, kisses, handshakes, back slaps, smiles, applause, cheers, and words of acceptance and approval. Negative strokes are frowns, sneers, cold looks, blows, deprecatory gestures, and words of rejection and disapproval. TA also calls our attention to "crooked" strokes, which convey contradictory messages. One message might be from the Parent ego state: "Stop walking with your muddy feet on Mrs. Snarl's nice clean rug." The Child ego state could be conveying (by smile, smirk, wink, or tone of voice), on the other hand: "Isn't he cute, pretending he's a choo-choo train? Besides, Mrs. Snarl is an uptight bitch who should get her overly clean rugs 'humanized.' " ("Crooked" Strokes, incidentally, when met with by the actual child as a steady part of his social environment, can lead to the "double bind" situations which have been so theorized to be probable stimulating or precipitating factors in the onset of schizophrenia.)

Berne stated that "after stimulus-hunger and recognition-hunger comes structure-hunger. . . . The eternal problem of the human being is how to structure his waking hours. In this existential sense, the function of all social living is to lend mutual assistance for this project." To satisfy structure hunger the individual seeks social situations within which activities are programmed in such a way as to provide him with strokes, Berne contends. An emotionally withdrawn person may be living on "stored" strokes (which he replays for himself) or on fantasied strokes. The popularity of television and the long hours spent by many people with it may be a result of some kind of fantasized stroking process—the structure-hunger is satisfied (that is, surplus time has been filled), and all these TV "personalities" can be somehow fantasized as sending out recognition strokes to the "beloved viewer."

Leadership hunger is closely related to structure hunger. In fact, it is often not listed as a separate urge or need. But, as Holland indicates, a significant aspect of leadership is the ability to help others structure the time at their disposal, and the most valued leadership is that which effectively directs followers to structure time excitingly. This merges, then, into the excitement hunger, which is the search for the most interesting way of structuring time.

Berne wrote about four basic classifications for the short-term structuring of time in human social behavior, with two limiting cases. This made six kinds of social behavior for two or more people to choose from in a social situation. They are classified from the safest to the most interesting and exciting. The first is the limiting case of withdrawal, where each individual avoids overtly communicating with the other(s) and remains safely in his own thoughts. The second safest form of social action is rituals. Berne defined these as "highly stylized interchanges which may be informal or may be formalized into ceremonies which are completely predictable. The transactions which make up rituals convey little information, but are more in the nature of signs of mutual recognition."

After rituals, the next safest forms of social action are activities (work). Unlike rituals that are programmed from outside by tradition and custom, activities are programed by the intrinsic nature of the material with which the individuals are working. These transactions are typically Adult-to-Adult, geared to the subject of the activity.

The fourth kind of social behavior in Berne's hierarchy is pastimes. These are not as predictable and highly stylized as rituals, but tend to be a kind of repetitive form of behavior considered acceptable within the particular social circle in which the transaction takes place. More informal and individualized transactions than rituals, pastimes are designed nevertheless to minimize the possibility of exciting incidents and the arousal of emotions. Pastime-sharers are selected from among the group of ritual-sharers as people safe to spend more time with as "interesting," "sociable," and so on. At such social events as country club dances, cocktail parties, Shriner picnics, and psychotherapy workshops, these pastime-sharers gather in little transactional groups to share the lore of their pastimes and to help each other thus to structure time.

Pastimes are not always totally distinguishable from activities. The small groups that gather before meetings or between sessions at a professional conference, for example, may be engaging in pastimes, but still occasionally exchanging some useful information (working).

Berne has observed that the confirmation of role and stabilizing of social position are important advantages obtained from pastimes. The roles of "peacemaker" or "tough guy" or "good girl" or "mother's little helper" can get confirmed through a series of participations in pastimes and come to be solidified in positions. Positions are simple predicative statements that influence all the transactions of the individuals who have taken them. Most such positions are taken very early in life (Berne said between the first and seventh years), before the individual is competent enough to make a serious commitment. "Unless something or somebody intervenes," Berne wrote, "the individual spends the rest of his life stabilizing his position and dealing with situations that threaten it: by avoiding them, warding off certain elements or manipulating them provocatively so that they are transformed from threats into justifications."

In the fifth category of social behavior as related to the short-term structuring of time, safety is pretty much left behind and excitement and drama come to the fore. This category of social behavior is the game, which is an ongoing series of complementary ulterior transactions progressing to a payoff. Activities, rituals, and pastimes are candid, but a game is dishonest, involves conflict (while the former involve nothing more than contest), and has a dramatic outcome.

Beyond games lie what Berne termed the other limiting case of what can take place between people: the sixth form of social behavior, termed intimacy. Berne defined bilateral intimacy as "a candid, game-free relationship, with mutual free giving and receiving and without exploitation." He goes on to say that intimacy can, of course, be one-sided: one party may be open and freely giving while the other is engaged in games.

In one of his later books, Berne also pointed out that sexual activities often cover the whole six-point continuum of social behavior. Such activities can occur "in withdrawal, . . . be part of a ritualistic ceremony, . . . be all in a day's work, a pastime for a rainy day, a game of mutual exploitation, or acts of real intimacy."

GAMES AND SCRIPTS

Transactional analysts understandably take considerable pride in TA's relatively clear-cut, operational terminology and the small size of its specialized vocabulary. Berne at one point said that there were really only five words that needed to be particularly understood in TA specialization: Parent, Adult, Child, game, and script. We will now look more closely at TA games and then move on to a consideration of scripts.

As we observed earlier, Berne defined games as sets of ulterior transactions that are repetitive in nature and characterized by a well-defined psychological payoff. He went on to indicate that because the agent pretends to be doing one thing while he is actually doing something else, all games involve a con. But for a con to work, the respondent has to present some kind of weakness (which Berne called a "gimmick"), like fear, sentimentality, greed, or irritability. After the respondent's weakness is "hooked," the agent pulls some kind of switch in order to get his payoff. TA writers indicate that the switch is generally followed by a moment of confusion for the respondent, and then the game ends with both players collecting their payoffs (which are feelings, not necessarily similar, in both agent and respondent).

As an example of a game, we will use the first one ever analyzed by Berne. It led him, in fact, to his concept of games. It is called "Why Don't You—Yes But," and is commonly played at parties and various kinds of groups. The content of this particular playing of the game came from one of my own psychotherapy groups.

GEORGE: I'm not getting ahead in my profession because I don't publish. For a geologist, it's publish or perish.

EVA: Why don't you write something, then? You yourself have said you have a lot of research data you've collected, and I can tell by the way you talk that you would be able to write satisfactorily.

GEORGE: Yes, but I can't even think, let alone write at home. The kids are always raising hell. My wife is permissive and doesn't believe in making kids go to bed at a reasonable hour.

MARTIN: So stay down at your office and write. As a senior staff member, you can use your office all night if you want to, can't you?

GEORGE: Yes, but then my wife would say I was neglecting her and the kids.

EVA: Oh, come off it, George. Your wife isn't so insensitive to your professional needs that you couldn't make her understand your need for some temporary period of time to work nights writing at the office.

GEORGE: Yes, but they have all electric typewriters at the office, and I've never learned to use one. I'd probably ruin one and then have to pay for it out of a family budget that is already in sad shape. The kids . . .

MARTIN: Oh, for Christ's sake, George, if secretaries with doubtful I.Q.'s can master the electric typewriter, I think—with special intensive instruction and all that crap—you might be bright enough to use one without destroying it.

GEORGE: Yes, but . . .

At this point, the therapist intervened rather than letting the game go on indefinitely. It is probable, however, that George would have won the game: that is, that the interchange would have reached a point where everyone ran out of suggestions and left George's Child triumphant. George showed annoyance, incidentally, in having the therapist somewhat spoil his victory over the "sensible Parents" in the group.

This game usually proceeds smoothly in social situations of various sorts because at the social level both the agent and the respondents are relating Adult-to-Adult. Although the ego states are different at the psychological level, they are nevertheless complementary, with Parent to Child ("Why don't you . . .") and Child to Parent ("Yes, but . . .").

Games are so popular and much practiced, according to Berne, because there is so little opportunity for intimacy in contemporary American social life. Even where opportunities for intimacy occur, many people avoid it (especially if it is intense) because they feel ill-equipped psychologically to handle it. For many people, then, games are apparently necessary and desirable. "The only problem at issue," Berne once said, "is whether the games played by an individual offer the best yield for him. In this connection it should be remembered that the essential feature of a game is its culmination, or payoff."

In the game just presented, it is obvious that there were many satisfactions along the way for George—strokes in the form of solicitous attention (even though after a while some members of the group were becoming irritated with him, they were still giving him a lot of attention) and other satisfactions from successfully rejecting the solutions offered by group members. As noted, his major payoff was aborted by the therapist. (This was done, incidentally, for the therapeutic purpose of getting George to become aware of his rationalizations and circumventions. The therapist believed this was more likely when George became frustrated in his payoff rather than when he enjoyed it.)

The satisfactions that group members got out of playing "Why Don't You—Yes, But" were at first in being helpful (they hoped), then in feeling superior to poor old excuse-ridden George, and finally in their expressions and feelings of annoyance and contempt. Payoffs can be in the form of negative feelings as well as positive ones.

Berne maintained that games not only serve the function of structuring time satisfactorily, but that they are necessary for people with psychic instability to stave off despair and perhaps psychosis. He noted their frequent appearance in marital situations in which the psychotherapeutic improvement of one spouse (which is to say, he gives up destructive games) may lead to great confusion, anxiety, depression, or other psychopathological manifestations in the other spouse (because the games were important for maintaining equilibrium).

On the other hand, the hope of psychotherapy is to help people to move from the "necessity" of games to the greater satisfactions of intimacy. In Berne's words, "the rewards of game-free intimacy . . . are so great that even precariously balanced personalities can safely and joyfully relinquish their games if an appropriate partner can be found for the better relationship."

Rituals, activities, pastimes, and games are ways of structuring time to avoid boredom and to get maximal satisfaction (or so it seems to the individuals engaged in the structuring) out of each situation. But Berne and other TA writers have shown that the individual also has a bigger (preconscious) life plan: the script. He uses the latter to structure longer periods of time (months or years or a lifetime) and to fill them with activities, rituals, pastimes, and games which further the larger blueprint (the script).

Transactional analysts believe that most people develop their scripts between the ages of three and seven and carry the plans from that point onward about what kind of persons they will marry, how many children they will have, what their children will be and do, what will constitute success and failure, and so on. Only trivial behavior tends to be left out of the script and decided by reason, according to TA. The Child ego state takes charge of the script in the adult and shields it from the penetrating knowledge and logic of the Adult. The more prolonged and difficult aspects of TA consist of direct intervention in the scripts of persons whose blueprints lead them in self-defeating circles or step by step toward destruction. Obviously when a person's script calls for good relationships and successful outcomes and his life is moving along satisfactorily according to such a script, TA intervention is unnecessary.

Berne brought out in one of his later writings that even without therapy more sensitive and intelligent and perceptive people gradually dissolve the childhood-derived illusions, and that this leads to crises at various stages of life. "Among these crises are the adolescent reappraisal of parents; the protests, often bizarre, of middle age; and the emergence of philosophy after that." Berne went on to say that grim efforts to maintain the illusions may in later life lead to spiritualism or depression and that abandonment of the illusions (without therapeutic assistance in working out less self-defeating alternatives) may result in total despair.

PSYCHOTHERAPEUTIC APPLICATIONS OF TRANSACTIONAL ANALYSIS

One outstanding characteristic of TA in its clinical applications is that it is contractual in nature. The patient is asked to define just what it is that he is seeking in therapy. He is asked, in effect, by the therapist: How will either one of us know when we are making headway and when our task can be concluded because sufficient progress has now been made? If the goal of treatment is not acceptable to the therapist, he will refuse to enter into the contract with the patient. On the other hand, if the patient is particularly confused and disturbed, the therapist may agree to enter temporarily into a kind of custodial contract (Parent-Child), which will be renegotiated later when the patient is better able to exercise his Adult ego state.

Although transactional analysts do not completely eschew individual therapy, TA evolved primarily as a group treatment. When a new member enters the group, other members as well as the therapist and the specific patient are fully informed regarding the nature of his contract. The therapist needs also to be aware of the nature of his own contract in the group and to keep both himself and the group steadily informed about what his own Parent, Adult, and Child are doing.

Holland has written that transactional analysts have tended to borrow their group techniques from many sources such as Gestalt therapy, psychodrama, and Bach's blend of Lewinian and psychoanalytic techniques. He goes on to suggest that this may well be indicative of a lesser inventiveness of TA adherents at the process, as contrasted with the theoretical level of psychotherapy. As Holland implies, however, such borrowings (differing in both degree and substance from one TA therapist to another) do not in any way negate certain valid generalizations about characteristic TA group procedures.

TA groups usually contain eight patients and one therapist (Berne was quite firm about the undesirability of a co-therapist in TA because of all kinds of complications likely to result in the Parent, Adult, Child configurations and interactions). For these nine people, there are, of course, in TA terms, the equivalent of twenty-seven people in the room, for each of the nine will be at various times interacting with three different primary ego states. Hence, a tremendous number of transactions are possible, and a patient who enters a group will stimulate others with his ego states and be stimulated by theirs. And the TA therapist has the responsibility of observing these multifarious transactions and to sift out each patient's characteristic ways of transacting with others.

TA is a direct and active therapy. It is usual, early in group proceedings, for the therapist to undertake structural analysis and to differentiate for each patient when he is thinking, feeling, and behaving as a Parent, Adult, and Child. Both verbal and nonverbal behavior is pointed out as the group proceeds and identifies with the three ego states. The TA assumption is that awareness of which particular ego state is functioning in the group at various times and in response to various stimuli is a necessary series of steps for the patient to go through in order to fulfill his contract successfully.

Although the realignment of awareness and ego state may be all some patients need to meet their contracts, usually much more is needed. The group goes on to the analysis of transactions.

Bibliotherapy is usually a part of a TA group procedure, especially in the structural analysis phases, in order to enable patients to supplement their first-hand group experiences with ego states with what they can learn from the TA literature (especially books by Berne and Harris). Attendance at TA workshops and other educational events, if such are available in the area, are often recommended as accompaniments of the reading and group therapy. Tape recordings are also used to help patients to hear differences in tonal quality and vocabulary as they appear in group members in their P, A, and C ego states.

TA therapists are strongly committed to the proposition that the mental life of the patient is largely available for his conscious control. If the patient wants to change, he can. The question is whether or not he is willing to give up payoffs he is now getting from various games in order to move toward intimacy and spontaneity. Most patients have been strongly conditioned to the contrary: namely, that all sorts of covert and overt behavior is outside their control. Thus part of the therapist's work in a group (often significantly helped by other group members who have learned that change is possible) is to convince a patient that he is not the helpless victim of any of his ego states. He does not, for example, need to go on in punishing himself with strictures from his Parent or in being led into labyrinths of self-defeat by the impulses of his Child.

In the course of the analysis of transactions, including crossed transactions, in the group, TA is likely to get into the diagnosis of games and scripts. It is usually found that the predominant game an individual plays in the group tends to block the fulfillment of his contract in group treatment. After the therapist (and members of the group) have helped the person to become aware of his game and the purposes it is serving him, the therapist allows him to choose whether or not (at least for the time being) he wants to continue the game. Part of the analysis of the game includes perception of its place within the patient's script. Games are not readily given up by the patient, and he is likely to experience a depression at their abandonment (in TA terms, the Child experiences a loss).

Not only the group locus for treatment but also the basic emphasis of TA is on the interpersonal rather than the intrapersonal. As we have seen, rather than directing attention toward what goes on inside the isolated individual, the TA therapist is looking at the relations of individuals—their transactions, especially those that are crossed and ulterior. Because of this, a great deal of TA psychotherapeutic work in recent years has been centered on problems of marriage, the family, management, industry, and other important interactional areas in our society. Individual treatment problems have not, however, been neglected by TA adherents: four areas in which significant contributions have been made are schizophrenia, alcoholism, criminal behavior, and mental retardation.

Although strongly active and directive as a therapeutic approach, TA also tends to be informal, casual, and equalitarian. An effective transactional analyst certainly is no pompous pedant. This is probably partly because of the contrary model set by Eric Berne (who trained most of the successful TA therapists or, in some instances, trained their trainers) and partly because of the intrinsic nature of TA: a therapist cannot be too dignified and formal and aloof as he involves himself in group interactions with his own ego states hanging out, so to speak. The therapist must use his Adult in order to perceive and diagnose ongoing transactions; his Parent must be available to the Child of the patient in various crucial situations; and the therapist's Child needs at times to be attuned to and reactive with the Child of the patient (especially where humor and laughter are appropriate both for tension relief and perspective in understanding).

One set of criticisms of TA from psychotherapists of other persuasions runs along the line that it is overly simple, superficial, and palliative. Such a criticism fails to establish any evidence that more is accomplished by any other system in either the understanding of human behavior or its therapeutic treatment by abstruse terminology, depth probes of the unconscious, and alleged personality reconstruction. (But then, the transactional analysts likewise have no real proof on their side.)

Another kind of criticism is along the no-proof line: namely, that when all ego states are understood, transactions (crossed or otherwise) analyzed, games and scripts charted, and contracts fulfilled, do most patients function less self-defeatingly—more effectively and enjoyably—in their daily life? The transactional analyst answers this question in the affirmative, but so do primal therapists and Gestalt therapists and reality therapists about the patients who emerge from their processes. None has scientific evidence, so the no-proof criticism applies no more to TA therapists than to any other breed.

SUMMARY

The key concept of transactional analysis is the tripartite division of personality into Parent, Adult, and Child ego states. Although this is reminiscent of superego, ego, and id, TA is not just a rewording of psychoanalysis. TA is most effective with a different set of problems than that which psychoanalysis deals with, Berne contended, and is especially adapted to group treatment.

Structural analysis, the process by means of which ego states are identified and clarified, is the foundation on which the system of transactional analysis rests. The ego state known as the Child has been preserved pretty much intact from childhood and is dominated by what Freud called primary process thinking. A person with his Child is beset with stimulus-bound behavior, but still, this ego state is what brings fun to life.

The Parent is a kind of copy of the real or surrogate parent of the person's childhood. When there is an informational or emotional block between the individual and external reality, the Parent takes over as an ego state that is a kind of repository of "suitable" behavior patterns to be followed.

The Adult emerges gradually through the years as the person comes more closely to validate his environment and his interactions with this environment. TA presents the Adult ego state as a logical data processor for making decisions and predictions.

TA therapists consider some of the presenting problems of clinical patients as falling into the structural analysis category. The most elementary of these problems is where the individual is not capable of discerning his ego states and confusedly slips from one state to another. Such confusion can usually be cleared up quickly in order to enable the patient to apply his acquired understanding of ego states to the next steps of therapy.

Another common structural problem is contamination. This is a condition in which the Adult ego state has its conceptions of reality seriously clouded by irrational beliefs that stem from either the Parent or the Child. Decontamination, an early and persisting therapeutic need in TA, is considered effected when the patient is able consistently to identify the ego state of origin for the sentiment expressed.

Exclusion is another structural problem. It is a patient's tendency to hold rigidly to one ego state and shut out the other two. The therapeutic condition that is the opposite of exclusion is stabilization. This is the person's ability to change easily and volitionally from one ego state to another.

In the analysis of transactions, an important question is whether or not the stimulus and response are complementary or crossed. A complementary transaction (and resultant satisfactory communication) exists when the response to a previous stimulus is addressed to the ego state that was the source of the stimulus and is emitted from the ego state to which that source addressed itself. Any other form of response produces a crossed transaction and will lead to conflicted and often disrupted communication.

TA hypothesizes various hungers at the social level of human behavior. One of these, recognition hunger, is met in the course of human interaction by what Berne termed "strokes." An exchange of strokes, which can be positive or negative, constitutes a transaction.

Another important social urge is called structure hunger, which leads the individual to seek social situations within which activities are programmed in such a way as to provide him with strokes. Four ways of short-term structuring are defined and discussed: rituals, activities, pastimes, and games. These are limited on each end of the continuum of social behavior by withdrawal and intimacy.

Games take a very important place in Berne's analysis of transactions. They are defined as sets of ulterior transactions that are repetitive in nature and characterized by a well-defined psychological payoff. Games are so popular and much practiced, according to Berne, because there is so little opportunity for intimacy in contemporary life and because many people feel ill-equipped to deal with it when it does occur. Not only, then, by the TA view, do games serve the function of structuring time satisfactorily, but they also stave off despair and perhaps psychosis for the emotionally unstable. TA, however, aims to help people to move from the "necessity" of games to the greater satisfactions of intimacy.

In addition to the short-term structurings of time, individuals have long-term blueprints, which are called scripts. TA directly intervenes only in those scripts that are leading individuals toward self-defeat and destruction.

An important characteristic of TA is that it is contractual in nature. The patient and therapist together agree on the goal of therapy. The attempted fulfillment of the contract is usually undertaken in a group setting, so other group members as well as therapist participate in the patient's movement toward his goal.

TA groups usually have eight patients and one therapist, and the therapy is often direct and active. TA is based on the assumption that the individual can consciously change, including his self-defeating games and scripts.

Some of the areas in which TA has been applied are marriage, family, management, and industry. TA therapists have also tackled such special problems as schizophrenia, alcoholism, criminal behavior, and mental retardation.

Although psychotherapists of other persuasions have criticized TA for being simple, superficial, and palliative, its results seem to compare favorably with those of other systems.

SELECTED READINGS

BERNE, ERIC, *Games People Play.* New York: Grove Press, 1964.

———, *Principles of Group Treatment.* New York: Oxford University Press 1966.

———, *What Do You Say After You Say Hello?* New York: Grove Press, 1972

BERNE, ERIC, CLAUDE M. STEINER, and JOHN M. DUSAY, "Transactiona Analysis," in R. R. M. Jurjevich, ed., *Direct Psychotherapy*, Vol. I. Cora Gables, Fla.: University of Miami Press, 1973.

HARRIS, THOMAS A., *I'm OK—You're OK.* New York: Harper & Row, 1969

HOLLAND, GLEN A., "Transactional Analysis," in Raymond Corsini, ed. *Current Psychotherapies.* Itasca, Ill.: F. E. Peacock, 1973.

6

GROUP THERAPIES

The Encounter Movement

In our introductory chapter on group therapies, we mentioned that this chapter will deal with groups that are on the borderline of psychotherapy and go under many different names, such as sensitivity training, human potential, personal growth, encounter, etc.; and that varying kinds of activities, processes, purposes, and structures may also go under the same name. When a person enrolls, for example, in a group for "personal growth," he cannot be at all sure that what will happen in that group will bear much resemblance to what is happening in somebody else's personal growth group down the street or in the next county.

Although it may not be possible to give a wholly orderly and comprehensive account of the encounter branch of the field of group psychotherapy, a quick look at the history of the small-group movement might give us our bearings. This history is cursory and does not credit all the people who first used a word or a process (there is disputation about historical bylines, but it often seems as if J. L. Moreno—see Chapter 9 in *36 Systems*—first used terms like "encounter" and "here and now" and many of the processes now going on in encounter groups).

Psychotherapy has been a major influence on the small-group movement from the outset. For a time such away-from-mainstream psychotherapeutic developments as Moreno's psychodrama and sociodrama, the theories of the Tavistock Institute in London (based on Melanie Klein's idea that group and therapeutic processes are reenactments of age-old myths), and the work of Redl and Bettelheim and others with children and adolescents, blended in with other forces then encompassed in a rather vague area known as group dynamics. Some of these other forces were personnel management (beginning particularly with the Westinghouse group counseling program), sociological and social psychological studies of institutional groupings, and work with servicemen in World War II and with veterans in the aftermath of the war.

In the immediate postwar period a great impetus and focus of the group intervention process came from the work of the National Training Laboratories (NTL). The NTL program, using techniques and theories developed by Kurt Lewin and continued after his death by his students (and students of his students), began informally in 1946 and was soon officially organized as NTL at Bethel, Maine. The major discovery of the NTL people, which has become the here-and-now core of the encounter process, was that apparently deep, powerful, and important things happen to people when the relationships within the group comprise the main content of the group work.

The T-group (training group) of NTL and the Group Relations Conferences of the Tavistock Institute in England (where somewhat similar experiences augmented by wartime and postwar developments with servicemen had taken place) originally placed emphasis on the study of the dynamics of groups as such and only incidentally on what happened to the individuals within the group. Tavistock has pretty much maintained that emphasis, but NTL has shifted considerably in the direction of individual dynamics. Some authors (see, for example, the Appley and Winder reference) use the term "T-group" in its original and pure sense of a group whose focus is on social action or organization development as distinguished from personal growth (for which they usually employ the term "encounter group"). Even though the notion of individual dynamics has been adopted by NTL, it has been on a relatively conservative basis, and there is a continued emphasis on group efficiency and group progress. This is particularly true of the groups conducted for management training for government and industry. A similar emphasis is found among other organizations throughout the country, which often carry the terms "training laboratories," "human relations," "industrial relations," or "management awareness" in their titles.

The great push for individual-centered groups, however, came with the foundation of the Esalen Institute in California, which was followed by imitative human-potential centers all over the country. The group techniques Esalen used were similar to those of NTL, but were called "encounters" and were directed much more toward individual development than group action. Esalen (and the other centers) also encouraged experimentation of all sorts. The experimentation often derived from Indian, Chinese, Japanese, Persian, astrological, mystical, and physiological-therapeutic sources as well as from various imaginative psychologists and psychiatrists (including, for a time, Fritz Perls and his Gestalt approach). Esalen kept the encounter idea as its central one, received a lot of national publicity, and spearheaded a movement that became symbolic of the life style of the young and young middle-aged American of the educated middle class. Carl Rogers, first heading the Western Behavioral Science Institute and later (after he and a group of followers split from the Institute) leading the Center for the Study of the Person, helped a great deal in giving further impetus and status to the encounter group movement.

The general setup of the individual-centered or encounter group is, on the average, ten to fifteen people in a face-to-face group. Several meetings are usually packed into a relatively short span of days or weeks. If the encounter group emphasizes fairly continuous meeting over a weekend, it is designated as a marathon group. If it meets for a day or an afternoon and an evening, it is called a mini-marathon. Marathons will be more fully discussed in a later section of the chapter. The techniques used—designed to stimulate open, intense, honest, and highly personal give and take among group members—include not only verbal interchanges (to which conventional group psychotherapy is pretty much confined) but also various nonverbal devices such as touching, massaging, holding, hugging, dancing, exercising, playing games, eyeball-to-eyeballing, acting out of dreams and fantasies, etc. The purpose of all these activities is to loosen people up emotionally, help them get rid of their inhibitions and resistances, and "peel off their hang-ups."

Social scientists and their followers (often calling themselves existentialists and humanists, and usually not specifically defining these terms) who have criticized the current American culture usually agree in including among its most grievous faults the frustration of the average citizen's desires for love, intimate interaction, and self-actualization. The encounter group movement is conceived by its proponents to be one of the few effective answers to the depersonalized image that a person develops of himself as he grows in the large, crowded, technologized, and computerized society of today. As Carl Rogers has expressed it, "the person who has entered into basic encounter with another is no longer completely isolated. It will not necessarily dissolve his loneliness, but at least it proves to him that such loneliness is not an inevitable element in his life."

In one sense, then, the encounter group movement may be considered as a counterculture rebellion. This rebellion is against not only the general culture of the society referred to in the foregoing paragraph but also the subculture of psychotherapy. This includes an attack on the alleged competence of the professional psychotherapist and on the training and education that was supposed to have produced this alleged competence. Conventional systems of psychotherapy have also been labeled irrelevant at best by some encounter advocates because they do not provide people what they need to escape the effects of the general culture: namely, freedom to relate and grow and directly express feelings.

Some psychotherapists have responded to such criticisms by incorporating some of the encounter methods into their treatment repertoire. Others have counterattacked with suggestions regarding the ineffectiveness, impermanence, and even nonexistence of the alleged benefits associated with encounter groups and regarding the irresponsibility of the leaders of these groups. Such evidence as there is about changes effected by encounter groups will be discussed later. The charge of irresponsibility is partly tied to the fact that some encounter practitioners are untrained or relatively untrained in discerning serious emotional disturbance and partly associated with the lack of screening processes for the admission of members of a group and their follow-up after they leave the group.

Kurt Back has pointed out that traditionally the psychotherapist has assumed special responsibility to guide the patient through difficulties to achieve the beneficial changes desired and to help him in case of any unforeseen undesirable consequences. "In encounter groups," Back says, "the responsibility ends with the final session. The here-and-now atmosphere does not carry any further." He goes on to say that "even the professional group leaders have a laissez faire attitude toward possible breakdown and other detrimental effects."

This would seem to be true of many encounter leaders. William C. Schutz, for instance, who has been one of the main moving forces of Esalen, stresses that choosing to go to an encounter group is always a voluntary act and that a leader must routinely announce that the group member alone is responsible for everything that happens to him during the life of the group. Schutz justifies this on the basis that an expectation of strength tends to bring out the strong parts of people. "If the group leader assumes much of the responsibility for the patient," Schutz has written, "this tends to infantilize and elicit the weaker parts of him." In any case, all choices of a group member about himself are his, Schutz says. "He may choose to have his brain washed, or to be driven crazy; he may or may not choose to be bored, or to resist all efforts to open him up; he may allow himself to be physically injured, or to reveal his sexual intimacies. These are his choices."

Some encounter group leaders have also tried to avoid the problem of responsibility that rests on a psychotherapist by contending that encounter groups are not psychotherapy. The initial goals of the T-group fell rather neatly into exploratory research and education in group process, but most encounter groups are clearly directed toward personal growth, self-knowledge, and peak experiences—goals that would readily describe forward-looking psychotherapy. The encounter groups also attract people who are in psychotherapy or who would probably enter psychotherapy and turn to these groups as a substitute. Testimony of many encounter group leaders indicates that there is no attempt to screen out patients from nonpatients. All professional practitioners of encounter seem to agree that quite seriously disturbed patients do not belong in encounter groups, but they have no surefire methods for discerning such patients in advance (enrollment is generally impersonally effected by the payment of a deposit) or of carefully routing him out of the group after sessions begin.

Arthur Burton (certainly a responsible and experienced psychotherapist as well as an encounter group enthusiast) has contended, on the other hand, that encounter groups appeal mainly to the relatively undisturbed in the educated middle class and implies that the concern about the mishandling of the seriously disturbed in the encounter experience is largely a straw man consideration. "Psychotherapy is no longer for the diseased," Burton has written. "Some form of it is demanded by large numbers of college students, management and supervisorial personnel, religious people, the formerly married, the unmarried, the sadly married, the literate, and the artistic and creatively inclined. . . . Its tenets are being offered as a new method of general education—of emotional rather than cognitive learning. It is freedom's approach to growth—and the possibility of being in a world which now severely curtails existence."

Burton goes on to say that those whom society has labeled "average" or "normal" often resented being placed "in that existential limbo, resented the fact that their alienation, their loneliness, their despair, and their anxiety were ignored *because* they were normal. The normal have at times even produced symptoms to gain the center of the stage—the existential neuroses —but the entire question of the meaning of a flowering symptom is now a complex and confused one. A psychic symptom is today no longer a symptom but a sign that life lacks joy."

Although some of the practitioners of encounter do not readily admit it, the influence of the movement has tended to be antiscientific, anti-intellectual, and antirational. Only feelings and personal experiences are usually trusted; the more intense the feeling or the experience, the more intense the associated conviction. In Back's words, "The stance of the movement stresses feeling, the strong experience *as experience,* and also the gratifications that come out of this experience. We have seen how, despite the scientific language, the ideology promotes in many ways a return to nonscientific thinking. . . ."

One of the chief ways that encounter groups, once assembled, get moving into the feeling-experience area is through structured exercises. Lieberman, Yalom, and Miles, in their study of encounter groups, define a structured exercise as "a leader intervention that includes a set of specific orders or prescriptions for behavior. These orders limit the participant's behavioral alternatives. If a leader said, for example, 'Go around the room and tell each member of the group what you think of his behavior in the last twenty minutes,' he would have outlined a structured exercise." These authors go on to state that as the encounter movement has grown, so has also the use of structured exercises. In fact, widespread dissemination of "package experiences" in the form of structured exercises has become common in the movement.

Lieberman and his associates found that whether structured exercises are used often, seldom, or even not all has little bearing on whether or not individual learning takes place. The prestige of the leader and his group is enhanced, however, by exercises. Participants indicated in the Lieberman-Yalom-Miles study that they believed their leader was more competent if he used exercises and were more enthusiastic about how much they had learned. Perhaps exercises enable group leaders to emulate the charismatic founders of various types of encounter groups, these authors infer: "Exercises offer a solution to the problem of transferring charisma, democratizing its magical properties. Anyone can learn to use them and thereby gain, if not a semblance of charisma, at least the appearance of technical proficiency. Exercises truly make the encounter movement egalitarian—all can be leaders and some can be gurus, for the skills are simple and the manuals are many."

In another context, Franks and Wilson (see references at the end of Chapter 4) comment critically on the widely held assumption that group cohesiveness is somehow sufficient in itself to lead to therapeutic improvement. They correctly point out that there is an extreme paucity of evidence for this proposition.

Adherence to this assumption can explain why structured exercises are strongly believed by encounter leaders to enhance individual learning and why Lieberman and his associates could find that "they are less effective in general than more unstructured strategies" (even though, because of the complications of the data by other factors, this had to remain an inference) and at the same time added to group cohesiveness. The same authors go on to state, however, that even though individual learning is not helped by structured exercises, "the demonstrated power of exercises to increase cohesion may also explain their popularity. If, as many have speculated, encounter groups have taken hold because there are fewer and fewer sources of communion in contemporary life, the experience of momentary togetherness, without the concomitant responsibility required by communion in the real worlds of religion, family, community, or corporation, may for many be enough to be worth their participation in an encounter group."

Whether with or without structured exercises (and usually with, as indicated in the foregoing account), the encounter group leader tries to get the members of the group interacting intimately with one another as soon and as persistently as possible. John Mann has described the whole process in energy terms. He writes that our socially guided experience has cut us off from our energy endowments: "We are taught to distrust our own vitality and to limit its expression. Every defense, every emotional tension, every situation we avoid, drains us of energy. Further, resistance itself requires energy. Our personality is in part an energy-binding system that limits our access to our own resources."

The leader of the encounter group, as Mann conceives him, has the primary responsibility of helping the members of the group to experience and learn to control (rather than to continue to deny and repress) the energies within them and among them. "From this point of view," he continues, "any technique is appropriate if it enables us to contact either the defense limiting our energy in a particular area, or helps us to contact the energy itself so that we can experience it and learn to live with it, like an unruly animal whose existence we have denied, but who appears, nevertheless, when we finally accept the possibility of its existence."

As Back has pointed out, after the early warm-up exercises of the group, one person usually volunteers to spill out his difficulties "since people have come in great part in order to bring up some of their own problems. . . . The personal problem that a person brings up can then be discussed at length and breadth, acted out, interpreted, and spun out according to all the techniques" that the leader and the group have at their disposal.

Although encounter leaders have often said that they follow the procedure of letting an individual have the attention of the group as long as he wants it, there is the unstated corollary "and the group (including the leader) wants to give it." Usually the transition is easy, with attention gradually shifting to an individual who has become actively involved in the first person's problem (perhaps in playing the role of a family member, a friend, or an antagonist). In this way, as the group proceeds, attention usually shifts gradually and gives everybody a chance in the limelight. Most leaders insert structured exercises (such as a body lift or a trust fall) at points at which one or more members feel neglected or rejected or when group interest seems to flag.

Back gives a graphic description of the kind of things that happen after the group has gone through some of its initial stages: "The group becomes ritualized, and people start to know what they can expect from each other. Thus, gradually, stronger emotions are being shown, and people who were holding back for a while are ready to emote at the slightest provocation. Stimulus and response are sometimes quite incongruous to each other. An exercise of rhythmic clapping (different people trying to clap different rhythms) suddenly caused one of the members to jump up, fall down on the floor, and give a very emotional appeal about his loneliness, his lack of understanding people, and especially his relation to his wife. It was quite obvious that he had been waiting for an occasion of this kind, and the slight heightening of emotion which rhythmic behavior can produce gave him a chance to release his feelings."

Back also gives an excellent description of how the structured exercises discussed earlier are worked into the ongoing encounter group process (he is talking about encounter centers, of which Esalen is the best known example, when he refers to "places," but the fame to which he refers applies equally to leaders as to centers): "Such a sequence might begin with some of the exercises for which the places are famous, such as beating pillows or other physical exercises, or some game such as imagining oneself as a flower or with another name. Activities of this kind raise expectations that something is going to happen, and under these conditions something is bound to happen to someone. This event then becomes the content, and other people start bringing in related experiences, or react to the way the person expresses his own problems, until the sequence of effects is wound up again. A new exercise might start a new routine of the same kind."

Jack R. Gibb has pointed to four aspects of personal growth which he considers of critical importance and which can be considerably moved toward by persons who commit themselves to the encounter group experience. The first aspect of growth Gibb describes is trust: the trusting person comes to have confidence in his impulses, his inner feelings, the people with whom he comes in contact, and his own motivations. The second aspect of personal growth is openness—"the capacity to open myself to communication in depth with the persons with whom I live. The open person communicates with his inner self, reveals himself and his feelings to others, and allows the feelings and perceptions of others to touch and to get to him." The third aspect, Gibb says, is self-determination—the person's capacity to find out what he is like, what he wants to become, and to come ever closer to being that kind of person. The fourth aspect of personal growth is interdependence. In Gibb's words, "the capacity to live and work with others, sensing my dependence upon them and achieving freedom and growth with them in overcoming self-defeating overdependence or rebellion. For me, it is in genuine interdependence that a person finds his greatest growth and his deepest experiences of fulfillment."

What happens when personal growth of the positive sort described by Gibb does not occur? How many members of the group have serious problems in their lives on which an encounter experience has a negative effect? How many are actively harmed? It is difficult to know, but serious researchers are in agreement that the observations of encounter leaders themselves are bound to be biased in a favorable direction. According to the best evaluation they can make of available data at the time they published their book (1973), Lieberman, Yalom, and Miles decided that "across all the encounter groups studied, the ability to effect change is modest when compared to that of psychotherapy" (and here they referred to outcome studies that have been made of various conventional forms of psychotherapy). In their advice to potential participants in encounter groups, these authors state that "one's chances for clear positive benefit are only about one in three. A person who feels, essentially, that he or she is in psychological distress should ordinarily be considering counseling or psychotherapy rather than an encounter group experience."

Lieberman and associates further suggest that if the potential participant, after looking over encounter group offerings, decides to enter a particular group, he should try to "avoid the traps of overoptimism, blind trust in the goodness of the group or the leader, and being out on the edge of the group. Avoiding these traps permits—but does not guarantee—achievement of positive learning goals." To achieve these goals, by the way, these researchers make a recommendation that is directly contrary to the admonition of almost all encounter leaders that feelings are the only thing that really are important: namely, "For those who maintain an active, *thoughtful* stance toward what is occurring in the group and in their own awareness, durable gains are more likely."

In his studies of encounter activities, Back seems to have arrived at more bitter conclusions about what he considers the evasiveness of many leaders concerning their responsibilities for group members. "Discussions by protagonists of sensitivity training typically start with a denunciation of the current intellectual, fragmented, technological, manipulating society, and a promise of a new way of life based on feeling, bodily enjoyment, and unity with nature. This exalted level is mainly inspirational and exudes a somewhat religious atmosphere. Questions about evidence or misstatement of fact are clearly inappropriate here. After this tone is set, the group leader can then take the professional route, quoting some results of training, testimonials of satisfied customers, and description of the training procedures. If his defense of sensitivity training as a procedure is challenged on the basis of the danger of the procedures in comparison with low evidence of success, the leader can return to the high road and deprecate these picayune concerns in the context of the aim of spiritual regeneration. If one dares to puncture this mood, however, there is always the comeback of comparing sensitivity training with other procedures of personal change, such as psychoanalysis; attacking the competition by pointing to the lack of hard research proving its effectiveness. Between claiming to be beyond evaluation and quibbling over the relative merit of their own and others' research results, the question of the responsibility of the sensitivity training leader remains unanswered."

In trying to evaluate the technological contribution to human change and growth being made by the encounter movement, Lieberman, Yalom, and Miles found that theoretical orientation did not correspond in any significant way to what a leader of an encounter group does in the sessions or to how much he helps people to change or grow. Of the four basic dimensions they found which described the activities of encounter leaders (stimulation, caring, meaning attribution, and executive function), only stimulation seemed to represent a distinctive contribution (because both education and psychotherapy have increasingly avoided excessive stimulation in recent years). Yet they found that this one unusual contribution of the encounter movement was not in and of itself productive and "leaders very high on this characteristic were not only modest in gain but high producers of negative outcomes. Thus a functional analysis of what encounter leaders actually do has isolated as characteristic of the encounter technology only one dimension, of which the efficiency for inducing positive personal growth is doubtful."

As they proceed further to analyze the encounter technology, Lieberman and his associates point to evidence which undermines the value of some of the experiences that have been systematically built into the encounter methodology "because they have been seen as the critical ingredients which are absent in contemporary everyday experience. None has been more widely acclaimed in encounter ideology than expressivity—the expression of warm, positive feelings or angry, hostile feelings. Yet, expressivity did not appear to be instrumentally related to gain or benefit from an encounter group. Even so hallowed an activity as self-disclosure needs to be accompanied by cognitive processes to maximize its benefit."

Lieberman and associates also hit such errors in the theories and the technology as the assumption that all participants in encounter groups need the same set of experiences and that, hence, a similar set of techniques will do for all. Worst of all, the authors think, are the magical expectations that have come to be attached to encounter experiences. "Encounter groups present a clear and evident danger," they write, "if they are used for radical surgery in which the product will be a new man. The danger becomes even graver when both the provider and the seeker share such a perception. Encounter groups are a disappointment if we place on them the burdens of the plight of modern man and ask why have they not done more."

Although these authors have been accused of having a strong anti-encounter prejudice (see, for example, the Schutz reference), they believe that—with the exercise of such cautions as their research has led them to suggest—"the ability of such groups to provide a meaningful emotional setting in which individuals can overtly consider previously prohibited issues cannot be ruled out as an important means for facilitating human progress. The notion, as simple as it is profound, that by creating a social microcosm based upon principles which are involving on the one hand and different from ordinary life on the other, remains sound. . . . Encounter groups, at their best, provide a setting for engaging in processes that are not usually available in the degree to which many apparently desire and perhaps need them."

SCHUTZ AND THE ESALEN ENCOUNTER

As had been mentioned, the Esalen Institute, located at Big Sur, California, has been the most important moving force in the development of the encounter group movement; fifty or more centers throughout the country have been inspired by its success. Encounter groups are by no means the only offerings of the Institute, for there have been workshops, seminars, lectures, and classes of all kinds in practically every subject that has any bearing at all on human behavior. Encounter, however, has been its central contribution, and central to Esalen encounter has been William C. Schutz.

Schutz has conducted groups extensively outside California and has written voluminously (we present only one reference to Schutz's works in the selected readings section, but this single chapter in Corsini's book will provide the serious encounter student with a full bibliography on Schutz and many other encounter writers). He calls his system "open encounter" to distinguish it from various other encounter groups (just as Carl Rogers distinguishes his system by calling it "basic encounter"). Because of his pre-eminence in encounter procedures at Esalen, his training of many present-day encounter leaders, and his undaunted enthusiasm for the encounter method as reflected in his personal leadership and his writings (one of his books on encounter methods is, for example, called *Joy*), Schutz is often considered the patron saint of the movement.

Schutz was one of the NTL people who early (1963 and 1964) introduced ideas of creative expression and personal growth into the National Training Laboratories programs and brought his ever-expanding and modifying methods (by this time including the techniques of Gestalt therapy, psychodrama, fantasy, massage, yoga, etc.) to Esalen Institute in 1967. With the assistance of other Esalen personages (including Fritz Perls, who was a co-founder of Esalen and a resident there until shortly before his death in the early seventies) and the prestige boost from enthusiastic Carl Rogers at nearby La Jolla, Schutz has been instrumental in the phenomenal growth of the encounter movement during the years from about 1966 to 1972. Since 1972, even Schutz admits, "the great wave of interest seems to be subsiding and a period of reflection and integration is setting in."

Schutz has described some of the main theoretical concepts on which his type of encounter group rests. First is the idea that man is unified—physically, psychologically, and spiritually—and functions best when these "manifestations of the same essence" are integrated.

Second, the integration needs to be accompanied and achieved by self-awareness. Schutz says that "a main purpose of encounter is to help a person become more aware of himself—to break through self-deception, to know himself, like himself, feel his own importance, respect what he is and can do, and learn to be responsible for himself. A person achieves these ends best through self-awareness."

A third basic concept of encounter, according to Schutz, is its voluntary nature. Presence in the group assumes not that one is sick or well, psychotic or normal, neurotic or happy, but that he is shooting for such encounter goals as more joy, self-acceptance, and awareness.

Fourth, as we mentioned earlier in the chapter, Schutz emphasizes the responsibility of each member of the encounter group for himself. But this same sort of responsibility applies to the leader and produces Schutz's fifth theoretical concept of contract. The leader says, in effect, "You volunteered to enter this group, I volunteered to lead it. I'm responsible for what I do and what happens to me here and you are responsible for what you do and what happens to you here. Within the limits of my ability I will do what I choose to create conditions under which your individuality and human potential will unfold and grow. I'll probably make mistakes because I'm human too. It's up to you to learn how to take care of yourself, and to know what you need for your own growth both in this group and after. I have confidence that you can deal effectively with what will happen here."

A trust in naturalness is a sixth basic concept in Schutz's system. He says that encounter involves removing psychological blocks so that a person can unfold naturally; the incorporated body methods help remove the physical blocks so that energy can flow freely.

Finally, encounter is not just a therapeutic technique but a way of life. The encounter culture is part of the counterculture and offers an alternative to what Schutz calls the devious ways people relate to each other in the dominent culture. Honesty, openness, and the emphasis on feelings as well as thoughts are at the heart of the encounter way. Also, in Schutz's words, "whatever a man is, he is responsible for, and therefore he can change. He is not considered a victim of forces far greater than himself. The encounter culture focuses on enjoying the here and now. While not excluding pleasant memories or exciting anticipations, it recognizes that the now is all we ever experience."

In personality theory, Schutz has been considerably influenced by the body therapists. He thinks three factors prevent normal development of the individual: physical trauma, emotional trauma, and limited use. "The body develops," Schutz writes, "to the degree that it is used, to the degree that it completes energy cycles. The more of these complete the more highly realized is the person. The blockages slow the flow and build blocks into the physical structure. These blocks diminish the physiological functioning leading to reduced blood supply, less oxygen, impeded nervous impulses, reduced organ function, diminished intellectual capacity and eventually physical and emotional illness."

It follows that in encounter attention to the muscular system is considered of primary importance. "By holding muscles under tension," Schutz writes, "a person suppresses emotional feelings. This gives rise to an important rule of encounter: 'Whenever you can either talk about something or do it, it is preferable to do it.' "

In encounter brief gestures or passing facial expressions are seized on by the leader (and other group members) as representative of strongly suppressed impulses. The person is asked to repeat and exaggerate them (to offset his inclinations to inhibit them). Schutz says this does not mean that verbalizing is never of value (after the feeling is reached, talking about it may be illuminating), but that it is important to make sure first that words are not allowed to mask underlying feelings.

Schutz contends that an individual has three basic interpersonal needs manifested in behavior and feelings toward other people and rooted in his self-concept. Inclusion is the first need and refers to feelings about being important or worthwhile. Control is the second and encompasses feelings of competence (intelligence, appearance, practicality, and general ability to cope with the world). The third is affection, which refers to feelings of being lovable, "of feeling that if one's personal essence is revealed in its entirety it will be seen as a lovely thing."

Encounter as Schutz conceives it is based on dealing with the whole person as he manifests these three basic needs. Specific people and their needs are, however, reached in different ways. Contrary to the criticism expressed about encounter groups in general (taken from the studies of Lieberman, Yalom, and Miles)—that they do not take account of the individual differences of persons—Schutz stresses the use of a wide variety of methods in his groups. "No method," he writes, "works for everyone, so that the greater the repertoire of the group leader and the more acumen he acquires in knowing when to use which method, the more effective he is."

MARATHON GROUPS

A particular application of the encounter group idea to a kind of island in time—a group that remains in more or less continuous involvement for usually a minimum of 18 to 24 hours up to a usual maximum of 48 hours—is referred to as a marathon group. As Elizabeth Mintz has written, a marathon group does not deal "with anything except its chosen task, which usually is the expression and exploration of immediate feelings. These conditions create in the marathon, for most participants, a sense of timelessness which makes the present moment very real and intense. And for most participants, the intensity of the marathon experience operates to bring about personality changes, in the direction of self-understanding and self-acceptance, which often endure."

Many would argue with the latter part of the foregoing statement by Dr. Mintz: there seems to be no irrefutable evidence that marathons bring about significant and lasting personality change.

Mintz says that although there is a different atmosphere and drama in every group, the prolonged time dimension of the marathon brings about an identifiable sequence of events; the extension of time leads participants to become aware of their social pretenses and begin to question whether or not they are necessary. "Next," Mintz writes, "there is time to test how it feels to relinquish the social pretenses" and to observe "whether disaster actually follows the unmasking or whether it is possible to be liked and respected for one's natural self." The marathon allows persons time to assimilate such an experience, and to think about the possibility of leaving the pretenses behind when they go back to the outside world. "Because the individual participant is allowing himself to feel and behave with more sincerity and spontaneity than in his usual daily life, and because his companions in the group are also undergoing the same experience, there arises in nearly every marathon a feeling of warmth, intimacy, and mutual acceptance which is experienced as unique and beautiful and which is usually carried away from the group in the form of enhanced self-regard and enhanced regard for others."

Mintz has pointed out that the encounter-marathon combination seems especially powerful and can be adapted to a wide range of human needs related to community problems as well as personal growth. In dealing with community needs, the marathon seems helpful in resolving conflicts between various subgroups by facilitating the recognition of common human denominators between members of opposite factions.

Paul Bindrim first initiated a technique for further enchancing self-acceptance: namely, the nude marathon. Since this idea was introduced in 1967, many marathon encounter centers have included nudity. Bindrim and some other marathon leaders believe that nudity increases participants' ability to open up to each other emotionally and to achieve a greater degree of authenticity and transparency.

ARICA INSTITUTE

An eclectic group approach developed by Oscar Ichazo, a Bolivian, has spread steadily in the United States since 1969. In that year, fifty Americans (many of them from the Esalen Institute) went to Arica, Chile, to study for ten months with Ichazo. Shortly thereafter, he moved to the United States, and since 1971 Arica centers have been founded in half a dozen or so large cities and training programs in many more places. Ichazo thinks it is the job of the Arica program to train as many teachers as rapidly as possible to bring about a spiritual awakening necessary to save Western culture from its otherwise inevitable decline.

What the Arica Institute has developed is a kind of streamlined American cafeteria offering of techniques and disciplines, Eastern and Western, that will push the practical-minded individual toward enlightenment. Ichazo believes that every person begins life "in pure essence," in which state the individual is fearless and in a loving unity with the entire universe. Along about the beginning of the fifth year of life, the ego begins to develop. The child begins to lie, pretend, and otherwise imitate the adults in his life, and a contradiction develops between his inner feelings and the outer social reality to which he must conform. As a result of his adaptation to society, the individual develops ego consciousness (which is a limited mode of awareness and a turning away from reality) and personality (which forms a defensive layer over the essence and separates the person from the world).

Ichazo believes that the ego is also the principle of compensation for an imagined loss. When the child turns away from his primal unity with the world, he feels incomplete and looks for completion from the outside. It is this dependency on exterior things that makes man's ego, and his ego consciousness produces desire and fear. A person cannot find happiness until desire is extinguished and he returns to his essence (the nirvana or the Void of Buddhism).

The Arica methods offer a route back to the essence. In the words of a brief paper issued by the Arica Institute of Washington, D.C.: "We are born essential and in the natural process of learning we are conditioned by society into fixed patterns of faulty perception and inauthentic behavior. Thus, we move out of reality. Arica processes this conditioning so that we regain our essential self and yet retain all the knowledge we have absorbed from our culture. As the personality is processed, higher states of consciousness, which are normal, emerge naturally. Being, doing and living in the world become easy and joyful."

Arica Institute holds the view that the process of individual development is greatly facilitated by working in a group. Its literature states that "a group that does essential work together generates pressure inside itself which accelerates the psychic processes. Thus work that would take years for individuals can be done by a group in a very short time."

Ichazo's training introduces a system of mentations that trains people to think with their entire bodies rather than only with their minds. He has indicated that in his system ego is viewed as false or distorted consciousness, and the techniques he uses are designed to destroy ego-dominated thought.

"Short of enlightenment there is no way to harmonize and unify the psyche. When man is in essence he knows he is within the divine unity. Only then does the dreadful alienation of the ego with all of its defensiveness and fear disappear. There is no peace short of being within the divine consciousness."

Ichazo and his Arica followers claim not to be anti-intellectual. They believe, however, that modern Euro-American man has overeducated and overdeveloped the intellectual aspects of his life and that much of the Arica system must therefore be focused on breaking down these intellectual facets.

The contradictions within Western culture have reached such massive proportions, Arica members contend, that major change must be made or the culture will die. Ichazo optimistically feels that a major enlightenment is in process, that the whole society is raising its consciousness, that we are living in the time of a transformation, and that Arica methods will train leaders to bring this transformation to fruition.

SUMMARY

Small-group intervention has grown out of various influences, including offbeat psychotherapy, personnel management, certain sociological and social psychological studies, work with servicemen in World War II and with veterans in the aftermath of the war. In the immediate postwar period a great impetus and focus of group intervention process came from the work of the National Training Laboratories. The major discovery of NTL was that apparently deep, powerful, and important things happen to people when the main content of the group work is made the relationships within the group. This idea was later to become the here-and-now core of the encounter groups.

Group dynamics were (and to some extent still are) the emphasis in the T-groups of NTL, but in 1963 there began to be a shift to include attention to personal growth. The great push for individual-centered groups came from California in general and Esalen Institute in particular. The group techniques used at Esalen were similar to those of NTL, but were called "encounters" and directed almost exclusively toward individual development. Esalen (and similar groups that soon evolved) also encouraged experimentation derived from all kinds of sources directed toward finding effective answers to the depersonalized image a person is alleged to develop of himself in today's technologized and computerized society.

The encounter movement includes criticism of conventional psychotherapy for not providing people what they need to relate and grow and directly express feelings. Some psychotherapists have incorporated some of the encounter methods into their therapeutic approaches, but others have counterattacked the movement for its alleged ineffectiveness and irresponsibility. In answer to the charge of irresponsibility, some encounter leaders point out that people grow more mature when treated as self-responsible.

Others claim that they are dealing with normal persons, not really conducting psychotherapy and hence, do not need to be "responsible" in the same way as are therapists with patients.

Structured exercises are often used by encounter leaders to get the encounter groups going and to keep them moving. These consist of leader interventions that include a set of specific orders or prescriptions for behavior. Although the research available indicates no relationship between structured exercises and individual learning, they apparently add to the prestige of groups and their leaders and are enthusiastically received by participants. Group cohesiveness is usually associated with these exercises, but there is no proved correlation between such cohesiveness and individual learning.

Intimate interaction and honest emotional expression are encouraged by the encounter procedure. One encounter leader (Gibb) has described what the encounter experience does for him (and what he tries to transmit to participants in the groups he leads) in terms of trust, openness, self-determination, and interdependence.

Regarding the effectiveness of encounter groups, the best available data indicates that change effected is somewhat less than reported in studies of more conventional forms of psychotherapy. Lieberman, Yalom, and Miles estimate that an encounter participant's chances for positive benefit are only about one in three. Chances are improved, they found, when participants take a thoughtful and critical approach to an encounter experience rather than just letting their feelings hang out (as often recommended by encounter leaders).

Lieberman and associates (and also Back in another study) find the positive values of encounter groups considerably exaggerated. Such groups do, however, seem to provide worthwhile experiences for many individuals who are unable to find such experiences elsewhere in contemporary society.

As the generally recognized leader of the encounter movement, Schutz of Esalen Institute has worked extensively and written voluminously on the subject. The main theoretical concepts on which his system rests are the unity of man, self-awareness, voluntariness, self-responsibility, leader-participant contract, naturalness, and encounter as a way of life. Schutz believes that three factors tend to prevent the normal development of the individual: physical trauma, emotional trauma, and limited use; hence, he directs a great deal of attention to body tension and emotional expression.

Inclusion, control, and affection are, according to Schutz, the three basic interpersonal needs of the individual. These are manifested in behavior and feelings toward other people and rooted in a person's self-concept. Encounter is based on dealing with the whole person as he manifests these three basic needs.

Encounter groups that remain in more or less continuous involvement for a minimum of 18 hours and usually a maximum of 48 hours are called marathon groups. It has been contended that the conditions of the marathon bring a sense of realness and intensity to any given moment and effect personality change in the direction of self-understanding and self-acceptance.

The Arica Institute is based on the spiritual teachings of Oscar Ichazo, who believes that a following of his teachings will not only bring about fundamental personality change but lead the way to a spiritual awakening of Western culture. Arica methods, he feels, can change faulty perceptions and inauthentic behavior so that people can regain their fearless and loving unity with the universe.

SELECTED READINGS

APPLEY, D.G., and ALVIN E. WINDER, *T-Groups and Therapy Groups in a Changing Society.* San Francisco: Jossey-Boss, 1973.

BACK, KURT W., *Beyond Words.* New York: Russell Sage, 1972.

BURTON, ARTHUR, ed., *Encounter.* San Francisco: Jossey-Bass, 1970.

EGAN, GERARD, *Encounter: Group Processes for Interpersonal Growth.* Belmont, Cal.: Brooks/Cole, 1970.

GIBB, JACK R., "Meaning of the Small Group Experience," in Solomon and Berzon, *op. cit.*

GOLDBERG, CARL, *Encounter: Group Sensitivity Training Experience.* New York: Science House, 1970.

——, *The Human Circle.* Chicago: Nelson-Hall, 1973.

HOWARD, JANE, *Please Touch.* New York: McGraw-Hill, 1970.

LIEBERMAN, M. A., I. D. YALOM, and M. B. MILES, *Encounter Groups: First Facts.* New York: Basic Books, 1973.

MANN, JOHN, *Encounter.* New York: Grossman, 1970.

MINTZ, ELIZABETH E., *Marathon Groups: Reality and Symbol.* New York: Naiburg Publishing Corporation, 1971.

ROGERS, CARL R., *Carl Rogers on Encounter Groups.* New York: Harper & Row, 1970.

SCHUTZ, WILLIAM C., "Encounter," in Raymond Corsini, ed., *Current Psychotherapies.* Itasca, Ill.: F. E. Peacock, 1973.

SOLOMON, LAWRENCE N., and BETTY BERZON, EDS., *New Perspectives on Encounter Groups.* San Francisco: Jossey-Bass, 1972.

7

THE BEHAVIOR
THERAPIES

Although the behavioral point of view has long existed in the clinical field and although there was some early evidence of behavior therapy "schools" (notably Salter's and Wolpe's—see *Psychoanalysis and Psychotherapy: 36 Systems*), a real behavioral modification movement of considerable significance did not get underway until the early 1960s. Despite great resistance by established clinicians, the majority of whom were trained in some kind of psychoanalytic tradition, behavior therapy has become a major trend within the field of psychotherapy. This form of therapy not only has its devoted adherents, but the theory and practice of other forms of psychotherapy have been influenced by the behavior therapy trend.

As the title of the chapter implies, it is more accurate to discuss behavioral modification in the plural, for there are many approaches. I shall make no attempt to include all of the behavior therapies, but have chosen systems that I consider influential and representative in the field. The one exception is the Japanese Morita therapy, which is neither influential among nor representative of behavior therapies in the United States, but is included because of the widespread curiosity expressed about it.

It is difficult to determine just how the war between the behavior therapists and the analytically oriented therapists began. H. J. Eysenck is usually credited with sounding the opening battle cry with his article in 1960 in his *Handbook of Abnormal Psychology*, in which he pronounced all so-called "dynamic" psychotherapy a totally futile game played by nonrealists. Analytic clinicians reacted with great defensiveness to this proposition (and to other attacks that followed through the years from behavior therapists), and the general atmosphere that has prevailed between "dynamic" therapists and behavior therapists has been one of trying to prove each other's efforts completely worthless.

The general contention of behavior modification is that the medical model with which psychoanalytic and related systems of psychotherapy have developed is an erroneous one. In the behavioral view a symptom is not a result of some underlying disease process; and because there is no such process, it is absurd to believe that it has to be cured to eliminate the symptoms. To the behavior modifier the symptoms *are* the disturbance and are, hence, to be directly attacked.

The behavior therapies in general assume that the effective point for therapeutic intervention is the individual's environment. This assumption is based on the learning theories that attempt to specify the relationships between the individual's behavior and his surroundings. Therapeutic efforts try to effect improvements in this behavior by generating organizational patterns which automatically use and involve environmental resources.

A strong tendency still exists among behavior therapists to reject the concepts and rationale of the psychodynamic therapies and to place emphasis on direct treatment of the symptoms of the patient through the manipulation of his environment. Some of the rigidity of psychoanalytic rejection has softened among some behavior modifiers, and efforts have been made by some of the behavioral systems (most notably Stampfl's implosive therapy) to incorporate some psychoanalytic concepts of personality.

Eysenck, in his *Behavior Therapy and the Neuroses* (1960), brought together therapeutic techniques that were largely dependent upon a learning theory point of view. In the years since then three major emphases in behavior therapy have emerged: systematic desensitization, aversion therapy, and operant conditioning. We will consider these main trends before turning our attention to specific systems or "schools" of behavior therapy.

SYSTEMATIC DESENSITIZATION

Considerable clinical evidence exists to substantiate systematic desensitization as an effective method for alleviating fear and anxiety. It is not at all clear, however, what is the mechanism of change. Wolpe's belief, which at first dominated the field, is that if a response opposed to anxiety can be made to take place in the presence of anxiety-evoking stimuli so that a suppression of the anxiety responses is effected, the bond between these stimuli and the anxiety responses will be weakened. So that these competitive (pleasant) reactions will have maximum response strength relative to the anxiety response, desensitization is begun at the latter response's site of minimum amplitude. Desensitization then proceeds from one item to the next highest and substitutes in a progressive way relaxation responses for those of anxiety.

M. H. Lader and others have questioned Wolpe's explanation of what is happening in desensitization and have suggested that it is best understood as habituation of the fear response under conditions of low arousal. Stampfl (as will be seen later in this chapter) contends that the essential ingredient for securing extinction of fear or anxiety is as strong a stimulus as possible. His position is thus opposed to Wolpe's graded approach as well as to the ideas of Lader.

Kimble and others have raised the possibility that desensitization can be understood in terms of an interference model—that is, extinction occurs as the result of acquiring interfering responses. In this connection, Kimble suggests that only the behavior that has heretofore expressed fear may get extinguished by the interfering response, and the fear may remain to instigate other habits. The interference hypothesis seems less likely for several reasons, including evidence (produced by Lader and others in measures of the treated individuals' basal metabolism, autonomic variability, and rate of galvanic skin response) that fear itself shows diminution in time.

Operant conditioning, which we will soon discuss as one of the major trends in behavior therapy, is offered as another possible explanation of desensitization. By this explanation, the desensitization process consists of reinforcement by the therapist's positive comments and by the patient's own satisfaction in success as he goes through the step-by-step responses.

In one as yet unproven way or another, then, behavior therapists can and do desensitize patients with fear and anxiety; the percentages of success vary, but are usually quite high. The specific procedures whereby this desensitization occurs, as well as the explanations as to why it occurs, differ from one therapist to another.

AVERSION THERAPY

Aversion therapy is aimed at behavior defined as socially undesirable or contrary to the patient's own long-run interests (or both), but which usually has short-run satisfying effects for the patient. These behaviors include many forms of sexuality that are judged to be immoral, illegal, or "sick" by the individual's society (e.g., homosexuality, transvestism, fetishism, and other so-called perversions); self-indulgence in extremes which result in such personal and social problems as drug addiction, alcoholism, and obesity; and sociopathic and criminal behavior. Some habitual behavior, such as enuresis, where the short-term reinforcing effects (such as getting even with mother) are less obvious, is also sometimes treated by aversion therapy.

As the name implies, aversive—that is, punishing—stimuli are used in this type of therapy. When the patient (or society) wants to stop certain behavior that is in some senses reinforcing or gratifying to the patient, punishment of some kind is the most likely means of getting rid of that behavior. Aversion therapists try in several ways to make their forms of punishment more effective than the usual social punishment certain violators may encounter. The latter is often spasmodic (not applied to all violators and usually not consistently to any single violator) and timed long after the violating event.

In many senses aversion therapy is the reverse of desensitization. It is an attempt to make the patient sensitive to the undesirabilities of the behavior being treated. The therapist follows the behavior to be deconditioned immediately with (or presents concurrently) strongly aversive stimuli. It is hoped that after a number of such associations, the original behavior (or thoughts about it) will evoke pain or anxiety instead of pleasure. It is further hoped that when the patient seeks gratification, subsequent to therapy, he will be conditioned to turn elsewhere than to this formerly pleasurable behavior.

Aversion therapy is much less widely used and reported in the literature than desensitization, partly because of the tendency of therapists to shun a punitive approach and partly because relapses are much more likely in aversion therapy. In desensitization the patient and therapist are working together to help the patient get rid of something that is objectionable and often self-punitive (such as a phobia). The aversion therapist, however, is trying to establish a conditioned response that goes against the short-term reward system under which the person operates. The necessity (by law and ethics) for mildness and infrequency of administration of punitive stimuli plus the usual ready availability of conditioned stimuli that reinforce the old patterns (like alcohol for the alcoholic) also help to make relapses frequent in aversion therapy.

It is only fair to point out that aversion therapy is often a therapy of last resort for very difficult patients for whom other therapy has failed or who refused to undertake any therapy voluntarily. Even with the problems of aversion therapy discussed in the previous paragraph, its record for recalcitrant cases is often superior to that of other therapies.

Most aversion therapy that has been undertaken has used electrical or chemical stimulation. Other types of aversive stimuli that have been used or suggested include time out for reinforcement (especially with children in reducing disruptive behavior), satiation, traumatic respiratory paralysis, intense auditory stimulation, and covert sensitization.

Although there is certainly no consensus that aversion therapy is a highly desirable therapeutic technique, there has been renewed interest in it in the last few years and a growing agreement among behavior therapists that it needs further careful exploration. Its greatest promise seems to be as a treatment of sexual anomalies and perhaps of alcoholism.

OPERANT CONDITIONING

Although the distinction between classical and operant conditioning is not always as clear as the student might wish, generally in classical or Pavlovian conditioning the stimulus elicits and precedes the response. In a young child, for example, a loud and sudden noise will elicit a fear reaction. If a light is flashed and immediately followed by a loud noise (and this is repeated several times), the child will become conditioned to respond fearfully to the flashing light, which has now become a conditioned stimulus that will bring the fear reaction just as the unconditioned stimulus—the noise—previously did and still does.

In operant conditioning the sequence of stimulus and response is reversed. The individual first gives a response to a stimulus, an event (usually a reward) called the unconditioned stimulus or the reinforcement. Operant behavior is behavior that "operates" on the environment and produces some change in it.

The operant conditioning pattern probably occurs in other behavior therapy approaches. For example, in systematic desensitization, therapist approval is implicit as a consequence that influences the responses of the patient. And in aversive therapy, negative reinforcers are involved in producing desired behavior. Nevertheless, desensitization and aversion therapy are usually considered as having derived primarily from classical conditioning theories and experiments.

In operant theory, because the behavior operates to produce the reinforcement, behavior therapists speak of a contingent relationship between a behavior and its reinforcing events. The idea of contingency between behavior and reinforcement is an important one in operant conditioning, and the types fall into simple categories as follows: (1) behavior can be increased in frequency and maintained by the addition of positive reinforcers or the removal of negative reinforcers; (2) behavior can be extinguished or decreased in frequency by the removal of positive reinforcers, the addition of negative reinforcers, or the lack of any contingent reinforcing events.

The operant conditioning approach to treatment of the emotionally disturbed can be conveniently illustrated by reference to a great deal of work with persons labeled as schizophrenic. Behavior therapists first break the vague and broad notion of schizophrenia down into such important behavioral indications as social withdrawal, apathy, bizarre verbalizations, and disorganization of thinking. Then they create operant procedures designed to change these specific behaviors. Thus schizophrenia is treated by changing its component behaviors. This practice is characteristic of the operant approach to the treatment of any so-called mental illness.

Operant conditioning by token rewards is also a common procedure. In the "real world" of our materialistic culture, money is, of course, a major positive reinforcer. It is a "token reinforcer" because its value derives from the fact that it can be exchanged for other events and things that are reinforcing. Behavior therapists have done a great deal of operant conditioning in modifying deviant behavior in institutional situations with the token-economy program. This type of program involves contingent reinforcement with three aspects: (1) certain behaviors are designated as desirable (hence, reinforceable) by institutional staff; (2) a medium of exchange is created that represents other things—i.e., back-up reinforcers; (3) these back-up reinforcers are, of course, whatever things are desirable in terms of the life situations of the persons undergoing the operant conditioning (extra food, movies, weekend passes outside the institution, special jobs or statuses, etc.), and a system is set up for utilizing these tokens.

Token programs usually have as their goals the establishment of behaviors that will lead to (uncontrolled) social reinforcement from others. The individual learns that he, without assistance from a program, can control his own environment in a way that will attract positive reinforcement from others not dissimilar to what he achieved by aid of the operant conditioning program.

THERAPY BASED UPON MODELING PRINCIPLES

Bandura and others have developed a treatment procedure derived from social learning principles which is based on observing other people's behavior and its consequences. Bandura differentiates three important areas of psychological functioning that are strongly influenced by modeling: these are the transmission of new patterns of behavior, the elimination of fears and inhibitions, and the facilitation of expression of pre-existing modes of response. We will discuss these three areas, but first we will look at what Bandura describes as four interrelated subprocesses that determine whether or not exposure to the behavior of others will produce new modes of response in observers.

The first of these subprocesses is discriminative observation. Such an intentional process is itself influenced by incentive conditions, observer characteristics, and properties of the modeling cues. The therapist using modeling principles obviously cannot assume that simply exposing persons to modeled responses will automatically lead them to attend closely, select the most relevant events from the whole stimulus complex, or perceive accurately even those cues to which their attention has been directed.

A second important subprocess of observational learning involves the retention of modeled events. Modeled responses are acquired while they are occurring only in representational form and then can be later reproduced by recall of the original observations that have been retained in some symbolic form—either imaginal or verbal or a combination of the two. Because in human beings most of the cognitive processes that regulate behavior are primarily verbal rather than imaginal, the representational system must be elicited to obtain effective and long-term retention of modeled contents. The therapist needs to direct his attention to methods whereby especially verbal retention can be facilitated for persons undergoing attempted behavior modification via the modeling process.

A third basic component function involved in observational learning is the motoric reproduction process. This calls for the utilization of symbolic representations of modeled patterns to guide overt performances. In delayed modeling, behavioral reproduction is directed by symbolic counterparts of absent stimuli. Where complicated and numerous motor skills are involved, modeling needs to be supplemented by overt practice. This is particularly true in instances in which a person cannot observe many of the responses he is making, where the model's performance is governed by subtle adjustment of internal responses (as in speech learning), and where fine or delicately balanced skills must be mastered.

The fourth subprocess involved in modeling concerns reinforcement variables. These variables affect observational learning by exerting selective control over the types of modeling cues to which a person is most likely to attend, and they also affect the degree to which the person undertakes to translate such learning into overt performance.

One of the major areas of utilization of modeling to which we earlier referred is the transmission of new patterns of behavior. This sometimes involves the overcoming of behavioral deficits, as in various speech problems, autism, and schizophrenia and also, less extremely, in the acquisition of a wide range of new competencies. But sometimes the therapist may eliminate established patterns of maladaptive behavior by the use of modeling procedures designed to transmit, elicit, and support modes of response that are incompatible with the undesirable behavior. For example, several studies have demonstrated that constructive modes of coping with interpersonal problems can be successfully substituted by reinforced modeling for destructive and aggressive behavior among groups of children.

A second major area of modeling influences is the strengthening or weakening of the inhibition of responses that already exist in the behavioral patterns of observers. Observation of rewarding and punishing consequences that accompany the responses of models largely determine the influence that modeling exerts on behavioral restraints. Disinhibitory effects tend to follow observation of models who have engaged in activities without experiencing any undesirable effects, and inhibitory effects are likely to follow observation of models' behavior which produces negative consequences. Although modeling influences are seldom used to create inhibitions, they are often applied to reduce or eliminate disabling fears and inhibitions. The modeling treatments used in such instances utilize the principle of graduation to reduce fear arousal, involve concentrated exposures to modeling displays under protracted observation conditions, and provide extensive variation of model characteristics and intimacy of approach behavior and aversive properties of the feared object (in contrast with dispersed and haphazard presentations of modeling by parents, for example, in trying to help children overcome objectionable fears).

In addition to transmitting new response patterns and eliminating self-defeating anxieties and inhibitions, modeling principles are used in a third major area: namely, the facilitation of established behavior. This is generally behavior which persons fail to perform because of inadequate social supports rather than the presence of strong inhibitions. Although observers differ in the extent to which their behavior is guided by the actions of others, response-facilitating effects of modeling have been frequently demonstrated in diverse areas, including emotional expressions, preferences, and cognitive activities.

Bandura has pointed out that when inability to function effectively is due mainly to faulty or deficient behavior, modeling is not only the most appropriate, but often the essential means of developing interpersonal competencies. He has also called to the student's attention that modeling is used in therapeutic approaches under a variety of labels. For example, George Kelly's fixed-role therapy relies a great deal upon modeling procedures, and such procedures are extensively involved in Moreno's psychodrama, in role playing employed by various therapists, and in behavior rehearsal used in some other forms of behavior therapy. Bandura contends that the potency of modeling procedures (especially when supplemented with guided performance and appropriate reinforcement) derives mainly from the fact that clients learn and practice effective behavior under conditions that are similar to those they face in their regular environment.

SOME OTHER BEHAVIORAL APPROACHES

Before discussing implosive therapy and Morita therapy, several positions in the behavior therapy area need to be briefly discussed. Assertion-structured therapy, which was discussed in *Psychoanalysis and Psychotherapy: 36 Systems*, has been given a much more decided behavioral bent by its originator, E. Lakin Phillips. Phillips has indicated that although the use of a behavioral model may seem to neglect important phenomenological variables, it tends to be more economical at the conceptual level and more effective in producing behavior change at the clinical level. Both operant conditioning and cybernetics have been major influences in Phillips' revisions of his theory and practice in the direction, he reports, of more precision, objectivity, and parsimonious use of variables (see the Jurjevich reference).

Another development in the area of behavior modification is a system originated by H. A. Storrow which he calls "verbal behavior therapy." Storrow admits borrowing much of his theory, goals, and methods from other forms of behavior therapy as well as using some of the tools and techniques of dynamic therapy. He says that verbal behavior therapy differs from most therapeutic approaches in its focus on observable or reportable behavior rather than upon hypothetical inner dynamics and its focus upon the present rather than upon the past. Actually, however, this causes his therapy to differ mainly only from the older approaches, most notably the classical psychoanalytic.

Another approach, attitude therapy, developed by E. S. Taulbee and J. C. Folsom, seems to be mainly an adaptation of various behavior therapy procedures to hospital settings (see Jurjevich reference). Attitude therapy provides for and facilitates the use of reinforcing techniques, especially making use of key persons in the patients' lives as social reinforcers. The therapy is pointed toward reinforcing adaptive behavior, learning new behavior, and extinguishing maladaptive behavior. In effecting such behavioral changes the attitude therapist structures the environment by seeing to it that persons in contact with patients consistently and systematically apply certain attitudes. Foremost among attitudes prescribed are active friendliness (giving attention before the patient is able or willing to request it), passive friendliness (being available and alert but not pushing), kind firmness (this is particularly used with depressed patients and indicates that all personnel working with the patient are to insist that he carry out all tasks assigned no matter how much he may complain), matter-of-factness (a consistently casual and calm manner of responding to patients' expressions of distress and found to be especially useful with manipulative, acting-out, passive-dependent, and passive-aggressive patients), and no demand (for the violent, angry, and threatening patients, no demands are made other than they may not leave the treatment program without permission, may not hurt themselves or others, and must take medication).

Gerhard B. Haugen has developed a system of brief psychotherapy which is designed mainly for the busy general practitioner who wants to help his neurotic patients without referring them to a psychotherapist. Haugen calls his therapy "physiologic therapy for the neuroses," and it consists principally in applying the relaxation methods of Dr. Edmund Jacobson. His approach seems to differ very little from that described by Wolpe and others in the process of systematic desensitization. Haugen himself says that the main difference is that he places more emphasis on the basic physiologic state of the patient than do other behavior therapists.

IMPLOSIVE THERAPY

The theory and techniques of implosive therapy derive from the attempt of Thomas G. Stampfl, a psychologist, to develop a learning-based approach to psychotherapy which took into account traditional psychodynamic personality theory. Stampfl presented a paper on the subject at the University of Illinois in 1961 (although the techniques were originally developed in 1957).

Stampfl's basic notion is that neurotic behavior consists of avoidance responses that are learned and continued on the basis of anxiety reduction. Anxiety perpetuates neurotic symptoms; hence, Stampfl reasons, if anxiety can be eliminated, then the neurotic symptoms will also disappear. If, Stampfl further hypothesizes, the stimuli that elicit anxiety are presented in strong force in the absence of primary reinforcement (real occurrence of the feared event), extinction of the anxiety should take place. Stampfl started with patients suffering from relatively mild neurotic reactions, but later extended the technique to patients with severe symptoms of personality disorganization. Stampfl and others (Donald J. Levis, Robert A. Hogan, J. H. Kirchner, R. E. Smith, T. M. Sharpe, and R. Carrera) report that marked changes in symptomatology usually occur in one to fifteen implosive sessions and also report less success in very severe neurosis, psychosis, and character disorders.

The therapeutic procedure is designed to induce the patient to imagine the feared and avoided objects or situations in their most aversive anxiety-producing way. In addition, the therapist makes use of hypothesized repressed material. This is where psychodynamic conceptualizations are introduced, usually in such areas as aggression, sexual conflict, fears of bodily injury, feelings related to fears of rejection, and guilt associated with inappropriate behavior. The combination of the anxiety of the avoided stimuli and of stimuli related to repressed material produces a rapid buildup of what these therapists consider overwhelming anxiety (the "implosion") and a consequently rapid diminution of the anxiety-producing behavior. Following the initial implosions, other repressed material may be discovered and handled with additional implosions.

In implosive therapy (as in many other forms of behavior therapy), the ability to visualize is an essential requirement. In the implosive session, the patient is told to close his eyes and picture as clearly as possible scenes described by the therapist. He is asked to imagine key scenes of conflict and anxiety (selected by the therapist from the things the patient has told him about himself and from what the therapist knows about underlying psychodynamic areas of conflict) described by the therapist and encouraged to experience as much anxiety, tension, and emotion as possible during the session. The patient is also asked to cooperate by not engaging in actions that tend to help him to avoid intense reactions; these would include not opening his eyes, not thinking of other scenes, not asking questions, and not making unnecessary movements.

Stampfl, Hogan, and others report that the therapist is aided in the selection of appropriate cues by observing the reactions of the individual as the therapy proceeds. Usual responses reported are muscle twitches, clenching of hands, anguished grimaces, crying, and sobbing. These responses thus provide feedback telling the therapist that he is getting the desired reactions.

Stampfl has indicated that the theory underlying implosive therapy considerably derives from learning theory and from data of the experimental laboratory. These data indicate, among other things, that subjects can learn a wide variety of responses in order to terminate feared stimuli.

The implosive therapist assumes that human anxiety states can be understood in terms of the conditioning model of the laboratory, that past experiences of punishment and pain have changed initially neutral stimuli into anxiety-inducing stimuli, and that the memory or image of these experiences functions as stimulus patterns to set off anxiety reactions.

The relationship of patient to therapist is considered less important in the implosive technique than the experiencing of anxiety with significant conflicts accompanied by nonreinforcement of the primary stimulus (nonoccurrence of the feared event). Relief of symptoms after a patient has been assigned homework of imagining specific scenes without the aid of the therapist is one type of evidence cited to support the contention that the therapist-patient relationship is not highly important. Some success has also been reported from taped implosive sessions in which there is no personal contact with a therapist.

Although typically patients are reported to gain some insight into their problems in implosive therapy, insight is not considered an essential of this therapeutic process. In this way, implosive therapy differs from traditional therapy. It also differs from most other forms of behavior therapy in that it stresses maximum anxiety experience without giving the patient any instructions to relax.

Although implosive therapists stress the unimportance of the patient-therapist relationship, critics of the approach have pointed out that the use of the implosive technique in the hands of the unskilled could result in an increase in anxiety and associated disturbances. Similarly, a premature termination of the treatment session could increase rather than decrease anxiety. There is also the possibility that in the course of treatment, even by the skilled implosive therapist, there will be the inadvertent association of anxiety with stimuli not previously related to fear. This could condition avoidance responses in a patient which are as bad or worse than the ones extinguished.

Most of the support for implosive therapy thus far in the literature consists of the presentation of convincing-sounding cases by proponents. Some experiments reported by advocates are pretty well counterbalanced by experiments with negative results from critics. Many of the supporting data derive from experiments with students, and even proponents admit that such data are to be viewed skeptically. Unanswered questions remain about optimal length and frequency of therapy sessions, effects of intense anxiety on unrelated behavior, the actual role of the therapist (modeling effects, interest and enthusiasm, expectancy and suggestion effects, and so on), and the general efficacy of the implosive technique even in phobic conditions (where the core of the conflict is usually specific and often associated with a clear real-life experience).

MORITA THERAPY

In 1920, Professor Masatake Morita of the Tokyo Jikei Hospital developed a kind of psychotherapy that bears some resemblance to what in this country is called "milieu therapy" and also has some of the attributes of behavior modification. Morita therapy, still widely practiced in Japan, but very little elsewhere, is described here because of its particularly interesting aspects.

Psychoanalysis had reached Japan by the second decade of the twentieth century, and Freud's ideas had growing influence in the theoretical and academic areas of psychology and psychiatry. But as therapeutic treatment for emotionally ailing Japanese, psychoanalysis made little or no headway. Complicated cultural reasons for its rejection as a treatment modality have been offered by Freudians and non-Freudians alike, but Japanese impatience with a long and involved exploration of past events as causes of present symptoms would seem to be a considerable factor.

Morita therapy does not lend itself to an office practice. A person accepted for this type of therapy is confined to the hospital for a period ranging between one and two months. Patients most likely to be accepted (because of a high percentage of success with these types) are depressives, neurasthenics, and those suffering from obsessional fears and manifest anxiety. Persons least likely to be admitted into the treatment program are severe schizophrenics and basic compulsives.

Complete isolation from the outside world (until the last phase of treatment) is one of the characteristics of Morita therapy, which begins with a period of four to seven days of absolute bed-rest in a private room. Bed may be vacated only for eating and toilet activities, and all amusements and distractions (conversing, reading, smoking, watching TV, etc.) are forbidden.

Therapists of the Morita persuasion believe that this first period brings the patient into intimate touch with himself, his neurotic symptoms, his goals or lack of goals, and his need for constructive help in reorienting his life.

In the second period, which lasts from three to seven days, the patient leaves his bed for group counseling lectures, daily personal psychotherapy, and light work of various kinds. In the personal therapy sessions, the therapist goes over the diary the patient is required to keep and comments positively on actions and feelings that show progress toward non-neurotic behavior. The patient is encouraged to move ahead along the constructive lines that lead him away from his self-defeating behavior.

Although the patient is still not permitted to interact with any other persons than professional staff during this second period, the tedium of the first period is gradually relieved by reading (of the nonescape variety), bathing (an intense experience for the Japanese), light work tasks, and individual arts and crafts. The exhilaration of release from the complete isolation and stimuli deprivation of the first phase usually lasts only a few days, and then dissatisfaction sets in again. At this point the patient is ready for phase three.

The third period, also lasting from three to seven days, still excludes interaction with anyone other than staff, but permits an expansion of individual pleasures (including reading anything the patient wants to read). Vigorous physical activity of a type that is purposively directed is characteristic of this phase of the treatment. This includes gardening, chopping wood, repairing land and roads, and carpentry. Morita therapists consider this period important in helping the person with neurotic ailments to realize that he can work productively regardless of his symptoms. The patient's positive reinforcement derives from the tangible satisfactions inherent in purposive manual labor.

"Life-training" is the focus of the fourth and last phase of Morita treatment. Physical labor continues during this period, but there is also a reintroduction of the patient to the give and take of interpersonal relations (with fellow patients and gradually with members of the outside community). The directive reconditioning aspects of Morita therapy are most evident during the several weeks of this final period. In both the individual and group sessions, the patient's role is defined as listening and learning and then acting on the basis of his newly learned principles.

Many of the neurotics who present themselves for treatment are intellectual, introverted, and perfectionistic. They have low self-esteem in a fundamental sense (although perhaps arrogant covering defenses). They tend to center attention on their symptoms and to criticize themselves severely for the manifestation of these symptoms.

Much of the focus of the group counseling and individual therapy sessions is placed on the importance of action and the relative unimportance of the thoughts and feelings of patients. Just as in the earlier period they were taught that they could accomplish the goals of hard work with satisfaction regardless of their symptoms, they learn the same lesson in relating to others, especially through active participation in volleyball, table tennis, folk dances, etc. The patients are taught that it doesn't really matter very much whether their symptoms remain or depart, for goal-directed activity can be concentrated upon and accomplished in any event. Their ego-defensive and self-defeating preoccupation with their neurotic behavior is broken and their attention is increasingly directed toward external objectives.

As have many Western psychotherapies of the directive and behavioral types, Morita therapy has been accused of being authoritarian and of no value in helping patients to achieve inner directedness and insightful self-fulfillment. Like other sweeping generalizations about any psychotherapeutic system, whether made by friends or critics, these charges at this point have no research basis for proof or disproof.

SUMMARY

A major therapeutic trend that has gained momentum in the last decade and has come to be referred to as "behavior therapy" is discussed in this chapter. This form of therapy, in contention with the so-called dynamic therapies, is based on various aspects of learning theory and attempts directly to treat behavior through therapeutic intervention in the individual's environment.

Three major emphases of the various systems of behavior therapy are discussed: systematic desensitization, aversion therapy, and operant conditioning. Although explanations differ as to what happens in desensitization, the general process has been established as an often effective means of alleviating fear and anxiety. Aversion therapy consists of administering punishing stimuli to patients whose "unacceptable" behavior is in some ways gratifying to him. In many senses aversion therapy is the reverse of desensitization, because it is an attempt to make the patient sensitive to the undesirabilities of the behavior being treated. Aversion therapy is much less widely used than desensitization. In operant conditioning as distinguished from classical conditioning from which desensitization and aversion therapy are usually thought to have derived, when the individual gives the desired response to a stimulus, an event (usually a reward) occurs after that response. Operant behavior is behavior that "operates" on the environment and produces some change in it. Because the behavior operates to produce the reinforcement, behavior therapists speak of a contingent relationship between a behavior and its reinforcing events. In treating behavioral disorders by operant procedures, therapists break the undesired behavioral complex down into its component parts and proceed to change these component behaviors. Token-economy programs are described as one type of operant conditioning often successfully employed in institutional settings.

One of the systems of behavior therapy that has been developed by Bandura (among others) is therapy based upon modeling principles. Three important areas of psychological functioning in observers that are strongly influenced by modeling are the transmission of new patterns of behavior, the elimination of fears and inhibitions, and the facilitation of expression of pre-existing modes of response. How effectively new modes of behavior will be produced in observers of modeling is influenced by the subprocesses of discriminative observation, the retention of modeled events, motoric reproduction processes, and reinforcement variables.

When inability to function effectively is due mainly to faulty or deficient behavior, Bandura has pointed out, modeling is not only the most appropriate, but often the essential means of developing interpersonal competencies; and the potency of it as a therapeutic procedure derives mainly from its basic replication of the conditions of the regular environment.

Other systems of behavior that are briefly described are the assertion-structured therapy of E. Lakin Phillips, the verbal behavior therapy of H. A. Storrow, the attitude therapy of E. S. Taulbee and J. C. Folsom, and the physiologic therapy for the neuroses of Gerhard B. Haugen.

Because of its greater impact on the behavior therapy field, more attention is devoted to implosive therapy, a system devised by Thomas G. Stampfl. Stampfl's fundamental hypothesis is that the strong and forceful presentation of stimuli that induce anxiety in patients (and in what for them are problem areas as revealed in interviews) under circumstances in which primary reinforcement does not occur will lead to the extinction of the anxiety (and the neurotic symptoms perpetuated by the anxiety). The therapeutic procedure is designed to induce the patient to imagine the feared and avoided objects or situations in their most aversive anxiety-producing way, and hypothesized repressed material is used. Most of the support for implosive therapy thus far in the literature consists of the presentation of convincing-sounding cases by proponents, and to date there are many unanswered questions about the optimal length and frequency as well as the methods of effectively administering implosive procedures.

Morita therapy is practiced in a hospital milieu and consists of intensive directive reconditioning of the patient over a period of from one to two months. Although it falls clearly into the behavior therapies as far as its major procedures are concerned and as far as its rebellion against psychoanalytic procedures go, it is not to be viewed as part of the behavior therapy movement that has developed, principally in the United States, in the 1960s and 1970s.

SELECTED READINGS

BANDURA, ALBERT, *Principles of Behavior Modification*. New York: Holt, Rinehart and Winston, 1969.

BERGIN, ALLEN and SOL GARFIELD, eds., *Handbook of Psychotherapy and Behavior Change*, Part III, "Analysis of Behavioral Therapies." New York: Wiley, 1971.

FRANKS, CYRIL M., and G. TERENCE WILSON, *Annual Review of Behavior Therapy Theory and Practice: 1973*. New York: Brunner/Mazel, 1973.

HOGAN, R. A., "Implosive Therapy in the Short-term Treatment of Psychotics," in Harold Greenwald, ed., *Active Psychotherapy*. New York: Atherton, 1967.

JURJEVICH, R. R. M., *Direct Psychotherapy*, Part One of Vol. I, "Physiological and Behavior Therapy Approaches." Coral Gables, Fla.: University of Miami Press, 1973.

KONDO, AKIHISA, "Morita Therapy: A Japanese Therapy for Neurosis," *American Journal of Psychoanalysis*, 13 (1953), 31–37.

KORA, TAKEHISA, "Morita Therapy," *International Journal of Psychiatry*, 1 (1965), 611–45.

LAZARUS, ARNOLD A., *Clinical Behavior Therapy*. New York: Brunner/Mazel, 1972.

STAMPFL, T. G., "Implosive Therapy: An Emphasis on Covert Stimulation," in D. J. Levis, ed., *Learning Approaches to Therapeutic Behavior Change*. Chicago: Aldine, 1970.

STORROW, H. A., Introduction to *Scientific Psychiatry: A Behavioristic Approach to Diagnosis and Treatment*. New York: Appleton-Century-Crofts, 1967.

8

THE BODY
PSYCHOTHERAPIES

Whenever a different trend, emphasis, or system arises in psychotherapy, it is standard procedure for proponents of the "new way" to denounce all variations of the "old ways" as superficial, ineffectual, misguided, pessimistic, apathetic, etc. So it is with the advocates of the "new" body psychotherapies. They contend that all the "old" brands of psychoanalysis and psychotherapy are content to bring about, at best, a patchwork mending of the most obvious symptoms of patients. In contrast, say the body therapists, their therapies help patients to learn to listen to the wisdom of their own bodies, to express their intense and primitive animal energies, to "lose their minds so that they can find their senses." In the outlook of these therapists, cerebral or cognitive processes are treated as interferences or distractions for the "true messages" that emerge from the "deep core of being" of the individual in the form of emotions and feelings. In order to get at the precognitive affect of the patient, varying techniques are employed by the systems under consideration in this chapter to focus on here-and-now body awareness.

Five systems will be considered in this chapter: the Reichian orgone therapy (sometimes called vegetotherapy), bio-energetics (the Lowenian offshoot from Reich), primal therapy, gestalt therapy (briefly discussed in *Psychoanalysis and Psychotherapy: 36 Systems*, but here treated with particular emphasis on its body manifestations), and autogenic therapy. Gestalt therapy and autogenic therapy fail to fit neatly into the "body" categorization: Gestalt because it at times focuses on other matters than body awareness (especially in family and other group therapy) and autogenic because there is emphasis on brain-directed abreaction (but it is really the brain treated as a part of the body rather than as the locus of the conscious mind, which is rendered "passive" in the autogenic neutralization process).

As we have already observed in Chapter 6, Arica and encounter group procedures also place great stress on feelings and could just as logically have been considered in this chapter. Because of their exclusive emphasis on a group setting, however, they were given a chapter of their own.

REICHIAN THERAPY

Before developing his own brand of body psychotherapy, variously termed orgone therapy and vegetotherapy, Wilhelm Reich made significant contributions as a psychoanalyst, particularly in character analysis (see *Psychoanalysis and Psychotherapy: 36 Systems*). In the course of his development of character analysis, Reich came increasingly to believe that the libido (or life-energy flow) became blocked in neurotic individuals by the repressive forces of the ego defenses and that these repressive forces could be attacked (thus releasing the libido) much more effectively by body contacts than by psychoanalytic procedures. Specifically, Reich contended, there are seven rings of muscular armoring which correlate with the repressive forces of the ego defenses. If these rings are systematically approached by direct body-contact methods, the ego-defense system of the patient will be opened up and have powerful effects on the psyche. The first effects tend to be what Reich called painful vegetative sensations and intense negative emotions of rage, hate, hurt, and frustration. After the release of these sensations and emotions over a period of time, however, patients will then be released from their neuroses and able to experience the full delights in and trust of their functioning as an organism.

One of the characteristics of Reichian therapeutic procedure that most shocked conventional psychoanalysts and psychotherapists when it was first practiced from about 1940 onward is the characteristic requirement that the patient disrobe and lie outstretched on a couch or bed during the session. In the late sixties and the seventies, however, nudist groups of various sorts (including nude marathon therapy) seem to have considerably reduced the shock (or at least its verbal expression). Reichian therapists point out that the naked patient in the full close view and reach of the therapist is designed to focus the therapist's attention on the body behaviors of the patient and to enable him not only to see but to manipulate areas of tension when they arise. These manipulations, combined with deep-breathing exercises in which the patient is instructed, help him to achieve full organismic relaxation. Talking is minimal on the parts of both patient and therapist, and that which takes place is largely directed toward bodily-related phenomena.

Added to the offending image of the nude patients stretched out in front of and being massaged by the therapist, Reich and his followers further opened themselves to criticism from their colleagues by offering a very simplistic theoretical picture of the almost exclusively sexual nature of human nature. Reich offered the formula that a person's soundness of mental health may be judged solely on the basis of the frequency and intensity of his orgasms: that is, high orgastic propensity equals low armoring and low psychopathology. Cure of neurosis comes via energy release through orgasm.

Criticism of the foregoing point of view hardly needs to be belabored. The Reichians appear to ignore other basic physiological needs of human beings, and to waive aside entirely more sophisticated humanistic goals and values as well. The Reichian outlook, in the opinion of many, seems to make man a kind of animal-machine which specializes in super-effective eroticism.

BIO-ENERGETICS

An offshoot of Reichian therapy has been developed by Dr. Alexander Lowen. He calls his psychotherapeutic modifications of vegetotherapy, "bio-energetics" and has founded the Institute for Bio-Energetics where therapists are trained to practice this form of body psychotherapy. Although the emphasis is on the body as the route to relief of disturbances of the psyche as in Reichian therapy, bio-energetics makes less use of direct body-contact techniques in the course of the therapy and instructs the patient, instead, in emotional-release verbal techniques and various exercises.

Lowenian patients are not required to remove their clothing (although they may if they choose). Instead of lying on a couch or bed, the patient is usually asked to take a stress position (such as an arched position with the feet, elbows, and head on the floor), which is designed to reveal the presence of chronic muscular tension: that is, the more the tension the more stressful becomes the maintenance of the position.

Lowen departs from Reich also in not thinking that the orgasm is the sole key to emotional health. He believes, on the other hand, that the main task of therapy is to get a fast and intense energy flow to course through the organism. The patient's exercises are designed to uncover chronic restrictions in the breathing cycle, energy blockages, and muscular tensions. These are his armorings that are keeping energy from flowing through his organism. Though much of Lowenian, like Reichian, therapy is aimed at these armorings, Lowen does not believe, as did Reich, that the seven rings of muscular armoring must be dissolved separately ring by ring (from head to pelvis).

One of the Lowenian activity exercises (as distinguished from the exercises described as stress positions) is having the patient hit or kick the couch while yelling at the same time (perhaps a forerunner in body psychotherapy of Janov's primal scream therapy, which we will discuss later in the chapter). Lowen contends that this is a therapeutic procedure because it helps the patient let go of his usual controls and to release great amounts of energy that were up to this point tied to negative emotions. Creative verbalizations in the course of the yelling process (even if unintelligible) are viewed by Lowenian therapists as signs of breaking through the repressed emotions.

As indicated, Lowen does not fall into Reich's procedure of treating human beings as if they were orgasm machines, but it can perhaps be suggested that he gives the impression that mental health can be achieved by making the human organism function like a giant battery. The charging and discharging of energy with efficiency and precision is treated as synonymous with mental health. A hypermanic individual can by this perspective be viewed as having let go of deep and chronic blockages and fixations. Even if one accepts the notion that psychopathology consists of a kind of frozen rigidification of energy, Lowen appears to accept manifestation of the breaking of muscular armoring at a superficial level (what of the deep visceral rigidifications?). The Lowenian therapist seems to be set up to help the patient remove external blocks to the free flow of energy rather than in any way employ his (the patient's) inner resources (including his cerebral cortex) to function in a less self-defeating way.

In summary, then, it is perhaps fair to say that bio-energetics is a modification of Reichian therapy which makes the whole procedure less a matter of a single-tracked push toward super-orgastic expression and which calls for more activity on the part of the patient. But the patient is still conceived in simplistic terms, and his activity is still directed toward superficial goals (striated muscular tensions).

PRIMAL THERAPY

Arthur Janov, the psychologist who invented primal therapy, speaks of human beings' primal needs as follows: to be fed when hungry, to be kept warm, to be stimulated and held, to have privacy, and to be allowed to develop inherited potentials. When a primal need is denied (a child isn't fed when hungry, not held, not kept consistently warm, etc.), the result is what Janov calls primal pain. Such pain, he hypothesizes, remains encapsulated in the human system and produces layers of tension, which find some kind of outlet. But discharge of the tension along the way of life does not rid the individual of his primal pain. It remains, according to Janov, "as pristine, vivid, and hurtful" as when it began. But it stays buried (repressed), and the original feelings can no longer be recognized or consciously experienced. A day is reached in a child's life, Janov asserts, when he changes from being a child with certain suppressions to one who has effectively turned a good part of himself off. He has become neurotic and a likely candidate for primal therapy. Tension, then, is the pressure of primal pain disconnected from awareness, and both the pain and the tension can be undone only by living out the pain. The job of therapy, Janov says, is not to interpret but to aid someone to experience and thus to connect his history with his behavior.

Janov believes that neurosis is the symbolization of primal pain, a defending against pain that enables the human organism to avoid insanity or death. But having served a useful purpose for the fragile child, neurosis lingers and continues to protect the adult from a pain that need no longer be devastating (e.g., "my mother doesn't love me"). The only way neurosis can be eliminated is to help the individual feel what lies under the shield of tension. The neurosis has developed slowly as a result of humiliations, indifferences, insults, etc., and needs to be undone from the most bearable on through to the most unbearable hurts.

Janov contends that people do not have to relive each and every hurt, but only key scenes (called primal scenes), which represent the feelings involved in many similar events. Experiencing such key scenes is often terrifying; hence the primal scream in the primal scene. But it is also, according to Janov, curative, because the repression of that fear produced the neurotic behavior.

A primal need or feeling, Janov says, generalizes to the present because it has not been fully felt specifically in the past. The adult homosexual, for example, may be trying unconsciously to get many men to love him because he never specifically permitted himself to feel hurt because his father did not love him. His need to be loved generalizes to others, and these other outlets are neurotic because they are symbolic of the original. The neurotic does not rid himself of his self-defeating behavior, but keeps repeating it in a vain attempt to get out the unrecognized and undefined pain. He does not change, Janov says, because he cannot (without primal therapy, that is) experience the pain that will free and change him.

One of Janov's innovations which greatly aids the process of intensive experiencing for the patient is the requirement that the first three weeks of therapy be an individual, continuous, undistracted process. Psychophysiological readaptation is much more likely with this kind of schedule. By combining early memory associations with superficial breathing techniques and direct verbal confrontation, the patient is reported to be frequently able to experience vivid and poignant feelings from an early age. The therapist also engages in the intensity of the experience, for he sees no other patient during the first three-week period. The patient then continues to have abreactive-cathartic experiences in a group for six to nine months following the individual therapy.

According to Reichians and Lowenians, such painful experiences of emotional catharsis are mainly valuable for releasing bound-up libidinal or metabolic energy; but according to Janov, the major value is the full and awareful experiencing of the pain, which puts the heretofore split person back in touch with his whole being.

In laboratory studies not only by Janov but also by some independent investigators (see the Karle, Corriere, and Hart reference), physiological changes do occur in the course of the first three weeks of primal therapy (reduction in pulse rate and rectal temperature and changes in electroencephalographic readings), which supports the contention that there is a reduction of tension. It is not clear, however, whether or not these are more than short-term physiological effects, and these effects do not support Janov's contention that primal therapy is thus *the* cure for neurosis even if they do turn out to be long-term. It is quite possible that all abreactive therapies would show similar effects (such effects have been obtained with autogenic patients); reduction of tension is by no means proof positive that a person can function both physiologically and psychologically in a self-actualizing, super-normal way.

Aside from the short-term physiological changes, nothing is verified regarding primal therapy, including the very existence of primal pains and memories. Accumulated tension and its release (with resulting physiologically recorded changes referred to above) can be understood more simply and as adequately in the terms of the behavior therapist. It would be interesting, for example, to take pre- and post-therapy measurements of pulse, temperature, and EEG with patients subjected to three intensive weeks of Stampfl's implosive therapy. Also, it would be well to find out how the tension measurements of patients stack up after they are subjected to emotion-releasing therapy in groups run on an encounterlike basis.

It also seems only fair to point out that not all psychologists and psychiatrists agree with Janov's conception of what constitutes good emotional health. The descriptions given by Janov of post-primal patients sound impressive from a physiological standpoint, but what about their psychological functioning? The EEG readings indicate that their brains function less actively, after primordial emotion is violently felt and expressed. Any sensitivity and refinement of the conscience would be tied in with the production of tension and might thus be shunned by a post-primal person. Likewise, long-term goals and projects that call for disciplined pain and commitment would be avoided by the post-primal patient with a desire to maintain Janov's conception of good mental health. Janov's own descriptions of the emotional health of a post-primal person gives the reader the impression of an individual who behaves not too differently from one who has had a prefrontal lobotomy.

Janov has nevertheless served to shock traditional therapists out of their complacency with his introduction of a revolutionary therapy that challenges the premises of all other therapies. He has also made some considerable (though, as indicated, sometimes naive) effort to find a scientific base for his assertions about the nature of human beings and their problems. It is to be hoped that a great deal more research will be undertaken to see what does or does not happen to patients in all forms of therapy, certainly including primal therapy.

GESTALT THERAPY

Gestalt therapy is unlike psychoanalysis in a number of ways, but especially in its unconcern about the "why" of human behavior (even though its principal founder, the late Fritz Perls, was psychoanalytically trained). Gestalt focuses on the "how" and "what" of human behavior, and it belongs in this chapter on body psychotherapies because, among other things, it teaches the patient that in new awareness of previously ignored body functioning and changed experiencing of his bodily processes he will find answers to where he is, what he is trying to achieve, how he is trying to achieve it, what within him is standing in the way of where he purports to go, and how all these things affect his relations with others.

In technical terms, the gestalt therapist tries to help the patient from the outset to bring back into awareness his considerably desensitized sensori-motor-affective modalities. By asking such questions as "what is your foot now doing?" and "what do you feel right now in your gut?" and "what are you now aware of in your body?" the therapist puts the patient in touch with his immediate phenomenological field.

The chief emphasis of gestalt therapy is the "here and now." Once he is released from the blocks he has built up, the patient finds himself acutely aware of his sensory and motor and emotional activities; he may find himself perceiving things in the therapeutic situation which until then he has blocked from awareness. He may become aware of emotions which until that point in time he has denied. He may notice bodily tensions or motions that have previously escaped his attention.

By starting with the patient where he now is and encouraging him to experience fully his current "beingness," the gestalt therapist is attempting to start the patient on the road to self-acceptance. Effective personality change cannot arise except in a climate of self-acceptance, gestalt therapists (along with most other therapists) contend. The self can be accepted only when there is full self-awareness and self-experiencing; and it is the body, gestaltists feel, that provides the means to this state.

In searching for fuller experiencing of his current beingness, the gestalt patient is functioning similarly to the psychoanalytic patient who is looking for unconscious or repressed material under the tutelage of the analyst, but the process of searching is in each instance quite different. Although the psychoanalytic patient through catharsis or free association releases repressed memories and perhaps discovers what is unconsciously influencing his present behavior, the gestalt patient becomes aware of repressed memories or other unconscious material by focusing his awareness on what is currently happening to him in a sensori-motor-affective way.

What the gestalt therapist tries to show the patient is the incongruity (which is causing his present problem behavior) between what is called his perceptual foreground and his sensori-motor-affective background. The patient is asked to focus his foreground awareness upon the bodily movement or stance that is symptomatic of the conflict between two parts of himself. Symptomatic behavior tells the therapist that a patient has a "stuck" process that obstructs his integrated flowing. The therapist knows that these two estranged components must meet and find mutual acceptance for the process to flow again. By being helped to overcome his lack of awareness, the bodily tension is perceived and frequently also the psychological conflict that underlies it.

Awareness of current behavior is usually blocked, according to the gestalt therapist, in four major ways: projection, introjection, retroflection, and desensitization. Projection may or may not include considerable distortion of reality. It consists of the individual's attributing disowned aspects of himself to others. Introjection, on the other hand, is the process of passively incorporating what others in the environment provide. Both the projector and introjector are failing to be aware of and identified with the behavior in question—the former by ascribing it to the environment and the latter by not assimilating or integrating the adopted behavior with himself.

In the awareness blockage concept of retroflection, Perls is indebted to the Reichians, for Reich's "character armor" is hardened, long-term retroflection. It consists of the process of counteracting or balancing impulse tension by sensorimotor tension, of dividing oneself into the observer and the observed, of having part of oneself in opposition with another part of oneself. As the Polsters state (see selected readings), "What is needed to undo retroflection is to return to the self-consciousness that accompanied its inception. The person has, once again, to become aware of how he sits, how he hugs people, how he grits his teeth, etc. Once he knows what's going on inside himself, his energy is mobilized to seek outlet in fantasy or in action. He can face such prospects as whom might he like to sit on, whom might he like to crush in a wrestler's grip or hold in a soft embrace, whom would he like to chew out or whom would he like to bite." Before therapeutic intervention, the individual spends large amounts of energy in maintaining the impulsive tension and in maintaining the countervailing inhibiting tension; a great deal of his energy is expended in keeping the uneasy truce between the two forces within him.

Desensitization is the awareness block to the sensory functioning of the individual comparable to retroflection with the motoric functioning. Examples are auditory defects (such as chronically not hearing in certain situations and with certain people), visual difficulties (such as blurring and scotomata), lack of sensation in penis or vagina, smelling and tasting inadequacies, and so on. Desensitization is less accessible to direct observation than the body (especially muscular) tensions which manifest themselves in retroflection. It is, however, just as important as an impediment to awareness even though the therapist is more dependent on the verbal reports of the patient regarding its presence.

Gestalt therapists emphasize that psychopathology is bound up with unfinished emotional business and that this is lodged to a considerable extent within the character armor. The individual feels weak and divided; breathing and vocal expression are crippled; and energy is consumed, as noted above, in the battle of tensions.

In the course of the therapy, the gestaltist tries not to leave any unfinished business behind: each resistance is dealt with long enough presumably to release the energy invested in it for more constructive use. Resistance is recognized and identified with by the patient rather than in some way overcome.

The "body psychotherapy" of gestalt is emphasized by the lack of the therapist's attempt to see to it that the patient maintains any consistency of topic and to understand or analyze the content of what he is saying. The stress is on keeping him in constant contact with what he is doing, and his body is the main source of information for this.

Gestalt therapists do not confine their awareness facilitation to getting the patients to look at and accept bodily tensions and rigidities. Awareness is often focused on much intrapsychic and interpersonal material (especially interpersonal material in groups, family and nonfamily, where a very high percentage of gestalt therapeutic work has concentrated in recent years) that is only indirectly related to body tensions.

To Reichians and Lowenians on the one hand and to abreactive therapists (such as the primals and the autogenics) on the other, the gestaltist position fails to give full weight and potency of repressed unconscious material from which the patient has isolated himself. Until the wall (character-muscular armoring in Reichian and Lowenian terms) is broken down either by manipulations and exercises (Reichian-Lowenian) or by catharsis-abreaction (primal-autogenic), the patient is unable, according to these critics, to bring deep organismic blockage material into immediate awareness. Through gestalt therapy, the "real" body therapists maintain, the patient will make only superficial changes and will leave untouched the troublesome core regions deep within him.

Criticism of gestalt therapy from another source—namely, cognitively oriented therapists—contends that the gestalt approach is merely palliative in that it temporarily helps the patient to feel more in touch with his body and his feelings, but does not help him to solve or develop the tools with which to solve the real problems of his life. For the here and now, these critics suggest, the patient is likely to feel all aglow with accepting the fact that he hates his wife and is unhappy in his marriage and that's why, say, he has been grinding his teeth and having headaches, and now he won't have these symptoms any more because he has faced and accepted his resistances. But he still is no better equipped than he was before to change the self-defeating behavior in his marriage and the rest of his life. Such a patient needs help, cognitive therapists insist, to think through problems, to work out solutions to be tried and discussed in therapy, to formulate goals and methods of working toward them, and to develop a value system with which to integrate his life. Until this is done by some other therapeutic route, these critics contend, gestalt therapy will merely achieve certain temporary symptom relief.

AUTOGENIC THERAPY

A much more sophisticated, research-based, and technically complicated approach to abreactive psychotherapy than Janov's primal therapy is what has been recently introduced in this country by Wolfgang Luthe under the name "autogenic therapy." Although there has been a great deal of refinement of techniques and elaborate development of research data in more recent years, many of the basic clinical procedures were developed in Germany by the late Johannes Heinrich Schultz half a century ago. The first edition of Schultz' *Das autogene Training* [Autogenic Training] was published in Leipzig in 1932.

Autogenic therapy is a psychophysiologically oriented approach that requires case-specific adaptation. The training consists of mental exercises of passive concentration upon combinations of verbal stimuli designed to promote a shift to a specific psychophysiologic state that is known to be associated with facilitation of brain-directed functions of a homeostatic and self-normalizing (autogenic) nature.

The general theory of autogenic therapy holds that brain mechanisms know what to do in order to reduce or eliminate disturbing interferences generated by their own system and how to neutralize accumulated brain-disturbing material. Autogenic therapy is designed to give ample opportunity to the natural forces in the brain to re-establish functional harmony in a self-regulatory homeostatic (autogenic) way.

Central to autogenic therapy is autogenic abreaction, which is achieved following the development of an attitude of passive acceptance on the part of the patient. The brain-directed cathartic process takes over (after much training in various autogenic exercises), after which there is a continuous unrestricted (tape-recorded) verbal description of the phenomena elaborated and programmed by a trainee's brain and of the expression of affective psychophysiologic components (laughing, vomiting, crying, swearing, etc.). Interventions from either therapist or trainee are limited to overcoming resistances that develop in the pathway of a neutralization process already indicated by the brain.

Various homework assignments are given the patient (usually called the trainee in the autogenic therapeutic literature). He is required to listen to and transcribe his tape-recorded verbal descriptions, reading aloud the transcribed material and elaborating on a commentary which focuses on different aspects of the material obtained by autogenic abreaction. He also takes notes on his dreams and carries out unsupervised (tape-recorded) autogenic abreactions after he has achieved the technical competence necessary to do this.

The autogenic therapist believes that the autogenic abreactive process derives from self-regulatory brain mechanisms that are largely uninfluenced by insight-promoting interpretations. Luthe (and other body psychotherapists) thus makes a major distinction between this type of psychotherapy, which emphasizes techniques aimed at multidimensional psychophysiologic neutralization of the disturbing potency of already accumulated material, and others, which focus on insight, understanding, learning, transference, and similar therapeutic variables.

Greater self-understanding and self-realization are listed among the positive developments of autogenic therapy, but such developments are not achieved by direct interferences from either the therapist or the patient with the brain-directed process of autogenic abreaction. In Luthe's own words, "During autogenic abreaction, processes of brain-directed neutralization pursue, in a self-regulatory, computer-like manner, a well-coordinated brain-programmed pattern of activities which progressively reduce the pathofunctional potency of accumulated disturbing material and certain interference-generating systems." In his view, the inherent biologic forces accomplish the readjustment of functional deviations. Under supervision of the autogenic therapist (who is knowledgeable about how to aid the patient's brain in overcoming resistances, but who does not otherwise intervene in the autogenic abreactive process), the brain-directed dynamics of self-normalization are given adequate opportunity to continue their work. As this proceeds, more desirable levels of functional harmony are usually achieved.

Just as in primal therapy, physiological changes (temperature drop, lower blood pressure, EEG changes, etc.) which indicate a reduction of tension follow a brief but intensive training period. As noted in the section on primal therapy, it would be interesting to have similar tests run on patients subjected to noncathartic, nonabreactive therapies.

The reader will no doubt have discerned that autogenic therapy is certainly not to be undertaken by a therapist who has not been specifically trained in autogenic methods. Particular knowledge is needed in understanding the dynamics of brain-directed mechanisms which prevail under both normal and favorable and abnormal and unfavorable circumstances. As Luthe has said, "If a therapist is not sufficiently familiar with the variations and patterns of a variety of positively oriented dynamics of autogenic neutralization, he is prone to commit serious technical errors by mistaking positively oriented (neutralization-facilitating) dynamics for manifestations of negatively oriented (neutralization-antagonizing) forms of resistance."

Observations derived from this therapeutic modality by its few practitioners will very likely continue to produce interesting data. Out of autogenic therapeutic research—along with studies of sleep, hypnosis and other altered states of conscious control, learning of autonomic responses and biofeedback techniques, hallucinogenic drugs, Zen, etc.—new hypotheses about human behavior and its aberrations are sure to emerge. These, in the long run, will strongly influence all effective psychotherapeutic approaches.

SUMMARY

Five psychotherapies which emphasize factors and processes outside the individual's conscious control are discussed in this chapter. For want of a better term, they are called the "body psychotherapies."

After having made a significant contribution to psychoanalysis, Reich developed a therapeutic system of his own for dealing with the seven rings of muscular armoring which he contended correlate with the repressive forces of the ego defenses. If these rings are systematically approached by the direct body-contact methods of vegetotherapy (orgone therapy), the ego-defense system of the patient will be opened up, according to the Reichians, and the patient will eventually be released from his neuroses and able to experience the full delights of human functioning. Reichians seem, on the whole, to have an oversimplified conception of human behavior and to rest their therapeutic case on seeing human beings through the tensions of their character armoring to great orgastic satisfaction (which Reich equated with mental health).

Bio-energetics, created by Alexander Lowen, is an offshoot of vegetotherapy. Lowen has partially substituted various exercises for direct body manipulation of the patient, which is characteristic of the Reichian approach, and does not place the same emphasis on the orgasm as the symbol of mental health. In bio-energetics, however, the main therapeutic task is to get a fast and intense energy flow to course through the human being. This super-energized condition somehow drives all psychopathology out of the patient and renders him well.

Primal therapy is the recent invention of Arthur Janov. By this theory, when primal needs are denied in childhood, primal pain results. This pain, rather than fading away, remains and forms tension. Tension is the pressure of primal pain disconnected from awareness, and both the pain and tension can be undone only by being lived out and re-experienced through primal therapy. There are many objections to Janov's conception of good emotional health, but his revolutionary therapy has provided a refreshing shock to traditional therapies which hopefully will stimulate further scientific study of the nature of human beings and their problems.

Gestalt therapy focuses on awareness in "the here and now." Through self-awareness and self-experiencing (often of body tensions and actions the patient has disowned), the patient can arrive, gestaltists believe, at self-acceptance, in the climate of which effective personality change can arise.

Unlike the psychoanalytic patient who releases repressed memories presumably through catharsis or free association, the gestalt patient becomes aware of repressed memories or other unconscious material by focusing on what is currently happening to him in a sensori-motor-affective way. Such awareness of current behavior is usually blocked, gestaltists say, by projection, introjection, retroflection, and desensitization. In the course of the therapy, the gestaltist tries to deal with each resistance long enough presumably to release the energy invested in it for more constructive use.

The gestaltist approach, according to its critics, gives insufficient stress to the potency of the "wall" of repressed unconscious material and the difficulty of reaching it. To cognitively oriented therapists, the great emphasis on awareness and experiencing does little to help patients actually change their self-defeating behavior and deal more effectively with life.

The last system of psychotherapy discussed in this chapter, autogenic therapy, is relatively new in the American therapeutic literature, but dates back to 1932 in Germany. The general theory of autogenic therapy is that the brain mechanism knows what to do in order to reduce or eliminate disturbing material. Autogenic therapy is designed to give the natural forces in the brain the opportunity to re-establish functional harmony in a self-regulatory (autogenic) way.

SELECTED READINGS

BROWN, MALCOLM, "The New Body Psychotherapies," *Psychotherapy*, 10, No. 2 (Summer 1973), 98–116.

FAGEN, JOEN and IRMA LEE SHEPHERD, *Gestalt Therapy Now*. Palo Alto, Cal.: Science and Behavior Books, 1970.

JANOV, ARTHUR, *The Anatomy of Mental Illness: The Scientific Basis of Primal Therapy*. New York: G. P. Putnam's Sons, 1971.

———, *The Primal Scream*. New York: G. P. Putnam's Sons, 1970.

KARLE, WERNER, RICHARD CORRIERE, and JOSEPH HART, "Psychophysiological Changes in Abreactive Therapy—Study I: Primal Therapy," *Psychotherapy*, 10, No. 2 (Summer 1973), 117–22.

LOWEN, ALEXANDER, *The Betrayal of the Body*. New York: Macmillan, 1967.

LUTHE, WOLFGANG, *Autogenic Therapy*, Vols. I–VI. New York: Grune & Stratton, 1969–1973.

PERLS, FREDERICK S., *Gestalt Therapy Verbatim*. Moab, Utah: Real People Press, 1967.

POLSTER, ERVING and MIRIAM, *Gestalt Therapy Integrated*. New York: Brunner-/Mazel, 1973.

REICH, WILHELM, *The Discovery of the Orgone*, Vol. 1: *The Function of the Orgasm*, 2nd ed. New York: Orgone Institute, 1948.

9

SIX DIVERSE
THERAPIES

Psychotherapies that have developed on the American scene in the 1960s and 1970s that do not fall neatly into one of the chapter headings we have thus far examined (behavioral, body, group, family, and family-related) are treated in this chapter. Three of them (reality therapy, direct decision therapy, and confrontation problem-solving therapy) may be considered predominantly cognitive, and the other three (psychosynthesis, psycho-imagination therapy, and placebo therapy) tend to defy any kind of collective categorization.

It is by no means contended that once we have taken a look at these six therapies we shall have seen everything psychotherapeutically invented by man. We might modestly state that within this book and *36 Systems* we have described most of the really prominent therapeutic schools and nonschools (Fish, for example, says his placebo therapy is a nonschool) in contemporary American society. Some approaches we have not considered (such as the late Haim Ginott's methods of working with parents and teachers and children and the Parent Effectiveness Training movement) are more properly viewed as educational theories and methods. Some systems that are clearly psychotherapeutic strike me as either too obscure or too unoriginal to be worth treating. But there may be a few others that I just plain missed. If so, I apologize to the systems and their originators and wish them well.

Obscurity would not be a wholly unjust label to attach to many of the therapies treated in this chapter. Reality therapy is the one of the six that has gained most prominence, and we give it priority in place and space in the pages ahead.

REALITY THERAPY

Although he had been working since the late 1950s on many of the theories and methods, William Glasser, a psychiatrist, first used the term "reality therapy" in a professional paper on young offenders in 1964. In 1965 his book, *Reality Therapy*, appeared, and in 1969 the Institute for Reality Therapy was formed for training professionals in the use of reality therapy techniques and principles in school, clinic, court, church, and other social institutions. The educational efforts of reality therapists have been particularly vigorous and extensive: an offshoot of the Institute for Reality Therapy has been the Educator Training Center with programs throughout the United States and Canada called "Schools Without Failure." Glasser believes that education is the key to sound human functioning and that the Educator Training Center can contribute significantly to preventing delinquency.

Glasser has written that the foremost need of human beings is to love and be loved. "In all its forms, ranging from friendship through mother love, family love, and conjugal love, this need drives us to continuous activity in search of satisfaction."

"Equal in importance to the need for love," he continues, "is the need to feel that we are worthwhile both to ourselves and to others. Although the two needs are separate, a person who loves and is loved will usually feel that he is a worthwhile person, and one who is worthwhile is usually someone who is loved and who can give love in return."

(It is interesting to note that in rational-emotive therapy, with which reality therapy is often compared, to love and to be loved, though considered very desirable, are not treated as dire needs. And an individual's worthwhileness is treated as an axiom, not as something he earns by his good behavior, as Glasser implies.)

One of the first steps in reality therapy is to assist the patient to understand, define, and clarify his immediate and long-term life goals. He is next helped to become aware of the ways in which he blocks his own progress toward his goals. Involved here is assisting the patient better to understand alternatives. Part of the block of a person with emotional problems is often that he cannot see alternatives, and one of the functions of the reality therapist is to assist the patient in realizing that alternatives are usually abundant.

Once a person comes for psychotherapeutic help, according to Glasser, the therapist may assume that this person is lacking the most critical factor for fulfilling his needs: namely, a person about whom he genuinely cares and who genuinely cares about him. To obtain help in therapy, Glasser says, the patient must learn to develop this caring kind of involvement, first with the therapist and then with others. Once he is able to become involved and begin fulfilling his needs, his problem and its symptoms will disappear.

Reality therapists believe that it is important for the patient to feel accepted; thus warmth, understanding, and concern are stressed, and the patient and therapist become warmly involved (but not emotionally entangled).

Fulfilling the patient's needs, however, is a part of his present life; it has nothing to do with his past no matter how miserable his previous life has been. It is not only possible, it is desirable to ignore his past and work in the present because, contrary to almost universal belief, nothing which happened in his past, no matter how it may have affected him then or now, will make any difference once he learns to fulfill his needs at the present time.

In corresponding unorthodox fashion, reality therapy also rejects standard concepts and categories of mental illness. Glasser believes that most forms of mental and emotional disturbance derive from irresponsibility. Whatever the behavior symptoms may be, the reality therapist directs the patient's attention to their unreality and self-defeating nature and helps him discover new behavior which will help him fulfill his basic psychological needs without hurting himself or other people.

Responsibility is a concept that is fundamental in reality therapy. Glasser defines it as "the ability to fulfill one's needs and to do so in a way that does not deprive others of the ability to fulfill their needs." Reality therapy views the patient's problems as largely the result of his inability to understand and apply values and moral principles in his daily life. No basic change can occur in the patient's life, according to the reality therapist, until he faces the responsibility for his own behavior and begins to act on this responsibility.

Reality therapy also departs from the psychoanalytic emphasis on the importance of transference. According to psychoanalysis, the patient tends to transfer attitudes toward significant persons in his past to the therapist, and much significant insight and gain in awareness can derive from the patient's working through this transference. The reality therapist, on the contrary, thinks that this procedure simply adds to the already heavy load of misconceptions and reality distortions of the patient. The patient is encouraged to relate realistically to real persons (including the therapist) rather than to transference figures.

Another departure from other therapies is represented in the stress of reality therapists on allowing the patient to talk about whatever he likes. "In the early part of therapy anything is open for discussion. If the individual talks about a subject other than his problems, this is not seen as a resistance but rather as worthwhile. . . . Many people who enter into therapy with a reality therapist are often surprised when they find themselves talking about a wide variety of subjects. . . . The therapist reassures the patient that these conversations *are* worthwhile and that, in discussing such things, they are closer to solving problems than if they talked about problems exclusively."

One of the major principles of reality therapy is to concentrate on the behavior of the patient rather than on his feelings. "If a patient states: 'I feel miserable and depressed,' rather than: 'Tell me more about it' or 'How long have you felt this way?' the reality therapist responds by saying: 'What are you doing to make yourself depressed?' " In this way the reality therapist is not denying feelings or their importance, but he is showing the patient how feelings are related to behavior.

Glasser and Zunin go on to say that they find that patients begin to regard themselves and their symptoms in a new light when told of the normalcy of their depressive feelings in the wake of the behavior that they describe.

"Patients take a totally different view of themselves and their symptoms when told (if applicable) that the therapist would be much more concerned about them if they . . . did not experience depression or loneliness. This principle pinpoints behavior and not feelings as the problem. The therapist might even ask the patient why he is not more depressed. . . . When they begin to outline the various things that assist them from becoming even further depressed, we begin to understand their islands of strength and can then assist them in becoming aware of their own assets."

According to Glasser, it is necessary for the reality therapist to teach the patient that therapy is not primarily directed toward making him happy. "Happiness occurs most often when we are willing to take responsibility for our behavior. Irresponsible people, always seeking to gain happiness without assuming responsibility, find only brief periods of joy but not the deep-seated satisfaction that accompanies responsible behavior."

Although most therapies avoid getting involved in the question of morality, reality therapists believe that it is their job to face the question of right and wrong with their patients and get them to judge the quality of what they are doing. "To the best of our ability as responsible human beings we must help our patients arrive at some decision concerning the moral quality of their behavior. . . . We believe that almost all behavior which leads to fulfilling our needs, within the bounds of reality, is right, or good, or moral behavior, according to the following definition: When a man acts in such a way that he gives and receives love, and feels worthwhile to himself and others, his behavior is right or moral."

However, even with their stress on morality, reality therapists do not believe in punishment. They point out that punishment has proved itself ineffectual in getting people to change their behavior. Patients already have a failure identity, which punishment only encourages. Though excuses for further failure are not accepted, the reality therapist must avoid confirming the patient's failure identity by critical and deprecating remarks. A specific failure is accepted as a matter of fact, and the notion of the patient's being a general failure is strictly avoided. "To the extent that the reality therapist eliminates punishment and does not accept excuses for failure, helping the patient substitute reasonable value judgments and make plans in accordance with those value judgments, helping him to make a commitment to follow through with his plans, he is truly assisting individuals to gain a success identity."

Patients in reality therapy are taught not only the limits of the therapeutic situation but also the limits and nonlimits life places upon the individual. Reality, in other words, is constantly emphasized. Some patients have even been found to work more effectively when they know that therapy will consist of a specific number of visits (especially in marriage and family therapy).

Confrontations (especially in the "no excuses" stand against irresponsible behavior), constructive arguing or intelligent heated discussions (which can support the patient's self-concept as an individual who has something of value to say and defend), and occasionally verbal shock therapy are also employed in reality therapy.

Glasser and Zunin have defined the therapist's goals in reality therapy in terms of concepts and values of individual responsibility and meaning (which the patient is encouraged to establish for himself). One of these concepts is that man is self-determining and becomes, within the limits of his own inherited endowment and the environment, what he makes of himself. Every man, according to reality therapy, has the potential for being responsible or irresponsible. The way he comes to behave (that is, responsibly or irresponsibly) depends upon decisions rather than conditions (note the similarity here with Greenwald's direct decision therapy).

In a summary statement these co-authors state that the single outstanding need of a human being is for an identity (the belief that we are someone in distinction to others). The basic-need routes to a success identity are love and self-worth. If these fail, a person will turn to delinquency and withdrawal (or "mental illness"), which are pathways to a failure identity (an outstanding feature of which is loneliness). "Through accepting responsibility for one's own behavior," Glasser and Zunin conclude, "and acting maturely to constructively change their behavior, individuals find they are no longer lonely, symptoms begin to resolve and they are more likely to gain maturity, respect, love and that most important success, identity."

PSYCHOSYNTHESIS

Roberto Assagioli, an Italian psychiatrist, has developed a system of psychotherapy which has gradually gained some following in the United States. There is a Psychosynthesis Research Foundation in New York City which has translated and disseminated Assagioli's writings for many years, but the biggest push of recognition has come with the absorption of some of his ideas and methods by the encounter movement.

Assagioli has written that "a distinctive characteristic of the psychosynthetic treatment is the *systematic* use of all available active psychological techniques . . . which means a use made according to the specific plan of the treatment and directed towards clearly envisioned aims. Therefore it is not a mere eclecticism as it might appear from a superficial view."

The basic technique stressed by Assagioli, which he says helps and makes possible the use of all the others, is the arousing and development of the will. Skillful and successful use of the will consists in regulating and directing all other functions toward a deliberately chosen and affirmed aim. The will is conceived of as including five phases: (1) motivation—goal—deliberation; (2) decision; (3) affirmation—command; (4) planning; and (5) direction of the execution of the plan. All of these can be used eventually by the properly guided patient.

Another technique that Assagioli rates as being of the utmost importance in psychosynthesis is the transmutation and sublimation of the biopsychic energies, particularly of the sexual and aggressive drives. He considers that the psychosynthetic process offers the means by which the energy that often goes into these drives can be directed and used for creative activities and achievements.

While redirecting the sexual and aggressive energies, psychosynthesis also encompasses a group of procedures aimed at the "awakening, the releasing and the employment of the potent superconscious spiritual energies, which have a transforming and regenerating influence on the personality. This release may be compared to that of the intra-atomic energy latent in matter."

Assagioli has compared psychosynthesis with existential psychotherapy. It shares the method of starting from within, with the self or presence of the individual. The idea of identity, with this orientation, is of primary importance. He also accepts the concept that each individual is growing or actualizing successively many latent potentialities and that there is a central importance in meaning: "particularly of the meaning which each individual *gives* to life, or is *looking for* in life." Further similarities Assagioli lists between the two types of therapeutic systems are the recognition of the importance of values (especially ethical, esthetic, noetic, and religious values); the responsibility of the individual for choices and decisions and for understanding his motivations for these; recognition of the depth and seriousness of human life and the place of anxiety and suffering in it; and the emphasis on the future and of its dynamic role in the present.

Assagioli points as well to certain differences in emphasis and the inclusion of factors not taken into sufficient consideration by other therapies. First, psychosynthesis includes a careful analysis of the various phases of the will (such as deliberation, motivation, decision, affirmation, persistence, and execution) and uses many techniques "for arousing, developing, strengthening and rightly directing the will."

Assagioli goes on to state that "a second point of difference from some existentialists concerns the nature of the self and the search for self-identity. In my opinion, the direct experience of the self, of pure *self-awareness*—independent of any 'content' of the field of consciousness and of any situation in which the individual may find himself—is a true, 'phenomenological experience,' an inner reality which can be empirically verified and deliberately produced through appropriate techniques."

A third difference is what Assagioli calls "the recognition of the positive, creative, joyous experiences which man may, and often does, have along with the painful and tragic ones." He compares these to what Maslow referred to as "peak experiences," such as self-actualization, achievement, and joy, and claims that these states are made possible through psychosynthesis methods.

Fourth, the experience of loneliness is not considered in psychosynthesis to be either ultimate or essential, but rather as a stage or temporary subjective condition. "It can and does alternate with, and finally can be substituted by the genuine living experience of interpersonal and interindividual communications, relationships, interplay; by cooperation between individuals, and among groups—and even by a *blending,* through intuition, empathy, understanding, and identification. This is the large field of interindividual psychosynthesis, reaching from the interpersonal relationship of man and woman to the harmonious integration of the individual into even larger groups to the 'one humanity.' "

Psychosynthesis also makes deliberate use of a large number of active techniques for the transformation, sublimation, and direction of psychological energies; the strengthening and maturing of weak or undeveloped functions; and the activation of superconscious energies and the arousing of latent potentialities.

The sixth point of difference noted by Assagioli is that psychosynthesis, unlike most existential approaches, works toward the conscious and planned reconstruction of the personality. The role of the therapist, though active at first, becomes more catalytic as he becomes a model to the patient; finally, he is replaced by the patient's true self.

Psychosynthesis begins with each patient by ascertaining his unique existential situation and the problems connected with it. This stage includes the use of various psychoanalytical procedures. "The harmonization and integration into one functioning whole of all the qualities and functions of the individual must be aimed at and actively fostered—the central purpose of psychosynthesis. Such harmonization and integration both allows and requires the constructive utilization and expression of all the liberated and activated drives and energies of the personality."

Although Assagioli recommends psychosynthetic didactic training (as in psychoanalysis) for therapists or educators who are undertaking any applications of the method, he believes many benefits can derive from a self-application of the procedures he describes in his book. In fact, he declares that psychosynthesis, however learned, will, when diligently practiced, lead to inner growth and self-actualization.

DIRECT DECISION THERAPY

After having worked for many years within a psychoanalytic frame of reference, Harold Greenwald, a psychologist, has gradually evolved an approach to psychotherapy which he calls direct decision therapy (DDT). The therapist confronts the patient with the constant choices in life he faces; he directly points out to the patient the decisions he is constantly making (and implementing) even when he believes he is successfully avoiding decisions. Greenwald believes that the most important aim of therapy is to help the patient make a decision to change and then help him to carry out that decision. Direct decision therapy is often quicker and more effective than other approaches, he contends, because it makes alternative choices more explicitly recognized and achievable for the patient.

Greenwald distinguishes between a person's wanting to and choosing to change. Probably an overwhelming majority of the people who consult a psychotherapist wish to solve their problems; but translating that wish into a decision to change means that the person must become aware of the costs of change. Usually the costs include his having to give up certain covert advantages associated with the continuance of the problem, as well as going through various kinds of self-disciplining difficulties in achieving the behavioral change. If a person really *decides* to change, however, and has intelligent direction in methods of implementing the change, even the most difficult problems respond very favorably.

In trying to help patients make decisions in the present that will lead to desirable change, it is important for the DDT therapist to try to find out the context in which the *original* decision was made—the decision that is now producing self-defeating behavior. It is also vital to find out whether or not patients have alternatives to the way they are living. "Once in a while," Greenwald writes, "they are so stuck and have such blind spots about their lives, that they can't see any alternative, any other way of living. Sometimes it's important to start exploring the other possibilities. I tend to believe that the greatest growth in an individual, the best development and the best chance of his not having these kinds of problems again come if I let him find the other choices rather than try to sell him on another choice. . . . The decision he arrives at *himself* is the most valuable for the individual, because one of the things I'm trying to help people learn is not just how to deal with their immediate problems, but a whole way of dealing with life in general."

Helping people focus on what happens when they do not carry out a decision has proved to be of therapeutic valuable in DDT. Greenwald has patients examine what the payoffs were for them in not sticking with their decisions to bring about understanding regarding not only the failure, but how more effectively to implement the decision in the future.

The process of helping people with decisions, Greenwald says, starts the first moment he sees them. He asks them to decide how long they want to come for therapy, stressing that they need not stick to a rigid timetable, and often even persuading them that a long time is not necessary, as it would be in classic psychoanalysis.

Greenwald has offered a number of suggestions for the person who wants to proceed to deal with his problems without the help of a therapist. In many ways these suggestions state clearly what he tries to accomplish with patients who actually enter therapy.

First of all, he suggests that the self-helping person sit down and think through (or, preferably, write out) as clear and complete a statement as possible of the nature of his problems.

Second, the person is asked to examine his past decisions—the ones that have produced the kind of behavior that now constitutes part or all of the problems. He is asked to look carefully at "the attitude that causes you unhappiness or the inability to get as much satisfaction and pleasure as you would like and believe you can achieve."

Third, the self-helping person is asked to list the payoffs for the past decisions that are behind the problem. These may be actual positive gains or the avoidance of anxiety. But in either case, they are still continuing payoffs that are helping to sustain the presumably undesired behavior that the person would (allegedly) like to change.

For further understanding, Greenwald next suggests that the person scrutinize the context in which he made the original decision. Just as the therapist needs to understand the social and phenomenological frame of reference in which the patient's earlier decisions were made in order to comprehend how they relate to the patient's life, so must the self-helping person work to achieve this kind of self-knowledge.

Fifth, Greenwald recommends that the person look closely at the alternatives to his past decisions. What were the other possibilities he can recall at the time he made the decision? What other possibilities can he now see in light of the new and different context of which his life is a part today?

The sixth recommendation is for the person to choose an alternative and decide to put it into practice. He goes on to write, "Do not confuse a wish with a decision. If you say, 'I would like to lose weight,' this is very different from a decision to lose weight and to pay the dues—the anxiety, the deprivation, the annoyance of dieting. Also, if you decide to lose weight, remember that this is not a one-time decision. Every time you sit down to eat, every time someone offers you anything to eat, you have to decide all over again whether you want to eat what you know will add to your weight or whether you want to be slim, attractive, and healthy."

Finally, the self-helping person should support himself in carrying out the new decision. Because of the ease with which people can make desirable resolutions and then fail to carry them out, this is the most crucial part of the DDT process. A further decision is required to implement the decision and to try to stick with it. Greenwald cautions, however, that the person must try not to be perfectionistic in his expectations of himself and to realize that failures are natural, and that when he slips all is not lost.

Rather than calling this a whole new system of psychotherapy, it is probably more accurate to call it an emphasis or type of focus within the general systematic framework of cognitive therapies. Except for the extreme body-and-emotion-stressing therapists, most present-day psychotherapists concern themselves with many of the same concerns, theories, and methods that Greenwald considers under the title of direct decision therapy. It would seem that rather than a new system of psychotherapy, Greenwald, by clearly emphasizing the importance of decision making in life and in the therapeutic process, has brought a common bond to our attention that serves to unify the approaches of allegedly diverse therapies. The flexible therapists of many "schools" of treatment can probably be helped to make the most desirable decision about what methods to use with particular patients by taking account of Greenwald's emphasis that the whole point of therapy is to help the patient learn to choose independently and wisely and to implement his choices effectively.

PSYCHO-IMAGINATION THERAPY

Joseph E. Shorr, a California psychologist, in looking for methods of understanding each patient's unique phenomenological world, has devised various techniques that elicit the use of imagination with the results of almost immediate increase in awareness of conflicts by both patient and psychotherapist, and also pointing the way toward an effective resolution of these conflicts.

Shorr has written that psycho-imagination therapy "puts great emphasis on how the patient has been defined falsely by others and how he must learn to define himself in line with his true identity. It is also an open system which allows the therapist to create newer approaches as they become necessary— within the framework of a self-and-other theory."

At first Shorr proceeded with general imaginative situations such as having patients imagine themselves in a meadow or imagining a cloud or feeling that they have strong telepathic powers and are in touch with someone in a foreign country. But it gradually became clear to him that though these general situations were useful in indicating the type of imagination a patient had and the nature of certain insecurities, they did not reveal the main internal conflict areas. He found then that by stressing the specific situation with patients and encouraging them to indicate their choice of action within the situation these main conflict areas were revealed.

Following are a few of Shorr's imagination situations that help a therapist and his patient see conflicts. He stresses that there is an infinite number of possible situations and particular ones are appropriate for particular patients.

1. Imagine yourself taking a shower with your father. How would you feel? What would you say to him? What would he say to you? (Alternate this situation with mother, or siblings.)

2. Imagine yourself waking up as a baby. How would you feel? What would you do?

3. Imagine your father is standing next to you. Whisper something into his ear. What does he reply? (Vary this with whispering into mother's ear, or significant others.)

4. You are a necklace around your mother's neck. What do you feel? What do you want to do? Now your mother puts her hand on you. What do you do and what do you feel?

5. You awake in a field and there are footprints over your body. On what part of your body do the footprints appear? Whose footprints are they?

6. Imagine that there's a large blank screen on the wall. What do you see on it? Bring someone else onto it.

7. Imagine you are looking up at a balcony. Your father comes out and looks down at you. What does he say to you? What do you say to him? (Alternatives: mother, or significant others.)

Another way of entering the phenomenological world of the patient is to ask him what image is aroused when the therapist says certain key words (such as love, loneliness, abandonment, self-worth, shame, conflict, closeness) abstracted from his own statements. These images, Shorr contends, especially when combined with such imaginary situations as the examples quoted above, increase the probability of effecting awareness and change in the patient.

Another technique that Shorr finds helpful to use in conjunction with the imaginary situation is existential questioning (which he also calls the self-and-other questions). "An existential question is that which elicits how a person views himself, and how he feels others define him." He notes that some questions seem applicable to nearly all patients and others occur to him spontaneously with particular patients. "One of the more general questions relating to the self is, 'You can call me many things, but *never* refer to me as what?' "

In order to get a glimpse into a patient's inner world, the therapist can ask the patient whether he or she makes a difference to anyone or comes first with anyone. He also cites that "an effective way of helping someone to define their relationships with others is to ask, 'Whom are you accounting to?' or, 'Who defines the relationship between you and your father?' (or any significant other). A closely related question to the last one, which can be used either as an alternative or as part of the cross-checking in another session with the same patient, is, 'Do you know where you stand with your mother?' (or any appropriate significant other). With a very insecure patient it may be suitable to ask, 'What did your parents endorse in you?' or even, 'What did your parents fail to confirm in you?' "

What Shorr calls the most-or-least method represents another way of trying to sharpen the awareness of a person's self-image and the concept of his basic attitudes and values. He states that patients often assume false identities allocated to them through the unconscious strategy of their parents. These may take the form of an idealized or a despised image. "In an effort to assist the patient to become aware of his own despised image or the rigid need to sustain the idealized image, and try to change it the following kind of questions can be helpful: 'What is the most immoral thing a person can do?' 'What is the biggest lie you have ever told?' 'What is the most jealous you have ever been?' 'What was the most unfair demand put on you?' 'What was the most often repeated statement made to you by your mother (father)?' "

Shorr points out that most-or-least questioning can also serve to reveal the guilt in a person. "Inevitably, either of the aspects of false identity is locked into guilt. If someone identifies with the despised false image then he feels guilty; if somebody falls short of the idealized image, the guilt will be compounded."

Although at first he was disinclined to ask a question that seemed as if it were an item from a test, Shorr found the sentence completion technique (which he calls finish-the-sentence technique) very valuable in therapy. He says that it is the spontaneity of the question and answer that makes it "both phenomenologically accurate and full of feeling, usually surprising the patient by the degree of intensity as well as content." This method is particularly useful with a patient who is amnesic about his childhood and who has difficulty with an imaginative situation; he may be asked "to supply ten different endings to such a question as, 'I strongly resent _____.' Out of a list of such examples as: 'stupidity,' 'my ulcer,' 'my boss,' 'my wife's back-seat driving,' and 'my family,' I will ask the patient to pick the one item that he feels most strongly about, and to proceed further into his feelings and awareness."

Shorr has asserted that even though psycho-imagination therapy generally involves an active directive approach, supportive measures are used when needed. The approach, he feels, is very sensitive to where the patient is and takes into account his resistances and hesitancies. The method has been used mainly with neurotic populations and with a few depressed and schizoid patients, but not yet with psychotics, alcoholics, or drug addicts. (Shorr indicated at the time his book was written in 1972 that he hoped to undertake work with such groups in the future.) He has used the techniques extensively in group therapy.

For the growth and expanding awareness of the therapist, according to Shorr, it is important that he ask himself the same questions and imaginary situations that he proposes to the patient. "With both the patient and the therapist attempting the feeling response to the same question or situation (not, of course simultaneously), greater authenticity is bound to occur."

Much more than conventional procedures, psycho-imagination therapy gives intensity of meaning to Sullivan's concept of the participant observer, according to Shorr. "It seemingly takes more of the resources of the therapist and the patient. There are fewer 'dead' spots in the sessions. The therapist not only listens but also experiences the patient's communications at many different levels."

In psycho-imagination therapy, Shorr contends, the therapist has greater opportunities for creativity—he can use various forms of self-and-other questions, finish-the-sentence questions, most-or-least questions, and imaginary situations to get the patient to respond and react. "Instead of the patient trying to fit into a prescribed theory of therapy, the therapist is trying to envisage and assess the unique system of the individual. It is phenomenology in action."

CONFRONTATION PROBLEM-SOLVING THERAPY

A Chicago psychiatrist, Harry H. Garner, has developed a confrontation technique in psychotherapeutic treatment which has a problem-solving rather than either a permissive or coercive approach. He developed this technique as a tool when he realized the difficulty with which old learned patterns, which once had adaptive value, are unlearned. "In the learning process," he writes, "motivational pressures and the subjective needs of the individual have created goal-seeking behavior directed at satisfying the needs of hunger, love, and urge toward mastery. The responses that brought satisfaction were repetitively carried out until they become automatic responses no longer requiring problem-solving. The person accepts his adaptations, when effectively repeated over a significant period, as unaltera-ble. Indeed, he reacts with resistance to alteration even when the pattern of behavior becomes obviously maladaptive."

Garner's basic method is to confront the patient with directive statements reflecting some aspect of his problems and following each statement by a question that tries to determine what the patient thinks about that statement. This provides a method by which the therapist can keep tabs on the patient's understanding and reactions.

Although he admits that controlling a patient through methods that seem to re-establish an authoritarian parent-child relationship is likely to be considered regressive, Garner believes that, correctly applied, the control of the therapist "reassures the patient that his own controls will be strengthened by an external control and thus helps relieve an acute panic state and anxiety. Authoritarian directives intensify transference phenomena and the tendency to repeat a behavior pattern previously executed without questions as to its significance. However, the patient is invited to work out a mutually satisfactory solution to conflicts rather than being simply instructed or left to wander on alone by the question, 'What do you think or feel about what I told you?'. The question creates a desire in the patient to test the significance of the control and to evaluate these further on a realistic basis. In other words, it tends to foster reality-testing instead of fostering transference neurosis."

Of the utmost importance in the use of the confrontation technique is obviously the therapeutic relevancy and the skill with which the therapist selects reactive material for the patient in his confrontation comments. Statements should be made to the patient either with the intent to work on a limited therapeutic focus or to drive through to the resolution of a core conflict that has been suggested by the longitudinal life history of the individual. In the latter area "the confrontation statement may be focused on the traumatic situations of infancy and childhood. Traumatic experiences have usually been considered to be: deprivation, overindulgence, rejection, hostility, excessive domination, restriction to excess, overprotection, seduc-tiveness, ambition, actual physical injury." In a more limited therapeutic focus, Garner points out that "the establishment of a previous stable state may be all that the patient seeks or all that is realistically desirable as a goal for therapy. The confrontation statement is used to support the defense when the reality-testing function has been so impaired as to create such distortions as wish-fulfilling illusions, projections, hallucinations, delusions, exaggerated overdetermined hostility, and aggressivity."

There are many other ways and situations in which the confrontation technique is appropriately used. For example, the focus of the confrontation statement may be based on the urgency of a required environmental change or, on the other hand, on the need to undermine vicious cycle patterns, such as those which diminish the patient's feeling of self-worth. Further, "the confrontation may be chosen to focus on a maladaptive assumptive system and the question, 'What do you think or feel about what I told you?' challenges the patient to explore, affirm, or disprove the assumptive set and to modify, correct or replace it."

Confrontation statements may be directed primarily at present interactions (both in his daily life and in the immediate therapeutic relationship), at what he wants to do ("that which represents the anticipated actions and the resulting inner reaction or interpersonal experience"), or at a genetic reconstruction of the past. In Garner's words, "confrontation interventions by the therapist may be directed at getting more information for reconstruction of the past so as to better understand the present and the goal-directed striving of the patient. How the past attitudes are influencing present and intended performance so that the repetition-compulsion nature of his behavior can be better understood by the patient may be the therapeutic focus of confrontation statements."

Garner lays great stress on the value of the question "What do you think or feel about what I told you?" and, in fact, considers it a key to therapeutic effectiveness; it becomes a lever for exploring the patient's tendencies toward compliance and noncompliance, and also acts as a prod to the patient's reluctance to develop problem-solving attitudes. In addition, the question stimulates in the patient the awareness of the therapist's constant involvement in observing and interpreting reality, a tendency with which the patient comes to identify and to emulate.

A kind of flexibility of approach is possible with the use of the confrontation problem-solving technique, according to Garner. If the therapist has been going along with a supportive type of therapy to simply reduce symptoms and improve the patient's adjustment in family and community, "the goal can be altered at any time to one of further exploration by pointing out that his response to 'What do you think or feel about what I told you?' was one of uncritical compliance and that further exploration of the problem was another possible response. In psychotherapeutic work with patients, there is frequently a change in the patient's behavior or a decrease in symptoms and improvement in affect. The therapist not infrequently sees such change as improved reality-testing whereas in actuality it is uncritical compliance to what the patient feels the therapist wishes."

Flexibility in the patient is also encouraged by Garner's therapeutic procedures. The confrontation technique tends to disrupt the patient's tendency for repetitive nonadaptive types of behavior: "ability to learn, to classify new experiences according to past experiences, to discriminate and evaluate differences, and to use reasonable judgment in modifying behavior and characteristics is restricted in the mentally ill person by a repetitive tendency to react on the basis of past adaptations. The question, 'What do you think or feel about what I told you?' forces the patient to evaluate and discriminate and to classify his experiences and, in a sense, it demands reasonable judgment and learning responses. It produces a push toward surrender of neurotic behavior or disarranged thinking and behavior for a flexible pattern of functioning or for establishment of an automatism that is less frustrating, uneconomical, and otherwise poorly adaptive."

The confrontation approach is also seen as helpful in correcting incorrect perceptions. There is a tendency for incorrect perceptions not to be corrected on the basis of new experiences because anxiety often creates an avoidance reaction to any appropriate re-evaluation of the incorrect perception. "The repetitive confrontation virtually demands a correction of incorrect perceptions, at the same time offering a supportive relationship which decreases anxiety and feeds back to the capacity to correct perceptions. The importance of perception and perceptual errors is attested to by the frequency with which the patient does not perceive what he has been told."

Blocking of the capacity for abstract thought, seen most notably in schizophrenic patients, can be reduced or broken down by the confrontation and the repetitive factor, according to Garner. Some patients build up rigid walls to protect themselves against the anxiety they feel about such abstract thinking called for in generalization of concepts, volitional acts, and thinking in terms of principles. In these cases, the therapist must "establish contact with the patient through the regularity and reliability of his intrusion."

In a kind of summary statement concerning the desirabilities of his therapeutic approach, Garner has written that "confrontation statements tend to encourage the expansion of the discriminatory, reflective, reality-testing and socially oriented thought processes, and behavioral tendencies of the individual. They also make the patient aware of the obligatory, insatiable, stereotyped nature of his thoughts and behavior, and the desirability of an effort at explanation. They lead to the uncovering of that which has been preconscious or unconscious. They create positive and negative reactions related to transference phenomena, a tendency to stimulate working through of conflictual areas, and hasten the corrective emotional experience. . . . The confrontation technique, through encouraging an awareness of alternatives of choice of freedom and individuality, furthers the extension of abilities and a tendency toward healthful living and release from illness."

PLACEBO THERAPY

Some of the ideas about the component of faith in psychotherapy first explicitly formulated in 1961 by Jerome D. Frank, a Baltimore psychologist and psychiatrist, have been borrowed, expanded, and modified by Jefferson M. Fish, a young New York psychologist. In his words, "the proliferation of such schools of therapy, whose persuasive names are intended seriously, prompted me to call my creation placebo therapy, a nonschool of persuasion whose therapeutic title is intended ironically."

Based on social influence principles, placebo therapy is offered by Fish as a strategy for getting the maximum therapeutic impact from whatever specific techniques the therapist uses to change his patient's personality and to resolve his problems. Fish believes that many of the most important processes that take place in therapy are unrelated to the theoretical orientation of the therapist.

In analyzing what takes place in the therapeutic transaction, Fish sees an interaction between two believers, the healer and the one to be healed: the former usually studies to become a therapist only if he believes in psychotherapy, and the latter generally comes to be treated with the faith that psychotherapy will cure him of his "ailments." Of the three treatment stages—pre-therapy, therapy, and post-therapy—the first is considered to be the most complex, mainly because then "the therapist must accurately predict his patient's response to the placebo communication. For example, if the therapist formulates a placebo which is not believable, the therapy stage will be a failure."

In formulating a placebo, the therapist must take into account many factors about the therapeutic setting and also about both the patient and himself. He next must make a careful assessment of the problem areas of the patient and of the patient's strongly held beliefs (areas of faith). "Usually," Fish writes, "a belief in psychotherapy as a scientific procedure is sufficient for therapeutic purposes. However, regardless of the originality or banality of the patient's beliefs, the therapist must take care to understand them in order to formulate a helpful placebo."

The next step in the process as Fish conceives it is the therapeutic contract. "The contract usually takes the form of a statement which appears ridiculously obvious to the patient, such as 'If I understand what you've been saying, you'd like to feel more confident in social situations; and if you attain this confidence, you'll feel the therapy has achieved its purpose.' Once the patient approves such a statement, therapy can begin." (In its emphasis on the importance of the therapeutic contract, placebo therapy is reminiscent of transactional analysis.) Fish goes on to say that the crucial message communicated from the therapist to the patient by the therapeutic contract is that he (the patient) is not crazy, but merely has a set of problems which, when dealt with, will render the patient "cured." "The contract itself serves as the placebo, and the patient's belief in psychotherapy enables him to change his belief about himself."

With the completion of understanding the preconditions of therapy, assessing the patient's problems and beliefs, and agreeing on the therapeutic contract, the therapist needs to build an effective placebo communication. According to Fish, communication is necessary to "activate one powerful set of the patient's beliefs (his faith) to change another set of his beliefs (*his problems*). Placebo therapy can thus be seen as a form of spiritual judo in which the therapist uses the power of the patient's own faith to force him to have a therapeutic 'conversion' experience."

The healing ritual is the next step. The therapist presents the ritual in two parts: the first part is telling the patient (with what will for him be a believable rationale) some procedures that he can follow to conquer his problems. The second part is experiencing the cure. "The important point," Fish says, "is that the patient must be persuaded that it is what *he* does, not what the therapist does, which results in his being cured. This belief is crucial because it implies that the patient is the master of his behavior rather than its servant."

Various psychological forces push the patient who follows the therapist's self-help instructions in the direction of change. Fish describes these forces as follows: "The patient's expectations of help tend to improve his condition. Then, his knowledge that he is receiving expert attention is likely to increase this improvement. His need to maintain his other areas of faith, which have been included in the rationale for the healing ritual, tends to force him in the direction of therapeutic change. This pressure is in turn increased by his realization that, if he does not change, the money, time, and effort devoted to therapy will all have been wasted."

With the kinds of pressure in operation, some change (sometimes dramatic) almost always takes place; such change can be used as evidence of progress toward the fulfillment of the therapeutic contract. This sense of progress increases the pressure for further change and contributes to a greater degree of movement toward the contractual goal.

After the contract is fulfilled, a number of forces, according to Fish, help to maintain the "cure." "One is the feeling of self-mastery which results from the patient's view that he himself has produced the change. Second, his awareness of his new level of functioning leads him to think of himself and the world in a new light. These new attitudes in turn make it unlikely that he will resume his old behavior. Finally—and this goes back to the pretherapy stage—the therapist should have arranged the therapeutic contract in such a way that the behavioral transformation which takes place will be warmly received within the patient's immediate environment."

In discussing placebo therapy (and the book he has written about it), Fish admits that focusing attention on the faith involved in psychotherapy may have the opposite effect from the one he seeks. A book, he acknowledges, that stresses the irrational faith of both patients and therapists may lead them to question their hereto unquestioned faith, and effective faith-healing necessitates a true-believing therapist and patient. In drawing attention to the omnipresence of faith in psychotherapy, he is trying to help therapists deliberately to use their patients' faith to help them. "If, after reading this book, a therapist attempts to contain or eliminate the role of faith in his psychotherapy rather than to use it as it already exists, my efforts will have been wasted. If a patient reads this book and uses it to keep his therapist from 'putting one over on him' rather than to strengthen his belief in his therapist and what he says, placebo therapy will have become a self-defeating prophecy instead of a self-fulfilling one."

SUMMARY

This chapter discusses six therapies that cannot be neatly included within the categories dealt with under other chapter headings. Reality therapy is based on the assumption that human beings have two outstanding basic needs: the need to love and be loved and the need to feel worthwhile both to themselves and others. To fulfill the need to be worthwhile, a person must develop and maintain satisfactory standards, so much of reality therapy is directed toward helping people to function in accordance with their moral values. Moral behavior is emphasized as acting in a way that will enable one to give and receive love and feel worthwhile to oneself and others.

Reality therapy does not concern itself with the unconscious, but rather with helping people to fulfill their conscious needs. Similarly it is not concerned with standard concepts and categories of mental illness, but holds that most forms of mental and emotional disturbance derive from irresponsibility. No basic change can occur in the patient's life, according to reality therapy, until the individual faces the responsibility for his own behavior and begins to act on this responsibility.

Psychosynthesis stresses the arousing and development of the will as the basic technique to induce personality change. The transmutation and sublimation of the biopsychic energies (especially the sexual and aggressive drives) which releases energy for the will to use and direct for creative activities and achievements. In addition, psychosynthesis allegedly awakens, releases, and utilizes superconscious spiritual energies which transform and regenerate the personality.

Although psychosynthesis has much in common with existential psychotherapy, it differs in its careful analysis of the various phases of the will, its emphasis on the direct experience of the self, its recognition and encouragement of positive and joyous experiences, its reaching for experiences of the larger community of man, its use of active techniques for personality change, and its work toward the conscious and planned reconstruction of the personality.

After ascertaining each patient's unique existential situation and the problems associated with it, psychosynthesis uses various active techniques to activate and develop desirable latent aspects of the patient's personality. At the same time, a harmonization and integration into one functioning whole of all the qualities and functions of the individual begins to take place.

Direct decision therapy emphasizes the importance of the individual's choices in life. The main role of the therapist is to help the patient to make and implement constructive decisions. Suggestions made to individuals to help them with their decision-making include (1) making a clear and complete statement of the problems, (2) examining past decisions that produced present self-defeating behavior, (3) listing payoffs for past decisions, (4) scrutinizing context in which the original (problem-causing) decision was made, (5) looking closely at alternatives to past decisions, (6) choosing an alternative for the present time and deciding to put it into practice, and (7) developing strong support for carrying out the new decision.

Greenwald's system is of value because it stresses the importance of helping patients recognize problems, learn to choose better ways of dealing with them, and make the decision to implement them.

Psycho-imagination therapy uses imagination to tap the patient's phenomenological world to reveal the nature of major conflicts and point the way toward effective resolution of these conflicts. The therapist starts with general imaginative situations for the patient and then moves into techniques that question the patient's responses and reactions, revealing to both of them problem areas and making clear paths to resolution of these problems.

In the confrontation problem-solving approach to therapy, the patient is confronted with directive statements reflecting some aspect of his problems and then with questions that try to determine what he thinks about what has just been said. Confrontation statements may be directed primarily at present interactions, at what the patient wants to do, or at a genetic reconstruction of the past. Great stress is laid on the value of the question "What do you think or feel about what I told you?" because it serves to explore the patient's tendencies toward compliance and noncompliance, and prods his reluctance to develop problem-solving attitudes, and stimulates involvement in observing and interpreting reality.

Placebo therapy stresses the component of faith in any system of psychotherapy. To get the maximum therapeutic impact from any techniques designed to resolve a patient's problems, it is necessary that there be complete belief on the part of both therapist and patient, as well as a contract stating the exact aims of the therapy. Both the carefully selected method of "cure" and the contract serve as a placebo that enables the patient to have a "therapeutic 'conversion' experience."

SELECTED READINGS

Assagioli, Roberto, *Psychosynthesis*. New York: Viking Press, 1971.

Fish, Jefferson M., *Placebo Therapy*. San Francisco: Jossey-Bass, 1973.

Frank, Jerome D., *Persuasion and Healing: A Comparative Study of Psychotherapy*, rev. ed. Baltimore: Johns Hopkins Press, 1973.

Garner, Harry H., "Confrontation Problem-Solving Therapy," in R. R. M. Jurjevich, ed., *Direct Psychotherapy*, Vol. I. Coral Gables, Fla.: University of Miami Press, 1973.

Glasser, William, *Reality Therapy: A New Approach to Psychiatry*. New York: Harper & Row, 1965.

Glasser, William, and Leonard M. Zunin, "Reality Therapy," in Raymond Corsini, ed., *Current Psychotherapies*. Itasca, Ill.: F. E. Peacock, 1973.

Greenwald, Harold, *Decision Therapy*. New York: Wyden, 1973.

Shorr, Joseph E., *Psycho-Imagination Therapy*. New York: Intercontinental Medical Book Corp., 1972.

10

CRITIQUE
AND OVERVIEW

What has happened to psychotherapeutic theories and techniques in the 1960s and 1970s? Where is psychotherapy headed as part of contemporary American culture? What generalizations validly emerge from the many therapeutic approaches we have considered in this book? It is to such questions as these that we will address ourselves in this final chapter.

One change that is quite evident from psychotherapies of an earlier era is that the "process of healing" is no longer a predominantly secretive one-to-one enterprise. Various kinds of group and family therapies are in the ascendancy, and these involve a simultaneous multiplicity of patients and often therapists. Even those therapies that still lean heavily on the dyadic relationship (which seem now to constitute a distinct minority of ongoing therapeutic transactions) have generally opened their doors to inspection via direct observations for students and researchers (sometimes with one-way mirrors) and recordings on audio- and videotapes.

Another important change in psychotherapy in the last decade or so is that the phrase we used in the preceding paragraph, the "process of healing," has become quaint. As a result of the influence of the encounter movement, of behavior therapy and learning theory, various cognitive therapies (reality, rational-emotive, and direct choice, for example), family and group therapies, and humanistic trends (of which client-centered therapy is a notable example), the whole idea of a psychotherapist's directing his attention to the "healing" of a "sick" mind has been wiped out of most of psychotherapy. Interestingly, one would need to turn to the remnants of classical psychoanalysis, on the one hand, or to the newly conceived primal therapy (with its return to abreaction and the catharsis of traumatized and repressed emotions) on the other, in order not to be considered hopelessly old-fashioned in discussing the "process of healing."

What has been substituted for the idea of curing sick minds in psychotherapy differs as one moves among the groups that have contributed to the change in this concept. The reality therapists contend that they are dealing primarily with irresponsibility on the part of the patient. The behavior therapists are helping the individual to extinguish self- (or society-) defeating

159

behavior and to learn and reinforce behavior defined as self-enhancing and socially desirable. The rational-emotive therapist says that he is teaching the patient to discern irrational and unrealistic internalized sentences that are leading to self-defeating emotions and behavior and to substitute more rational and realistic evaluations that will reduce or remove problems of living. The Gestaltist speaks of restoring awareness of previously ignored bodily functions in order to clarify life purposes. The encounter movement people (and related humanists) talk about personal growth, self-fulfillment, and self-actualization.

It would be a mistake to infer from the foregoing that there has been simply a change in terminology and that psychotherapists are doing essentially the same things to and with patients that they did when they were "curing mental illness." The whole medical model of a psychotherapist treating a sick patient is fading. Even the term "patient" seems to persist more out of habit—and because no one has come up with an acceptable alternative; "client" is thought by many persons to be too firmly associated with lawyers. Few therapists seem to think any longer of patients as really ill persons who need "treatment" in the medical sense of the word.

Two major factors seem currently to be operating to slow down the complete departure of psychotherapy from the medical culture. One is that an important minority of psychotherapists, the psychiatrists, still emerge from the medical tradition and from years of medical training. Although psychiatrists who are full-time psychotherapists admittedly almost never use their medical knowledge or license, some of them feel a defensive need to justify their medical background as exceedingly important in "treating the whole patient." Honest and discerning psychiatrists have privately admitted to the author that the medical background serves only as a prestigious economic advantage in the therapeutic marketplace. It nevertheless accounts for much of the persistence of the medical-illness strain in psychotherapy.

The other major factor that keeps psychotherapy from entirely freeing itself of the medical model is insurance. Because private insurance companies in the past decade have agreed to cover a sizable percentage of psychotherapy costs in their policies on health care, psychologists as well as psychiatrists contend that the psychotherapy they are practicing is the treatment of various types of mental and emotional illness. Such ideas as solving personal problems, self-actualization, learning to deal more rationally and realistically with crisis situations, overcoming self-defeating behavioral tendencies, and enhancing personal growth and understanding clearly do not fit in with an insurance company's idea of health care treatment. Hence, much hypocrisy exists: psychotherapists know that they are trying to help people to function more effectively and enjoyably in today's very complex social environment, but they write and talk about treating "mental illnesses" for insurance purposes. This hypocrisy will probably be increased and compounded if a national health insurance under government sponsorship goes into effect.

A rational argument could, of course, be made for providing people with insurance, whether private or public, to cover the cost of psychotherapy in times of crisis. When a person is having difficulty coping with life problems, is dissatisfied, depressed, or distressed with the tenor of his life, is confused and uncertain regarding courses of action he wants to take in regard to his occupation or his marriage or some other important area of living, believes that he is caught up in self-defeating behavior patterns, or feels lonely and unloved and desires reliable and unexploitative human relationship—when a person has a need of this sort, why is it not as legitimate for him to have financial help in meeting it as when his physical health is threatened? Why must the social and psychological problems of living be cast awkwardly and inaccurately into the terminology and styles of thinking of and treating physical illness in order to "legitimatize" financial assistance via insurance? Behavioral problems can be just as real and just as incapacitating as physiological problems, but their nature is quite different and so is their treatment.

The perpetuation of the medical model and tradition in psychotherapy is only one of the hypocritical and misleading representations of the art. Another is to think and speak of psychotherapy as a "science." As the first nine chapters of this book testify, psychotherapy consists of many varied procedures whereby individuals generally called therapists try to help or inspire individuals generally called patients. Even in those very rare instances in which any procedure (within any set of procedures) has been established as definitely effective in relation to some specifically described therapeutic goal, that obviously does not make the particular set of procedures a science. To be a science, psychotherapy would need to be "a particular body of knowledge distinguished by the special set of operations employed in gathering empirical facts and by a distinctive set of constructs employed in interpreting the data" (from English & English, *A Comprehensive Dictionary of Psychological and Psychoanalytical Terms*). It is quite clear that neither psychotherapy as a whole nor any system of psychotherapy meets these criteria. Psychotherapists nevertheless assemble in professional conferences they designate as "scientific meetings." They write for "scientific journals" in "scientific language" and refer in this language to "scientific results." And most therapists seem to think of themselves (and sometimes even their fellow therapists) as scientists engaged in a predominantly scientific enterprise.

It is this pretense at science that probably leads to much of the nonacceptance of psychotherapy in academic communities, where help could be forthcoming in the study of its operations and constructs and their alignment with empirical facts. But more than any damage that derives from turning away potentially helpful friends is what may happen over a period of time to the personality of a psychotherapist who is a sciosophist. It is the psychotherapist's personality that is supposed to serve as a model of rationality, sincerity, and honest dealing with reality, and yet this very personality is not infrequently a reservoir of self-delusion and duplicity. Self-actualization and authenticity of personality are not likely to be transmitted by some osmotic process by pretenders of health treatment and science to those who seek their help.

Not all the scientific claims, of course, are made by psychotherapists who at the same time stress the importance of the therapist's authenticity of personality. Janov, for example, makes no mention of the personality of the psychotherapist and focuses his attention entirely on enabling the patient to release repressed emotions through a process of abreaction. But his claims for primal therapy as a "science" rest to a considerable extent on pre- and post-therapy measurements of pulse, temperature, and EEG readings; these evidences, as we have indicated, do not prove what they are claimed to prove and thus are, at this point, as "unscientific" as are other systems for which no such measurements have been conducted.

If psychotherapy is not science and not medical treatment, what is it? Is therapy, as Jefferson Fish seems to imply, mainly a matter of faith healing? Not, in my opinion, with most therapists most of the time. I base my opinion on what I have directly observed of therapists (especially in workshops and other situations where I have functioned with them in co-therapy situations), what I have seen in movies and video- and audiotapes of therapists at work, what they report in case records, and what I have seen "before and after" many different kinds of therapy in many people. Seldom, if ever, have I seen the sudden and dramatic transformations of personality that would presumably be forthcoming under circumstances in which faith was a major factor. Therapists may talk expansively about their brand of therapy being reconstructive and deep and fundamental in the changes it effects as compared to some other brand, but talk is about all that is available regarding such changes (and even such talk is much less common among therapists than it was a decade and more ago).

Instead of the dramatic, sweeping, and sudden alterations in behavior that would signal "faith healing," the progress of patients I have directly and indirectly witnessed is almost always the long, slow, tedious behavioral change one would expect from problem solving, from gradual substitution of more realistic points of view for less realistic ones, and from the overcoming of firmly entrenched self-defeating habits carried like backpacks from childhood.

It would be highly desirable for researchers with a good eye for experimental design to set up a test of Fish's placebo hypothesis for several major types of psychotherapy. Meantime, I see no reason to buy Fish's general thesis that everybody in psychotherapy is riding the faith train and that they will ride it more efficiently by awareness and confession that that is what they are doing. Although there may indeed be a few faith healers with great charisma out there somewhere, the overwhelming majority of psychotherapists seem to be hacking away at quite pedestrian (but sometimes solid and lasting) behavioral changes in their not very inspired and not very worshipful flock of patients.

We have thus far eliminated the ideas of psychotherapy as predominantly medical treatment, science, or faith healing. Where does that leave us?

It leaves us with a definition of psychotherapy as *the process of presenting people with new learning experiences in such ways as to reduce their strong negative and self-defeating emotions and/or to enhance their realistic problem-solving abilities.* There are, it seems to me, four categories of psychotherapeutic approach within this general definition.

A. First is the approach that has a major focus on helping a person rethink or refeel past experiences in such a way that anxiety, guilt, and hostility are so reduced that he is able to take a quite different perspective about the present and future than he could when he was carrying all those negative emotions. The basic assumption of this approach is that once a person has unloaded the self-defeating feelings of the past and hence has nothing formidable in his way, he can proceed to deal effectively with the present and the future.

B. Another approach centers its attention on the feelings of the here and now. The assumption in this case is that by encouraging the individual to be aware of and overcome his current emotional blocks (whatever past experiences they may have arisen from), he will be able to go on to learn how to live an effective and enjoyable life.

C. A third way of trying to change an individual's negative emotional outlook is through environmental manipulation. The alteration of the stimuli characteristically presented to the individual is designed to change his emotional responses. Such stimulus alteration may be mainly effected by the therapist himself, in and through the therapy group, or in and through the persons with whom the individual lives (in his family or in an institution).

D. Finally, the main emphasis of the psychotherapy may be on the problem-solving or life-coping processes rather than on the individual's emotional reactions. The major assumption of this kind of therapy is that an individual who learns characteristically to think realistically and handle effectively the difficulties he encounters in life will begin to peel off the self-defeating emotions without any (or much) special conditioning process being necessary to help him rid himself of anxiety, hostility, etc.

We have then four categories of psychotherapy. In the therapies that fall into the first three, it is generally assumed that when a lot of self-defeating emotions have been reduced or removed, the person will be able to run his life in an effective and enjoyable way. Therapies of the fourth category make just the opposite assumption: namely, that once a person learns how to cope effectively with the difficulties of life, he will no longer be troubled and handicapped by self-defeating emotions (they will have been reduced or removed in the process of his learning to deal with reality).

Which approach works best? The answer seems to be that it depends on each particular patient and each particular therapist. Some people may be in such a state of emotional confusion and tortured mental distortion that the problem-solving method (D) cannot possibly get through to them. For them one of the first three approaches (or some combination) of emotional reshaping may be necessary and desirable. Other persons, on the contrary, may find their emotional confusion unrelieved (or even increased) by any of these three approaches and be very responsive to being taught explicitly how to cope more directly and ably with the reality factors in their life.

It would greatly increase the effectiveness of psychotherapy, in my opinion, to have intake interviews in which brief tests would be run on people who are seeking help. The tests (which could be in informal interview form) would try to determine which therapeutic approach would be most likely to help them at that particular point in their lives. Referrals could then be made to therapists whose approaches were compatible with the prospective patients' needs. If we could get reliable and valid statistics on patient-therapist incompatibility, I suspect they would not be too different from husband-wife incompatibility. Therapists and patients (like many spouses) often keep trying (and assuming that the other is not trying hard enough) long after an objective observer would declare the relationship stalemated or deteriorating.

What about self-actualization, self-fulfillment, joy of living, and all the more positive goals of psychotherapy? Although some psychotherapies (especially encounter groups) claim that such goals are achieved, most contend only that they will remove the obstacles in the path of the individual's achieving such goals. The implication (or sometimes statement) is that positive ends are attained by reducing or removing the negative emotions that are blocking the individual's natural tendency to experience and express positive emotions. Therapists in category D usually claim or imply that life enjoyment will be forthcoming once the individual learns how to cope effectively with reality. Although proof is lacking either to confirm or disconfirm such contentions, any more direct route to full life satisfaction is uncorroborated.

With our simple categorization of the four main areas of psychotherapy in mind, we can look back over the therapies we have considered in this book. The family therapies and, for the most part, the family-related therapies have their chief stress on environmental change as the route to emotional reshaping (category C). Most of the work of the family therapist is directed toward changing the family, and the family, of course, is a large and significant chunk of the individual's environment. By repatterning family interactions, the therapist is getting different stimuli transmitted and different reactions produced in each individual in the family.

Much the same is true with marriage therapy (and sex therapy, for which Masters and Johnson constantly stress the interactional responsibilities of the couple). The focus in such therapy amounts to providing the mate with the kind of stimuli that will bring responses which, in turn, are enjoyable stimuli for the other person. Likewise, the behavior, feelings, thoughts, and perceptions of children and adolescents are altered primarily through changing the stimuli of their significant environmental influences (therapist, parent, teacher, etc.).

There are a few strands of categories A and B that run through family and family-related therapies. Satir, for example, spends some time getting parents to rethink and refeel their own childhood experiences, but this is ultimately directed toward thus providing a different emotional environment in the family for their children. Some family therapists (Bell and Ackerman and the multiple impact therapists, for example) instruct family members in how to deal more effectively with certain problems (approach D), as is true of some of the family-related therapists. But the main emphasis of the therapies of the first three chapters is emotional reshaping through environmental manipulation.

The group therapies offer a mixed picture of emphases. The very use of group therapy itself, regardless of the orientation of the leader, is basically a category C (environmental reshaping) approach. The subemphases vary, however, with the therapeutic philosophy and technical direction of the group leaders.

Although their styles vary widely among themselves, the following groups place considerable stress on reshaping emotions by focusing on the here-and-now interactions (category B): Horneyian, existential, behavioral, Sullivanian, bio-energetic, peer self-help groups, and encounter groups. None of these methods fail to make full use of the fundamental environmental reshaping (C) nature of the group, but within the framework they seem, most of the time, to concentrate on a "here-and-now" (B) emphasis. These groups differ, of course, in what they see as the most promising techniques for here-and-now emotional reshaping. The encounter leaders and the bio-energeticists spend a great deal of time on the body and its tensions as a route to emotional reshaping. Assertive actions within the group are also utilized by these two camps, and here they are joined in a big way by the behavioral group therapists, who also place great stress on emotional reconditioning outside the group by homework assignments that are reported on by group members at the next group session.

Explicit instruction in category D—coping techniques and problem-solving procedures—are fairly often mixed in with the emotional reshaping processes in peer self-help groups. Although it is almost invariably disguised (often to the leaders themselves, for explicit instruction in any form seems still to be loathsome to therapists, other than Adlerians, who have emerged from any kind of psychoanalytic tradition), education in problem-solving seems to creep into Horneyian, existential, and Sullivanian group procedures from time to time.

The group psychotherapists who approach problem-solving and life-coping education with a zest (rather than the reluctance seen in many other systems) are the Adlerians, the rational-emotive therapists, and the transactional analysts. Although we have not considered them in a group context in our book, the reality therapists, the direct decision therapists, and the confrontation therapists (all of whom use group therapy) need also to be added to this list. The usefulness of the reshaped environment (the structures and functions of the groups themselves) for emotional reshaping is not ignored by these practitioners, but their primary focus tends to be on the therapist and other group members as means of helping the individual to learn to deal more effectively with the world about him. The transactional analysts also undertake a certain amount of here-and-now emotional reshaping in such ways as confronting the individual with his games and the various functionings of his Parent, Adult, and Child. In like manner, the Adlerians in their emphasis on encouragement of the individual, the reality therapists in their stress on a close and warm relationship between the therapist and the patient, and even the rational-emotive and confrontation therapists with their intense interest in helping their patients at times color their problem-solving (D) focus with emotional reshaping of the here-and-now (B) variety.

In addition to its use as a group method, behavioral therapy is primarily a matter of emotional reshaping through environmental manipulation. This emphasis is sometimes mixed with some here-and-now emotional reshaping, and among behavioral therapists with a cognitive bent, some problem-solving instruction is introduced from time to time.

When we turn to the body psychotherapists, we have the here-and-now emotional reshapers supreme in the Gestaltists, the Reichians, and the bio-energeticists. The primal and autogenic therapists, on the contrary, in their different abreaction-emphasizing ways are working toward a reshaping of the emotions by rethinking and refeeling the past. A little of this method (A) is undertaken by some of the encounter group leaders from time to time and likewise by the psychosynthesists, but this is not their major emphasis.

The psychosynthesists seem to have a little environmental reshaping and a little problem-solving in their mix, but the main emphasis is on reshaping the emotions by focusing on the here and now. This is also true of psycho-imagination therapy.

Placebo therapy, not even considered a system or school by Fish himself, does not lend itself to this four-category classification. To a certain extent (very limited, in my opinion), the "magical" influence of faith could make any of the four emphases work more impressively on any patient suggestible enough to think he had found the guru and the cure.

To summarize, this is the way the therapies we have considered in this book line up in the four categories of emphasis (the major emphasis is listed first and minor influences put in parentheses):

Family therapies—C (A, B)

Psychotherapy with children and adolescents—C (A, B)

Marriage and sex therapies—C (B)

Existential, Horneyian, behavioral, Sullivanian, bio-energetic, peer self-help, and encounter groups—B (C, D)

Adlerian, rational-emotive, transactional analysis, direct decision, reality, and confrontation problem-solving therapies—D (C, B)

Behavior therapies—C (B, D)

Gestalt, Reichian, and bio-energetic therapies—B (C)

Primal and autogenic therapies—A (B)

Psychosynthesis—B (C, A, D)

Psycho-imagination therapy—B (C, D)

Something that stands out in this summary is the frequent occurrence of emotional reshaping by environmental manipulation and, even more, emotional reshaping by focusing on the here and now. The latter is either a primary or subsidiary emphasis in all the therapies we have discussed and the former is likewise in all except primal and autogenic therapies. The direct problem-solving emphasis is of moderate significance, and the emphasis which consists of the rethinking and refeeling of the past is a definite minority approach found significantly only in primal and autogenic therapies.

The near disappearance of category A from the psychotherapeutic scene and the concomitant rise in prominence of category D may be considered one of the most important trends of the past decade or two. Psychoanalysis, which until about 1960 almost completely dominated the psychotherapeutic culture, has primarily used the deep exploration of the unconscious. It has involved the rethinking and refeeling of the past to the degree of contending that any other therapeutic approach was bound to be superficial and palliative. Even indirect teaching, let alone the often very direct instructional approach of therapies with the problem-solving emphasis, is considered obstructive to those who use the cathartic, abreactive, and reconstructive process of free associational psychoanalysis. However, for many therapists who still call themselves psychoanalysts (largely through the influence of ego psychology as a more recent development in psychoanalysis—see *Psychoanalysis and Psychotherapy: 36 Systems*), more directive procedures have become widespread.

Although representing a less dramatic reversal of procedures, the old psychoanalytic emphasis on rethinking and refeeling the past has been even more completely undermined and replaced by emphases which center attention on the feelings of the here and now and on environmental manipulation. Many of the group therapies (especially the encounter-type groups) strongly emphasize the here-and-now approach, and those that do not are oriented toward problem-solving approach. Family and family-related therapies have a predominant emphasis on environmental reshaping.

The psychotherapeutic scene in the sixties and seventies, then, tends to stress *group therapies* (with some use of categories B and D), *family and family-related therapies* (with category C emphasized), and strong (but minority) strains of *behavior therapies* (C) and *cognitive therapies* (D). On the edge (not really the growing edge, but more like remnant shoots of an essentially dead old tree) are close little clusters of emphasis on category A.

Therapies of the contemporary psychotherapy scene, then, are designed mainly for people who feel alienated from their immediate associates and frustrated in relation to their present and future goals. Relatively few people today feel the need for or have confidence in the effectiveness of a thoroughgoing analysis of their pasts, and only a small percentage of these few can afford the time and money required actively to pursue therapies that emphasize the use of category A techniques.

For people who seem too disoriented and disturbed to know what they want or need, institutionalization along with drug or electric therapy are still the usual procedures. Sometimes these methods are followed by psychotherapy utilizing methods from the last three categories, and other times these people are sent back to unchanged environments with unchanged feelings and unimproved life-coping capacities. Where psychotherapy has been undertaken either as a substitute for hospitalization (as in various family therapies) or as a concomitant of institutional commitment, good (but not spectacular) results, including fewer relapses, have been obtained.

Overall at this point—in the middle of the 1970s—we can say that various forms of psychotherapy have become established as society's aid for the friendless and the troubled. Loving associations among family and friends are sometimes mentioned by skeptics as better answers to feelings of alienation and frustration, but this, of course, begs the question. Psychotherapy is mainly for people who are bereft of or unable satisfactorily to cope with family and friends.

Although it is to be hoped that sooner or later our society will design an institution more effective than psychotherapy for meeting people's problems, this is the current (rather disjointed) answer—or, rather, we should say, this is the variety of answers. Out of this variety, we have no clear-cut evidence for saying that one therapy is greatly superior to another.

INDEX

171